NEWS AND THE CULTURE OF LYING

NEWS AND THE CULTURE OF LYING

PAUL H. WEAVER

THE FREE PRESS
A Division of Macmillan, Inc.
NEW YORK
Maxwell Macmillan Canada
TORONTO
Maxwell Macmillan International
NEW YORK   OXFORD   SINGAPORE   SYDNEY

The Free Press
A Division of Macmillan, Inc.
866 Third Avenue, New York, N.Y. 10022

Maxwell Macmillan Canada, Inc.
1200 Eglinton Avenue East
Suite 200
Don Mills, Ontario M3C 3N1

Macmillan, Inc. is part of the Maxwell Communication Group of Companies.

Printed in the United States of America
Printing number
1 2 3 4 5 6 7 8 9 10

Library of Congress Cataloging-in-Publication Data

Weaver, Paul
    News and the culture of lying/ Paul H. Weaver.
        p.   cm.
    ISBN 0-02-934021-7
        1. Journalism—United States—Objectivity.   2. Government and the
    press—United States.   I. Title.
    PN4888.O25W43   1994
    071'.3—dc20   93-41562
                                                                   CIP

This book is dedicated to
CECILE T. WEAVER *and* HAROLD F. WEAVER,
my mother and father, with love and gratitude

CONTENTS

CHAPTER 8

Fabrications

This is a book about the way journalists and officials fabricate an alternative reality that is covered in the media, reacted to by the public, and dealt with by government as if it were the same as the reality we experience in everyday life at home or on the job.

The process seems innocent enough at first glance.

Journalists need officials' events and information to make news stories. Officials need journalists' attention to gain public support for their projects and careers. The two engage in barter: Information, access, and events are given in exchange for news coverage, and vice versa. The trade leaves everyone involved seemingly better off. Officials get publicity, journalists get the raw materials of news, and the public learns what officials and institutions are up to.

The problem arises because, contrary to the way we usually speak of it, news isn't simply a report of what happened yesterday. It's a *story*, with characters, action, plot, point of view, dramatic closure. Moreover, it's a story about *crisis* and *emergency response*—about the waxing and waning of urgent danger to the community, and about the actions of responsible officials to cope. Thus, officials in search of publicity and journalists in search of news don't converge on just any sort of news event. They enact, select, and narrate events in the image of the genre's overarching drama of urgent public danger. In other words, they translate themselves and their projects into the language—and theater—of crisis.

In some circumstances, this self-translation involves little or no change. When a real crisis is at hand and officials are taking real steps to cope with it, the genre's focus on crisis and emergency response simply means that the media faithfully reflect what is actually happening.

But the news genre insists that crises and emergency responses are taking place every day and in every arena. As officials and journalists adapt to the news story's preconception of ordinary events as crises and the front page's preconception of ordinary days as times of great excitement and historical consequence, the actions they undertake and the stories they tell become fabrications. What's actually going on in the real world is the ordinary business of ordinary institutions. What officials and reporters converge on, therefore, are travesties, not real events. The news stops representing the real world and begins to falsify it. The barter transaction between newsmaker and journalist degenerates into an exercise in deceit, manipulation, and exploitation.

The officials and journalists involved are more or less aware of the falseness of what they're up to. However, disclosing that falseness would undermine the benefits they're seeking from the news process. Officials are looking for public approval and support. Telling the audience that they're playacting for the press wouldn't exactly further that goal. Journalists present themselves to the public as objective observers and reporters of the real world. Disclosing the fact that they're covering fabrications as news events would destroy the trust they're trying to establish. Thus, both newsmaker and news worker generally withhold any information or comment that would alert the audience to the real nature of the transaction between them.

When official and journalist script themselves into the genre's story of crisis and response, they enter the distracted, unhappy, bizarre world of government's emergency power.

Normal constitutional government is a stately, deliberate, often quite principled affair. Rules predominate, people and institutions have prescribed roles, powers are both conferred and limited, the objective of public processes is to represent and discuss and make general rules generally applicable. Whatever function isn't explicitly assigned to government is reserved to the individual. The presumption is that the private sector and individual rights come first and that government is their servant.

Emergencies and crises open up a giant loophole in this textbook image of constitutional society. When society's survival is endangered, the normal processes and perspectives and limits of representative democracy recede into the background and an authoritarian politics of urgent public problem-solving takes center stage. Representation and deliberation are put on hold since there isn't time to hear everyone out and anyway the objective isn't to formulate general rules generally applicable, it's just to get past the present disaster in one piece. Government by executive decree is the prevailing practice; the role of legislatures and courts is primarily to go along and give their blessing. The presumption in favor of the individual and private sector is in eclipse. Now the going-in assumption in public affairs is that society will bear any burden, pay any price, support any friend, and oppose any foe to assure the survival of democracy.

Even in the best of circumstances, emergency government is an often unattractive affair. Within wide limits, officials are free to do whatever they think is necessary, and they quickly fall out of the habit of explaining what they're up to. In wartime, it's truly said, truth is the first casualty. However, when the crisis is only simulated, as it is in the world according to the news genre, the level of mendacity and exploitativeness soars through the ceiling. Facts in the news generally remain true, that much being necessary to maintain the credibility of the entire exercise. However, sooner or later almost everything else becomes a fabrication. The public discourse degenerates into a farrago of invented crises, illusory programs, government interventions that make matters worse, benefits to the undeserving, punishment of the innocent, sneaky heroes, villains whose only offense is to be on the losing side, and lies of every size and description.

The word *lying* is harsh, but it's the correct term for the behaviors we are talking about here. A lie is defined as a misrepresentation of one's state of mind or belief as to what is authentic and true. When officials script and enact events and simulate sentiments for the media's consumption, they meet the simple dictionary test of misrepresentation. When journalists present these made-for-media impersonations as authentic news, they meet it, too. Journalists are almost always aware of what newsmakers and sources are really up to; it rarely happens that they are completely taken in by officials' lies.

Lest there be any misunderstanding, I had better say immediately that I am not talking here about the corruptions of truth and history that take place when journalists and newsmakers break the rules and falsify facts. I am talking about what happens when people *follow* the rules. In other words, this is a book about the behaviors that prevail and the consequences that flow when officials and journalists work *within* the framework of accepted practice, when everything is on the up-and-up, when the facts are right and the relevant people have been contacted and the story has been told straight. I am arguing that in such circumstances, officials and journalists are usually lying. They're pretending that the events they're enacting and narrating are bona fide actions taken on the merits in the normal context of the newsmakers' jobs, whereas in fact, most news events and stories are performances.

Take, for example, the past decade's news coverage of the Gramm-Rudman-Hollings program to eliminate the federal deficit.

In the hundreds upon hundreds of stories that ran on the subject, presidents, congressmen, public finance experts, and others were portrayed as saying and doing all the right things with respect to the vast and growing gap between what the federal government takes in and what it spends. They acknowledged the mind-boggling size of the deficit and the enormity of the problem it poses. They committed themselves to eliminating the deficit. They created and applied the elaborate Gramm-Rudman-Hollings procedure to reduce the deficit to zero over a multi-year period. When the effort faltered, the stories showed officials discussing alternatives and taking steps. To judge from the clips, in short, the deficit was a problem on its way to being solved despite difficulties.

In the budgeting offices of the executive branch departments, at the Office of Management and Budget, and in scores of committees and subcommittees on the Hill, however, a different story was unfolding. In these far-flung venues, via a multistage process stretching throughout the year, hundreds of major decisions were taken to spend at levels that, in the aggregate, grew much faster than revenues over the 1982-1992 decade. As a result, over the period in which the Gramm-Rudman-Hollings program was supposed to be cutting the deficit back to zero, the deficit not only didn't go away, it grew.

The vast majority of these deficit-generating actions went uncovered in the media. The press rarely reports the routine, obscure, seemingly undefinitive actions by which the federal government spends $1.5 trillion per year. Even the self-described newspaper of record, the *New York Times*, ignored most of the major annual authorization and appropriation votes.

Moreover, of the relatively few stories that did cover the actions that built the deficit, most treated them as *good* news. The events were written up, not as drops in the bucket of the national debt, but as benefits conferred by a bountiful government. When Congress voted to expand the deficit by cutting taxes and increasing spending during the Gramm-Rudman-Hollings decade, the news accounts focused on the *desirable* aspects of these steps—the economic benefits being handed out, the political support the policies enjoyed, the career progress being made by the measures' sponsors. The effect on the deficit was either ignored or covered perfunctorily as a subsidiary issue, a matter of secondary importance.

By the same token, news stories about proposals or actions to cut the deficit by reducing specific spending streams or raising specific taxes focused on the steps' *negative* aspects—the dislocations they would cause, the political opposition they were arousing, the social callousness of the conservatives supporting the moves. The stories ignored or played down the positive effect on the deficit such steps would have.

In other words, during the decade in which the federal deficit exploded to meltdown proportions, there were lots of news stories about government's taking steps to reduce the deficit, there were plenty of news stories about government's providing the people with the bounties of various tax cuts and spending programs, *but there were no news stories about government adding to the deficit even though that was what was happening.*

Thus, the fiscal actions government took in this period and the news reports the press ran about them amounted to a charade. The public's power to tax and spend was exercised in a way designed to create a misleading impression of advantage and benevolence. In some cases real benefits were handed out amid much fanfare and credit claiming, while the costs were carefully concealed. In other cases benefits were simulated, while a prior and controlling refusal to impose the requisite costs, a refusal that rendered the benefits illusory, was concealed. In no case were actions taken and reported in their real-world context in which there is no free lunch, benefits come with a price tag attached, and policy is made by striking a balance between anticipated costs and anticipated benefits. In all cases actions were taken and reported in an artificial, journalistic context in which costs and benefits exist in isolation from one another and in which, given proper self-scripting and stage management by newsmakers, all the news is capable of being good news.

The spending/taxing mess is a dramatic case, but it is not unusual. To the contrary, this line of news coverage illustrates a process that takes place more or less every time a news story is put together. The central fact about the interaction between news media and the people they cover is that *the people being covered know the media are watching and behave accordingly.* As a result, the actions the media cover as news aren't spontaneous events but self-conscious efforts to create favorable impressions. For their part *the news media are aware that newsmakers are performing, but they nonetheless treat newsmakers' fabrications as authentic actions,* covering or ignoring these performances as they see fit. They rarely go beyond the performance to unmask the plays and players or to describe events with reference to the self-conscious, self-serving effort at work backstage. Thus, both parties deny the manipulative nature of their roles in making the news, insisting instead that their actions are authentic, un-self-conscious, and taken on the merits.

The purpose of these performances is, or becomes, the acquisition of personal privilege and government-given advantage. For the news media, the advantage of the crisis-and-emergency-response genre that invites and validates the lies is that it attracts bigger audiences, and bigger audiences in turn mean more advertising revenues than could be provided by a less puffed-up, more candid concept of news. For officials, the crowd-pleasing images the news enables them to project are a terrific boon to, and often a necessary base of, their public careers. For groups and organizations seeking subsidies, protection, or other help from the political process, the misleading news images of crisis that they initiate or co-opt are often the only way to get inhibited constitutional institutions to provide the special-interest benefits they want.

This pattern of media-enabled fabrication is something I've become familiar with in my own work as a journalist, starting with the first story I ever wrote, for *Fortune* magazine.

I joined *Fortune* as a staff writer in the summer of 1974, a thirty-one-year-old ex-professor of political science and junior editor of the neoconservative quarterly the *Public Interest*. The premise was that with my background in politics and public policy, my sympathy for business, and my hostility to business's critics in a Naderish age, I was just the person to cover the new regulatory programs being set up in Washington, such as the Environmental Protection Agency and the Consumer Product Safety Commission. In keeping with this program, my first assignment was to report and write a five thousand-word story about the efforts then afoot in Washington to issue new limits on exposure to vinyl chloride, a gas from which a major plastic, polyvinyl chloride, is made. A few months earlier, a Kentucky doctor's discovery that a few of his patients at a polyvinyl chloride plant had died of a rare liver cancer had created a sensation, setting powerful regulatory and scientific forces in motion. As I got into the story, it came alive with an intensity I'll never forget.

My work was the essence of simplicity. I went to the institutions involved in the issue and observed what they were saying and doing with respect to it. I noted the names of people and organizations who were active, called for appointments, showed up at the agreed-on times and places, asked the obvious questions, and wrote down what they said in spiral-bound stenographer's notebooks. It was a thrilling experience. Everyone was willing to see me. I had a wonderful time chatting with important people about topics in the news. I was absorbing vast amounts of information.

Everyone I talked to was, in one form or another, lobbying or being lobbied.

The labor people and most of the scientific and agency types were urging the Occupational Safety and Health Administration to reduce its existing ceiling on vinyl chloride exposure—a dose of one hundred parts per million (ppm), set years earlier to prevent fainting and other nonfatal maladies—to zero. OSHA, they pointed out, was required by law to eliminate health and safety dangers to the maximum possible extent short of destroying the industry in question. While no data showed workers to have contracted cancer at dosages much below 100 ppm, one of the major theories of carcinogenesis held that any exposure to a cancer-causing toxin, however small, would cause cancer at some rate, however low, and thus that the only safe dose was zero. They further urged OSHA to require employers to meet the new standard by redesigning production processes to eliminate all human contact with the gas. Otherwise workers would have to wear gas masks and respirators, which, they argued, are disagreeable and potentially dangerous.

On the other side, business spokesmen and their scientists were arguing that a zero standard was unwarranted and would be ruinous. They pointed out that the vinyl-related cancers had involved ambient levels of 100 ppm or more, and they urged OSHA to set its new standard somewhere comfortably below 100 ppm and comfortably above zero. They also urged that employers be authorized to comply by means of gas masks and respirators since the cost of rebuilding existing plants would be astronomical.

In a couple of weeks, I understood most of what was going on. In a month I had the entire story down cold. And at the heart of the story, as I pieced it together from my interview notes, was a simple, hard-to-believe, yet undeniable fact: Just about everyone involved in the vinyl chloride affair was lying.

Lie No. 1 was that, though no one knew how big a dose of vinyl chloride it took to cause cancer or how much vinyl chloride a person could be exposed to without risk, all the participants were advocating specific levels as safe while attacking as dangerous the different levels urged by others.

Lie No. 2 was that the regulatory solutions proposed by the various sides would maximize the workers' safety at little or no cost to them. The truth was, however, that if you followed the zero-exposure camp's advice and rebuilt existing plants to eliminate all contact with the gas, workers would either lose income (while the plant was down for renovations) or lose their jobs altogether (because the company would shut down the old plant and build a new one at a more economic location somewhere else). If, on the other hand, you let the old plants continue operating unrenovated and merely required workers to use gas masks and respirators, the workers would be trading their old cancer risk for a new burden of discomfort, physical stress, and accident risk. Either way the workers were going to pay.

People were abusing the truth about vinyl chloride, I could see, for a simple reason. Rather than viewing the discovery that vinyl chloride causes cancer as a common problem that industry and union leaders had a common need to resolve if the manufacturing enterprise from which they made their livings was to go forward, each was trying to use the medical discovery as a lever with which to pry personal advantage out of other people's hides. This in turn was related to the fact that the people and organizations immediately affected were not the ones who were going to make the decision. OSHA was. Rather than talking and bargaining with one another within the sharply constraining context of their need to make a go of the business they shared in the long run, each of the vinyl principals was talking mainly to the scientists and regulators in Washington who, with little knowledge of and less interest in the industry, were going to impose a mandatory vinyl standard on the parties. Thus, rather than seek from OSHA a standard intelligently reflecting the many considerations involved, each was trying to define the vinyl problem in a way that would take the matter out of a deliberative framework and put it into an emergency framework in which government doesn't balance competing considerations but instead focuses on a single survivalist objective—workers' survival, the unions hoped, or the companies' survival, the industry urged. Whichever survival interest OSHA opted for, the effect would be to benefit one party at others' expense.

Members of the zero-exposure faction were looking to advance their careers as labor leaders or medical specialists, increase their budgets, broaden their research programs. Companies were hoping for a regulation that would restructure the industry to their advantage. Firms with new, low-exposure plants wanted a tough standard they could barely meet, and older plants couldn't meet, so that the old plants would be closed, the industry's capacity would shrink, and prices would rise. Companies with older plants wanted an easy standard that would enable them to avoid the huge costs and tough decisions involved in building new plants.

When the reporting was done, I sat at my typewriter and began to write. My spirits quickly fell. Reporting had been fun; every day, it seemed, I was encountering interesting people and fresh viewpoints. Writing was a nightmare. I agonized for days over the lead. Once I had it right, I turned with relief to the rest of the story, only to find that in spite of a brilliant outline I hadn't the faintest idea of where I was really headed. I tried all kinds of ideas, but nothing seemed to work. Eventually, a week after the story was due, a sympathetic phone call from my editor—when I first heard his calm voice on the line, I'd thought in a panic he was going to fire me—roused me to a frenzy of guilty all-night typing, and the next morning I had a manuscript.

The technical problems posed by my story were formidable. I had to organize my information in a flowing narrative that had a beginning, middle, and end; that had pacing and contrast; that was fair, yet made a point, yet also conveyed a maximum of information; that was novel but spoke wherever possible through colorful quotations from the people involved. To my surprise, however, meeting these requirements wasn't that hard. Once I figured out what to say, the story almost wrote itself.

What wasn't easy was figuring out what to say. And the reason it wasn't easy, I now see, is that I was torn between two completely opposing impulses.

On the one hand, I wanted to write the story my reporting had disclosed to me. I wanted to report to my readers that the discovery that vinyl chloride is a carcinogen had prompted everyone involved to lie about the problems at hand in an effort to turn the government's decision into a source of institutional advantage and personal gain. I wanted to write this not only because it was true but also because it was something I'd lived through. I'd come to the story through personal encounters with people and ideas and events, the encounters had challenged my picture of the world, and I had come to have an emotional as well as intellectual stake in my discoveries. I had a need to tell this story in much the same sense that water has a need to find the lowest level or air has a need to expand to fill a vacuum.

On the other hand, I felt an intense desire *not* to write the story my reporting had disclosed to me. I desperately wanted *not* to say that corporate executives and union leaders and scientists and regulators were lying to benefit themselves at others' expense. The idea of saying these things made me feel extremely anxious.

For one thing, my assignment was to write a story about the vinyl chloride issue—the problem, the facts, the different approaches to dealing with it, and so on. I worried that if I focused on the fact that much of what was being said about the subject was a pack of fabrications, I'd be undercutting the story. In effect, I'd be telling readers that the whole subject was a con, and this in turn would give people the impression that there was no compelling reason to read the story. People would be turned off. My boss would feel I hadn't written the strong, engrossing, issue-oriented story he'd asked for.

Moreover, I was reluctant to write the story my reporting had disclosed because I was having a hard time believing it myself. The notion that, up close and personal, regulatory politics were an exercise in mendacity and exploitation flew in the face of my picture of the American political system as essentially just and effective.

Finally, I worried about the consequences for my career if I wrote that everyone was lying. The people involved would indignantly deny the claims. There would be letters to the editor, hostile remarks to my boss, head-shaking professions of puzzlement.

And the negative responses wouldn't be confined to my sources. Everyone I knew who had helped my career—particularly the neocon professors and editors who had taught me, spoken well of me, commissioned articles from me, and given me jobs—would be troubled. The fact was I lived in a world in which a great many people were heavily invested in the sly, self-serving, sanctimonious lying I'd run into, and to expose it was to ask for trouble. In any event, I was not the sort to ask for such trouble. I had made my way by happily doing what teachers and bosses expected of me, not by being insensitive to them or disappointing them or defying them. I wanted to go on going along. I wanted to write a story about the Solomonic choice between health risk and economic risk the business participants in the debate were talking about and how these issues were being handled competently by effective institutions amid the normal play of pluralistic politics.

In the end that's more or less what I did. We called it "On the Horns of the Vinyl Chloride Dilemma," and it sounded an essentially complacent theme. A complex issue was being fought over hard, with some misrepresentation and adversarial posturing, but the likely outcome would be a compromise that the country should be able to live with. Indeed, the adversaries' exaggerations were a sign of healthy diversity and vigorous political competition.

The core reality I'd observed—the phenomenon of dishonest, self-destructive advantage seeking—I relegated to a short box that sketched the position-taking activities of a government regulatory institute that had proposed a standard of zero exposure without knowing anything about its economic effects, and of a company with old plants that lobbied for a permissive standard without knowing anything about its health effects but in full knowledge that it would prevent firms with newer, more efficient plants from getting a leg up. It was an effective, sassy little piece, but it misrepresented the central phenomenon I'd encountered as an amusing and colorful sidelight.

In opting to forget the story my reporting had disclosed and to go with the conventional account my business-journalism colleagues and neoconservative friends expected, I was crossing a Rubicon. I was submerging my discoveries and myself in the warm, murky shallows of groupthink. I was integrating myself into a human, occupational, and political community and allowing its standards to supersede my own. I was willingly cooperating with powerful others. At the time, and for some years thereafter, I was unaware of what had happened. I was conscious only of the profound anxiety the real story made me feel and the blissful sense of relief that descended on me when I wrote the story the conventional way and received the approval of all concerned.

The vinyl chloride principals' journalist-assisted poses of altruism and their pie-in-the-sky lies about the dose-response curve and the regulatory debate on the horns of a dilemma added up to a highly successful power grab. With these lies the professional regulators, medical researchers, union leaders, business executives, and journalists took the issue out of the hands and frames of reference of the workers and the marketplace that empowered them, arranging to have it dealt with by and on the terms of the authorities in Washington, D.C. OSHA imposed a version of the zero standard. The result: About 10 percent of vinyl chloride manufacturing capacity was closed, several hundred vinyl workers lost their jobs, and vinyl prices and profits rose smartly.

Fabricated politics and journalism of the sort I observed and participated in during my years as a working journalist constitute what I believe can fairly be described as a culture of lying. The culture of lying is the discourse and behavior of officials seeking to enlist the powers of journalism in support of their goals, and of journalists seeking to co-opt public and private officials into their efforts to find and cover stories of crisis and emergency response. It is the medium through which we Americans conduct most of our public business (and a lot of our private business) these days.

We encounter the culture of lying in the contrived statements of government and corporate officials trying to look good on the nightly news. We encounter it in a union leader's complacent advocacy of an action that will benefit his members in the short term but endanger their jobs and harm the U.S. economy in the long term. We see it in phony claims of danger to national security made by businesses seeking protection from foreign firms making better products at lower prices. We encounter it in the TV anchorman's unctuous pretensions to an authoritativeness no human being could possibly possess. We see its reflection in polls showing that the American people don't trust their leaders to tell the truth.

The culture of lying, as I am using the phrase, does not refer to all acts of public mendacity, only to those prompted by the news genre. Coexisting with this media-based culture of lying but distinct from it are other, more traditional kinds of lying—for instance, the dehumanizing lies of religious, racial, and cultural oppression, the self-protective lies of the criminal avoiding censure or punishment, the manipulative lies of the social parasite. Such non-media-related lies can arise as sequels to the media-generated kind. And officials desensitized by the news environment to the virtue of truthfulness and the vice of dishonesty may acquire a propensity for these other kinds of lying as well.

The culture of lying has engulfed the most solemn occasions and biggest issues of our time.

In 1964, during his campaign for the presidency, Lyndon Johnson said over and over again that he intended and planned "no wider war in Vietnam." He would never send "American boys to die in Asian jungles." It was his Republican opponent, Barry Goldwater, who was the dangerous, war-minded hawk, Johnson insisted. The election turned on this issue, Johnson was elected in a landslide, and within weeks the administration announced the military buildup that would take the U.S. troop level in Vietnam above 500,000. Years later, secret documents included among the so-called Pentagon papers released to the news media by Daniel Ellsberg showed that during the months in 1964 when he was pledging no wider war, Johnson and his staff were planning and intending precisely such a war.

It was a typical culture-of-lying sort of lie—technically modest enough to win easy acceptance, substantively large enough to provide adequate cover for the liar and his associates to smuggle advantage of compelling magnitude into the public's business.

The lie was a core element of Johnson's larger effort to define himself as the solution to the potential future crisis of Goldwater's hawkishness, while also, by taking an aggressive military posture against Communist expansion, denying political opponents any future opportunity to attack him as soft on communism. In effect, Johnson was translating a small real foreign-policy difference between him and Goldwater into a sequence of dramatic, made-up media postures—first a pledge to stay out of a war that he implied his opponent might start, then a decision to enter that war to prevent the opponent from depicting him as weak.

From a technical standpoint the act of dishonesty was arguably limited. Military and diplomatic staffs are always developing plans for this or that potential action. While it was apparently true that LBJ had personally asked for these war plans, he wasn't committed to going ahead with them, so it wasn't an out-and-out, black-is-white lie for him to say that he intended no wider war. Even if in his heart he did intend such a war, who could prove it? Did he himself know for certain what he was going to do before he did it? Until the attack was launched, he could always change his mind and order a stand-down.

In a larger sense, however, Johnson's little liberties with the truth added up to a gigantic misrepresentation that led to horrendous consequences for everyone involved, from LBJ himself and U.S. foreign policy to the shape of international relations for decades to follow. It was as big a lie about as big a subject as has ever been told in American history.

Seemingly little lies with big consequences have been the rule, not the exception, in our time. They are the way we get important business done in America.

Running for the presidency in 1960, John F. Kennedy charged that the complacency of the Eisenhower-Nixon administration had enabled the USSR to take a commanding lead in deployment of intercontinental ballistic missiles capable of delivering nuclear warheads on American targets. A secret Pentagon study demonstrated a dangerous "missile gap," Kennedy declared, and he pledged to close it and to establish U.S. superiority in ICBMs. The charge was plausible at a time when the Soviet nonmilitary space program was far ahead of our own, but it was untrue, and Kennedy knew it. There was no Pentagon study demonstrating a missile gap. The actual U.S. intelligence estimate was that, against a U.S. deployment of some one hundred ICBMs, the Soviet Union had perhaps five. Soon after taking office, Kennedy declared that apparently he'd been mistaken and he was happy to announce that there wasn't a missile gap after all.

"Read my lips, no new taxes," George Bush declared repeatedly in sounding what was the most important theme of his campaign for the presidency in 1988. A year and a half into his first term, Bush flip-flopped, saying that he'd changed his mind and was now prepared to seek a substantial tax increase as part of an effort to reduce federal deficits that had grown to crippling proportions. Circumstances had changed, he insisted by way of justification. But the circumstances he cited—the budget deficit, the magnitude of the savings-and-loan bailout, the weakening state of the economy—were the same ones his critics had anticipated, and he had rejected, in the debate during the campaign over whether or not to raise taxes. The pledge was a made-for-media posture intended to blur the negative of Bush's association with the horrendous Reagan deficit and to take credit for one of the desirable policies responsible for generating the deficit—the tax cuts. This posture was, of course, at odds with Bush's own historic preferences and positions. A member of the GOP's moderate wing, Bush had ridiculed Reaganite political economy as "voodoo." Predictably, once he was in the White House, he reverted to type, revealing a cynical media-oriented campaign posture as the lie it was.

The top executives of American corporations declare their support for private enterprise, free markets, and limited government in a seemingly endless succession of speeches, advertisements, and other communications. They oppose big government and denounce regulatory programs that distort the adaptive processes of the free market and arbitrarily impose legislators' values on consumers. Yet behind this facade of talk about freedom, most companies actively lobby for government interventions in the marketplace from which they hope to derive subsidies, tax breaks, advantages over their competitors, and other antimarket benefits. Business rhetoric about free enterprise is propaganda deployed to discredit individual policies business opposes for other reasons and to conceal the government-given goodies businesses seek at the expense of their customers and competitors.

We speak of the Great Depression as the result of the unbridled free market, and we imagine that it was cured by Franklin D. Roosevelt's New Deal. In fact, roughly the opposite is true. The

Great Depression, economic historians increasingly agree, was largely the result of a sharp contraction of the money supply by the Fed and by European central banks, plus the sharp falloff in international trade that resulted from the Smoot-Hawley tariff of 1930 and the tit-for-tat reactions by other major trading partners, plus regulatory programs to maintain wage levels that led employers to adjust to the downturn in economic activity mainly through layoffs. Moreover, the New Deal did little to help things. It was mostly an extension of what Herbert Hoover had already begun through regulatory regimes, stepped-up government spending on public works, and jawboning. And by the middle 1930s it was no more successful than Hoover's program had been in the early 1930s. Indeed, the nadir of the Great Depression came during FDR's presidency, not Hoover's; what got the United States out of the depression was its entry into World War II. Almost everything we were brought up to believe about the Depression-New Deal experience is the reverse of the truth.

After President John F. Kennedy was assassinated in Dallas in 1963, the government took the position (it has also been the position of the Kennedy family) that the president had been killed by Lee Harvey Oswald acting alone and from essentially irrational motives and that with Oswald's death three days later at the hand of another lone, irrational, apolitical assassin named Jack Ruby, the case of Kennedy's murder was closed. Unlike the cases sketched in the paragraphs above, this theory, though far-fetched, hasn't been proven false, due in part to the destruction of some evidence and to the government's failure to gather other evidence in the first place. Yet clearly it was a made-for-media posture, tossed together on the fly during the desperate hours following Kennedy's death and confidently marketed as the truth long before anyone knew for sure what had happened. Later, this fabricated explanation was given the imprimatur of a Warren Commission that, according to Edward Jay Epstein, didn't possess, and in some cases didn't even seek, all the evidence needed to verify the lone-assassin theory and discredit the alternatives.

As an exercise in media manipulation, the lone-assassin theory served Kennedy's survivors nicely. By closing the case without benefit of formal legal process, it protected Johnson's succession from potential questions and forestalled potential demands for drastic steps against nations and organizations linked to Oswald—for instance, the Soviet Union, to which he had defected; Castro's Cuba, with whose agents he had had contact; or organized crime, through his own assassin, mob associate Jack Ruby. Treating the killing of JFK as a closed case also protected Kennedy family members from potentially embarrassing revelations, some of which have come out anyway, such as JFK's obsessive womanizing or the long-standing ties of clan patriarch Joseph P. Kennedy to the Mafia.

The Kennedy assassination is a fascinating case of a made-for-media fabrication losing its credibility among the general public without being definitively discredited yet retaining the tepid support of top people in the White House, law enforcement, and the national press, which has skeptically covered some of the alternative viewpoints but never abandoned the theory that it accepted lock, stock, and barrel in the hours following the assassination in Dallas.

The public's continuing inability to believe the lone-assassin theory and its nagging sense that the assassination is an unsolved mystery have kept the question open. This in turn has cleared the way for any number of crusaders and kooks to pursue investigations and promulgate theories. The festering, heartbreaking mess that is the Kennedy case is a definitive instance of the culture of lying, illustrating not only an infamous official lie but also the political and cultural demoralization and paranoia that flourish when society's need for truthfulness from its institutions is trifled with.

As these examples suggest, the culture of lying occupies an odd dual status in American life.

On the one hand, it is a reality that works, at least in the political sense. Media-validated lies define what we take to be the nation's experience. They are accepted as facts of life, and people routinely act with reference to them. Thus, while the lies involved may be easy to shoot holes in intellectually, they're usually impossible to dislodge politically. Once put out by the press, the fabrications take on a life of their own. Thus, today Americans are still bemused by FDR's Great Depression myth even though they know that the 1930s weren't like that at all. They still buy into the big corporation's myth that it's a creature and apostle of the free market. People still speak anxiously of Barry Goldwater as a man who might well have involved the country in a terrible land war in

Southeast Asia; of defeated Reagan Supreme Court nominee Robert Bork as an enemy of minority rights; of withdrawn Clinton Assistant Attorney General nominee Lani Guinier as an opponent of representative democracy and majority rule.

On the other hand, the credibility of the culture of lying is practically nil. In the view of the large majority of the American people, the public discourse is a pasticcio of cheesy fabrications, the highest officials in the land routinely lie to the public they're supposed to serve, and fundamental processes of communication and answerability that make liberal democracy a reality have broken down. What's more, they're mad as hell about it. Public opinion surveys reveal massive public distrust of the elites and institutions involved in the culture of lying. The growth of this alienation is arguably the single most dramatic measured change in American attitudes since the advent of modern random-sample opinion polling after World War II. The following tables, from surveys by the University of Michigan, tell the story in a nutshell:

Question: I don't think public officials care much about what people like me think.

	1960	1970	1980	1990
Agree	15%	47%	52%	64%
Disagree	73%	50%	44%	23%

Question: Would you say that the government is pretty much run by a few big interests looking out for themselves or that it is run for the benefit of all people?

	1964	1972	1982	1992
Few big interests	29%	33%	61%	76%
Benefit of all	64%	38%	29%	20%

Question: Do you think that quite a few of the people running the government are a little crooked, not very many are, or hardly any of them are crooked at all?

	1958	1970	1980	1990
Quite a lot	24%	32%	47%	50%
Not many	44%	49%	41%	41%
Hardly any	26%	16%	9%	9%

The entire range of American institutions has felt the sting of this growing mistrust. The public schools that used to be the pride of the nation have become its shame; the chemical industry that we once prized as a source of scientific progress and better living is now feared as a generator of toxic side effects. But above all it's been top politicians and journalists who have attracted the negative feelings.

Question: I am going to name some institutions in this country. As far as the people running these institutions are concerned, would you say you have a great deal of confidence, only some confidence, or hardly any confidence at all in them?

1973*				1993*			
Institution	*Great deal*	*Only some*	*Hardly any*	*Institution*	*Great deal*	*Only some*	*Hardly any*
1. Medicine	54	39	6	1. Military	42	45	11
2. Science	37	47	6	2. Science	38	47	6
3. Education	37	53	8	3. Medicine	39	51	9
4. Organized religion	35	46	16	4. Supreme Court	37	52	13
5. Military	32	49	16	5. Major companies	21	63	12
6. Supreme Court	31	50	15	6. Organized religion	23	50	25
7. Financial insts.	32†	54†	11†	7. Education	22	58	18
8. Major companies	29	53	11	8. Financial insts.	15	57	26
9. Executive branch	**29**	**50**	**18**	**9. Executive branch**	**12**	**53**	**32**
10. Congress	**24**	**59**	**15**	**10. Television**	**12**	**51**	**37**
11. Press	**23**	**61**	**15**	**11. Press**	**11**	**49**	**39**
12. Television	**19**	**58**	**22**	12. Organized labor	8	53	32
13. Organized labor	16	55	26	**13. Congress**	**7**	**50**	**41**

* Responses are in percent.
† Responses to this item are from 1975, the first year the Michigan survey queried respondents about financial institutions.

Not only do politicians and the press stand lower in the public's regard than most other groups and institutions, but in an era of generally declining public esteem for institutions, they've fallen the farthest. And the few institutions that have risen in public esteem—the military, or science—are the ones with the narrowest connection to politics and journalism.

Confidence gainers and losers, 1973–1993

Net aggregate change in high and low esteem ratings

1.	Military	+15
2.	Supreme Court	+2
3.	Science	0
4.	Major companies	–9
5.	Organized labor	–14
6.	Medicine	–18
7.	Organized religion	–21
8.	**Television**	**–22**
9.	Education	–25
10.	**Executive branch**	**–31**
11.	Financial insts.	–32
12.	**Press**	**–36**
13.	**Congress**	**–43**

This sharp falloff in public confidence in the press reflects a spreading feeling that journalists and the media are contentious, unfair, inaccurate, and under the thumb of powerful institutions, according to a survey by the Gallup organization for the Times-Mirror Center for the People and the Press in 1989.

Question: In presenting the news dealing with political and social issues, do you think that news organizations deal fairly with all sides, or do they tend to favor one side?

Deal fairly with all sides	28%
Tend to favor one side	68%
Neither, don't know	4%

Question: In general, do you think news organizations get the facts straight, or do you think that their stories and reports are often inaccurate?

Get facts straight	54%
Inaccurate	44%
Neither, don't know	2%

Question: In general, do you think news organizations are pretty independent, or are they often influenced by powerful people and organizations?

Pretty independent   33%
Influenced by powerful   62%
Neither, don't know   5%

Question: As I read from a list, tell me whether or not you feel this group often influences news organizations in the way they report the news. [*Answers in percent*]

	Yes, influences	No, does not	Don't know
Business corporations	71	23	6
Conservatives	48	40	12
The federal government	74	21	5
Catholics	28	60	12
Jews	25	61	14
Liberals	52	37	11
Advertisers	71	24	5

In short, mistrust of politicians and journalists as conspirators in a system of public manipulation, once confined to a tiny ideological fringe, has entered the mainstream of American politics. Today it is associated with middle-of-the-road political values and majority sentiments and is rapidly rearranging the landscape of national politics. By 1992 it had become robust enough to be a credible base for a number of presidential campaigns. Ross Perot, who translated strong antipolitician, antipress, antideficit appeals into an astonishing 19 percent of the popular vote in the general election against Clinton and Bush, developed a distinctive center-right brand of a pro-constitutionalist, anti-culture-of-lying politics. Jerry Brown, the former California governor who campaigned largely on the claim that he didn't have conventional financial support and campaign staffing, did very well with a different strain of anti-culture-of-lying politics in the liberal-to-left range of the spectrum. This same mood was expressed by the passing of referendums in fourteen states to limit the number of terms in office elected representatives may hold.

The media themselves, of course, routinely deny the thesis I am propounding here and the public alienation that reflects it. They insist that they are in the business of purveying true and objective reports about significant events. They vehemently reject the notion that they are foisting a manipulative alternative reality on the public. They resent any judgment that their behavior might be undermining constitutional values. They *like* democracy and constitutionalism, they say; the role of the press as they see it is to be the servant and enabler of democracy.

This view of journalism as an objective mode of discourse—and its corollary, the image of the journalist as an observer and reporter *who has no point of view*—is the emblem and product of a historic shift that took place in the news business toward the end of the nineteenth century and that continues to characterize it roughly a hundred years later.

Previously, the news firm had been primarily in the business of selling information to readers. As part of their effort to gain and keep readers, many publications developed, owned up to, and sometimes even flaunted special points of view—Democratic or Republican, Protestant or Catholic, upscale or downscale.

However, with the rise of a mass urban society and the new consumer product manufacturing corporation, the underlying economics of the news business changed. Now news firms began to derive a rapidly growing share of their revenues from advertising sales. By World War I an average of three-quarters of news firm revenues came from ad sales, up from two-fifths a generation earlier. The nature of the news product underwent a corresponding change. Advertisers, wanting to reach the largest possible audiences, sought media that evaded audience-limiting points of view and stressed universalistic, audience-increasing postures. The news media quickly adapted to the needs of their biggest customer. Thus was born the concept of news as a story about crisis and of journalism as a purely factual discourse without point of view.

There is no such thing, of course. To observe or speak or think, in private or public, is to exercise a point of view. Thus, when the media stopped selling information to customers and started selling audiences to advertisers, they entangled themselves in a lie. They adopted a new point of view, the one embodied in the crisis-and-emergency-response scenario and the business strategy behind it, while pretending that they had abandoned point of view altogether.

Today, reflecting this institutional lie, working journalists have a divided and incoherent view of their role in society. On the one hand, they repeat—with more or less sincerity—the standard myths about objectivity. On the other, despite these professions of faith, nearly all journalists have a nagging, fugitive, contrary awareness of a reality that is sharply at odds with the myth. Most of the time this fugitive awareness is kept bottled up inside. Once in a while it is expressed, as it was with rare candor in an editorial by the *Washington Post* in the fall of 1981.

The occasion for the *Post*'s burst of self-revelation was a bitter little controversy touched off by an item in the *Post*'s Ear column reporting that President Jimmy Carter had bugged and tape-recorded the White House's official guest residence, Blair House, during the transition period when President-elect Ronald Reagan and Mrs. Reagan were staying there as the Carters' guests. According to Ear, the tapes revealed that Mrs. Reagan was irritated by what she perceived as the Carters' slowness or reluctance to leave the White House. The Carters were furious at the story, denied it hotly, and threatened legal action. In the editorial in question, the *Post* was making its official response to the brouhaha.

> There are a lot of "we's" at the *Washington Post*, but the one you are about to hear from comes about as close as you can get to being the basic, collective "we"—the voice of the *Washington Post*, speaking for the *Washington Post*. . . .
>
> Mr. Carter and Rosalynn Carter are upset about an item that ran in The Ear column last week. That item, which was accurately sourced, made a relatively modest point that had, nonetheless, a momentous implication for those who read it casually. The point was that a story was *circulating* (various unnamed hearers of it were alluded to) that Blair House had been "bugged" while the Reagans were staying there. . . .
>
> It is one thing, however, to read that item to say that such a tale is circulating and being given currency by estimable public figures who repeat it—and quite another to conclude from this that the place was in fact bugged and that the Carters did in fact perpetrate such a scheme. We weren't there. But everything we know about the presidency of Jimmy Carter suggests otherwise, that it was false. . . .
>
> [I]t always did seem to us and still does—especially as the values involved are being eroded in present-day Washington—that

Jimmy Carter was courageous and right in his refusal to play the bugging-taping game, in his insistence on rejecting the precedents for White House invasions of . . . privacy. . . . Mr. Carter's distinction in this area was real and it was rare, and he can hardly be blamed for wishing to see it maintained.

Perhaps it is foolish to expect people to read newspapers with rabbinical or juridical care, to sift out the fair from the unfair or the justified from the unjustified inferences that can be drawn from a collection of words, even when those words don't add up to what an angry subject thinks they do. The best we can do here, because we feel as strongly as Mr. Carter does about the importance of what he tried to do on this score while he was in office, is to be as blunt and clear about what that Ear item said as we know how. It said there was a rumor around. *There was.* Based on everything we know of the Carter instinct and record on the subject, we find that rumor utterly impossible to believe.

In other words, the *Post* was admitting that it publishes, without correction or other caution, news reports based on statements that it believes to be untrue. The *Post* was saying that it considers such reports to be up-to-standard journalism requiring no apology or correction or other remedial action. This is, in essence, what I am saying in this book. I am arguing that, precisely like the Ear column but on a much more massive scale, the news media routinely write up as real news actions and sentiments that they believe to be fabrications.

The difference between my view of the process and the *Post*'s concerns the moral status and political consequences of the practice. The *Post* seems to think that there's nothing wrong with printing news items making damaging assertions it believes to be untrue without giving some meaningful indication of that belief. I, on the other hand, am convinced that the practice is very wrong, that its negative consequences have extended a blight across the entire landscape of national life, and that American journalism is in acute need of rethinking and reform as a result.

Before getting on with the main body of this book, I'd like to say a few words about where I and my argument are coming from.

For one thing, the ideas in these pages are very much the product of personal experience.

They didn't start out that way, to be sure. My intellectual involvement with news began almost thirty years ago in the ivory towers of Harvard University, where I wrote a Ph.D. thesis on the politics of the press and, in particular, on the way the news genre itself, as opposed to the liberal or conservative politics of journalists, shapes public opinion and current events. A decade later, the thesis having evolved into the first draft of a book, it was clear that my premise was right; the genre *is* a key to the behavior and influence of the press. However, it was also clear that interviews, observation sessions, analyses of news texts, historical study, and other research methods I'd used had cast little light on the subject and that I had surprisingly little to say. I dumped the manuscript in a cardboard box, returned the advance to my publisher, and having learned that I liked doing journalism better than political science, quit my academic career and joined the staff of *Fortune* magazine.

Over the decade that followed, I worked as a writer, editor, Washington bureau chief, and, for two fascinating and fateful years, as a corporate communications staffer for the Ford Motor Company. Up close and personal, I found, journalism was not at all what it had seemed from the outside. In the media world, news events usually had a double identity. On the surface there was a made-up public story put out for the purpose of manipulating others in ways favorable to the story makers. Behind that was another story, known to those immediately involved and to outsiders with the knowledge to decode it, concerning the making of the public story and the private objectives it was meant to advance. The two stories, or realities, were often wildly at odds with each other. In the real world, the role of the press was to promote public illusions and private privilege.

This, I eventually realized, was the insight that had eluded me at Harvard. And the practical experience that enabled me to discern this reality also enabled me to test it. As I pondered the odd, disconcerting falseness of the news, I began to see connections with other striking patterns I observed in the news business—the strongly dominant role of the editor, for example, or the low level of self-consciousness of most news workers.

This book's basis in personal experience will manifest itself, in the pages to come, in frequent references to my own career. This goes counter to the prevailing practice in serious nonfiction writing, I'm aware, but it seems to me that I have little choice in the matter. It would be both absurd and misleading to write in an objective and impersonal voice, as if I hadn't been a journalist and hadn't learned from my experience.

Is my experience idiosyncratic? I would insist that it is not. As a writer and editor, I have worked closely with dozens of other writers and editors in a variety of publications. As a student of the media, I have met and interviewed scores of journalists and analyzed hundreds of news stories. There is, as I think about it, almost no relationship I haven't had with journalists: I have had close friendships with them, been married to them, been divorced from them, benefited from their patronage, suffered under their abusive supervision, brought them under my own wing as protégés, read their novels, corrected their mistakes, puzzled over their behavior, stayed up all night with them to close a story, called them to ask where the manuscript was, avoided taking their calls asking where *my* manuscript was, dealt with them as a source while working in a big company's public relations department, and so on ad infinitum.

Having kept company with journalists in such a variety of ways, I believe that my experience as a journalist is every journalist's experience. It isn't precisely identical with others', to be sure, but it is substantially similar. I feel well justified in writing about journalism on the basis of personal experience, and I expect that journalists reading this book will recognize much, though of course not all, of their experience in mine. In a sense, the culture-of-lying thesis is simply a distillation of the journalist's actual experience into a coherent picture of the social and political role of the press.

This book's grounding in personal experience also gives it an unusual time frame—not the two- or three-year slice of recent history that we normally think of as the present, but the entire three-decade period in which I've been studying or practicing journalism. My objective in writing the book has been to use the best material from the whole period, provided that it still seems typical of the way things work now. Readers will find events from the Clinton and Bush years cheek by jowl with stories from my reporting days in the 1970s and from academic research I did in the 1960s. An entire chapter explores the rhetoric of a thirty-year-old news story because it's an outstanding example of spot news writing and because time's passing affords a better perspective on the event involved.

A second thing that needs to be said about the origins of this book is that it also leans heavily on scholarly research. An insight is one thing, a thesis quite another. What made the latter possible in this instance was a rich trove of recent scholarship concerning media and related subjects. Just as many journalists will recognize the personal experiences I've drawn on, people who know this burgeoning literature will also find in these pages much that's familiar. Indeed, as it has taken shape, the notion of a media-enabled culture of lying can almost be described as a synthesis of most of the major strands of media-related research and criticism in recent decades.

Foremost among my intellectual IOUs stands the debt I owe to what in my opinion is the first really important book about media in America, Daniel Boorstin's sprightly, original critical history, *The Image*, written when Eisenhower was president and published the year Kennedy was inaugurated. It is as fresh and full of insight in Bill Clinton's nineties as it was then. Anyone interested in further reading in this subject is urged to begin with this outstanding piece of historical scholarship and cultural criticism. Boorstin, who coined the excellent term *pseudo-event*, was the first serious student to draw attention to the fabricated, manipulative, dishonest quality the news media introduced into American politics and culture. My goal in writing this book has been to follow in Boorstin's footsteps and carry the conversation he started a sentence or two forward.

Among other bodies of research and writing on which the culture-of-lying thesis draws, I want to mention the following particularly:

- Sociological studies of the behavior and attitudes of reporters, editors, and newsmakers. Books by Leo Rosten, Douglass Cater, Edward Jay Epstein, Herbert Gans, Leon V. Sigal, Gaye Tuchman, Stephen Hess, Robert and Linda Lichter and Stanley Rothman, and many others have provided an informational and analytic point of departure without which my own analysis of the dynamics of media-invited, media-validated lying would have been impossible.

• The massive literature that, through traditional criticism and modern content analysis, helps define news as a genre. I benefited enormously from the rhetorical theorizing of critic Wayne Booth; the social science studies of Todd Gitlin, Michael Robinson, Thomas McClure, and Robert Patterson; the book-length critiques of journalists like Edith Efron and Peter Braestrup and critics like Noam Chomsky; and the occasional writings of Edwin Diamond, Ken Auletta, Dorothy Rabinowitz, and other working media critics. Thanks to these many writers, we have become as familiar with the principles and patterns of the news genre—for instance, with the fact that news focuses on crisis and emergency response or that political news focuses on the horse-race issue of who's ahead and who's behind—as we are with Newton's laws or the table of the elements.

• The ebullient outpouring of historical writing that has given the serious student of media such a rich resource and daunting task. I refer not just to the scores of biographies and memoirs and institutional histories, on which I have drawn frequently, but also to the profoundly interesting and important historiography of the corporation, advertising and public relations, political and social modernization, and the late nineteenth- and early twentieth-century Progressive-era context in which these emerged—research pioneered by figures as diverse as business school professor Alfred D. Chandler, left-wing historian Gabriel Kolko, and neoconservative political theorist Jeffrey Tulis.

The culture-of-lying thesis also incorporates key ideas from the news criticism of both left and right. Along with left-wing theorists of media, I take the view that the late-capitalistic nature of the modern news industry—in particular the fact that the news firm's business rests primarily on selling audiences to advertisers rather than selling information to readers or viewers—is a root source of the culture of lying. A century ago the alliance between news and advertising remade the news story in the image of advertising. As a result, the news media empower sellers vis-à-vis consumers and officials vis-à-vis citizens.

The notion of a media-assisted culture of lying shares with conservative perspectives the view that journalism undercuts established authority. In my opinion, the advertising-oriented crisis-and-emergency-response story that fixes the media's attention so firmly on the actions and agendas of high officials, thereby empowering them, also interposes between officials and the public the intellectual mediation of the news story and the news worker. The media empower high officials, but on the media's terms. Officials pay a stiff price for the political bounties they derive from journalism.

A final point about where I'm coming from: While I am a critic of media and media politics, I am not a media basher. My sympathies lie with the journalist, and not only because I am myself a journalist and proud of it. Indeed, I believe that the journalist is the archetypal figure in modern society. His fate reflects the fate of democracy.

I take it for granted that man is a political and social being with a profound need to go forth into the community and its institutions, participate in their affairs, seek personal fulfillment in the making of a shared destiny, and in short act as a citizen. More than any other occupational type, the journalist enacts, empowers, and dignifies the private person's public role. Day in and day out, he or she goes into the world to observe, respond, think, and communicate about events of general interest—not as an expert or under color of any special authority, but precisely as a nonexpert and layman.

If, as I will be arguing, the journalist in our time is trapped in a dual role as both victim and victimizer, he is not alone in suffering this fate. The crisis of modern journalism is not a problem generated by a small group of malefactors making trouble, with everyone else an innocent victim. The journalists, while no angels, are hardly the only villains of the piece. The misdeeds they perpetrate are nurtured by the active cooperation of newsmakers and the passive connivance of readers and viewers. The drama that is the culture of lying involves us all.

Thus, though there is much about the news business that

invites dismay and demands reform, we should resist the temptation to simply denounce and diminish, and we should seek the calm and compassionate understanding that can be the prelude to reform. What is at stake here is nothing less than the fate of liberal democracy, constitutionalism, and indeed, true politics itself. In the concluding chapter I will suggest a number of ways in which journalism could be extricated from its unhappy status as the enabler and bearer of a culture of lying and reunited with its proper destiny as a pillar of liberal ideals. I do this, not because I expect a revolution in our journalism and politics anytime soon, but because I believe that in a situation as bad as the one we're in, people who are serious about liberal and democratic values have little choice but to think in terms of a radical reformation even if the chances of its happening are poor. The hope for journalism today is the same as the hope for liberal democracy itself—that the eclipse of the liberal spirit that has made the past century an often dark age will pass and that a rebirth of liberal, democratic, and yes, journalistic ideals will dissipate oppression in the century ahead much as these same ideals suddenly blossomed on the North American continent among the colonies of a distant autocrat during the decades leading toward 1776 and 1787.

Such a renaissance would involve large and complex institutional reforms, but the central change required would be a personal one, a matter of the heart. The culture of lying is, at bottom, the product of journalists' *self-censorship*. Newsmakers' lies rarely fool the journalists covering them, at least not for long; as I'll explain in a later chapter, the journalist has a powerful, little-known ability to figure out what the newsmaker is up to. The culture of lying is created by journalists' failure to tell stories that adequately reflect their experience as observers of events and gatherers of information. Curbing the culture of lying would thus entail no radical remaking of the journalist's skills or knowledge. It would demand only the rediscovery of the journalist's God-given need to be true to himself and a redoubling of his commitment to telling the story that is present in his experience.

CHAPTER 2

Pulitzer's Revolution

There's nothing accidental about the tendency of news to promote an illiberal and undemocratic politics. The genre was the
product of a broad movement in American civilization that, toward
the end of the nineteenth and in the early years of the twentieth
century, rejected most of the Founding Fathers' view of man and
society in favor of a new politics grounded in concepts adapted
from the physical and natural sciences and intimately connected
with the emergence of the corporation, urban society, and the
modern university. At the core of this transformation was a sharp
narrowing of the sense of citizenship and of the individual's relationship to society and a radical expansion of the centralized planning, management, and manipulation of human affairs. Besides
news, these same currents gave rise to other major modern institutions, including advertising and public relations, the manageri-
al/interventionist state, and the activist presidency.

The George Washington and Henry Ford of the revolution that
brought these changes to journalism was a self-made genius

named Joseph Pulitzer. Today the Pulitzer name is famous because of the program of prizes for journalistic excellence administered by Columbia University—and also because it adorns the building on the Columbia University campus that houses the Graduate School of Journalism, which Pulitzer's endowment brought into being in 1913. These are peculiarly inappropriate monuments, however, to a man who didn't go to college, had no special training in journalism, and was no pillar of responsible society. He was sui generis, a loner who did things his own way, unrespectable, controversial, reviled, rebellious—and, as I said, the man who, practically single-handedly, founded modern journalism.

Pulitzer (the first syllable is pronounced "pull," not "pew") was born in 1847 near Budapest into a comfortable bourgeois family that was shattered, during his teens, by the death of his father and his mother's remarriage. Joseph left home at seventeen, shipping out to Boston to join the Union army, the only military force represented in Europe that would have the scrawny youth. During his year in uniform, Pulitzer saw little action but lots of anti-Semitism (his paternal grandfather was Jewish, his mother Catholic), and after Appomattox the young non-English speaker made his way to St. Louis. There Pulitzer's skill at chess brought him to the attention of liberal publisher (and soon-to-be U.S. Senator) Carl Schurz, who offered him a job as a reporter on his German-language *Westliche Post*. Pulitzer, knowing nothing of journalism but needing work, said yes.

It was a match made in heaven. Pulitzer was an outsider given to sharp resentment of in-groups yet also intensely interested in social acceptance and success. Journalism was a magnificent way to pursue both motives. Covering the Missouri state capital for Schurz and Washington, D.C., for the *New York Sun*, he became a canny insider. He was elected to the Missouri legislature, married into the socially prominent family of Jefferson Davis, even won a seat in Congress (he resigned before his term was out). As an outsider Pulitzer developed muckraking news stories that exposed wrongdoing in high places and found large audiences. Not least, he parlayed his journalistic and social talents into a newspaper arbitrage business, acquiring and reselling an equity position in Schurz's paper for a thirty-thousand-dollar profit. With part of this money, he bought two failed papers, merged them as the *St. Louis Post-Dispatch*, quickly pushed his partner out, and held the property for the rest of his life. It was providing him with the income and social position of a rich man by the time he was thirty-five.

Then, on a spring day in 1883, while passing through New York City with his wife and children on the way to a vacation in Europe, Pulitzer learned that the *New York World*, a respectable Democratic paper that was operating in the red, was for sale. A few days later it was his for a $346,000 note payable in two years. Pulitzer canceled Europe, installed his family in a rented town house on Gramercy Park, and got to work attracting the readers who would provide the cash to pay for it all. The result was a revolution in the scale and nature of American journalism.

When Pulitzer bought the *World*, it had a daily circulation of some 11,000 and a Sunday circulation of 16,000. A year later the circulation had roughly quadrupled, the press run hitting 50,000 on weekdays and 60,000 or more on Sunday. In May 1885, two years after Pulitzer's advent, daily circulation was 125,000, and the Sunday circulation was 153,000.

Having engineered a tenfold increase in the *World*'s readership, making it roughly as large as the biggest newspapers in America's biggest city, Pulitzer, shifting into high gear, effortlessly blew past them. By 1895, twelve years after taking over at the *World*, Pulitzer had raised his combined average daily circulation to 540,000 and Sunday circulation to 450,000. On his twentieth anniversary as owner, the *World*'s combined daily circulation was 725,000, and its Sunday circulation was in excess of half a million. Over his career, in short, Pulitzer brought about a seventyfold increase in the size of his own newspaper and a fivefold increase in the size of the biggest newspaper in America.

He did it by making his audience feel the whole world was watching. From day one Pulitzer's policy was to stop writing stories about events in their institutional contexts and to start writing stories that would directly engage the values and the feelings of the people among whom Pulitzer was seeking his audience.

For example, the day before Pulitzer became the *World*'s owner, the newspaper's first page, forbiddingly dense with words and type, included a column entitled "Brooklyn News," in which the first item was a wordy note about the plans afoot in the

Brooklyn Common Council for a big celebration of the opening of the Brooklyn Bridge, scheduled for two weeks later. The item anticipated this event in the stuffy procedural language of government, naming the ten kinds of organizations and people who would be welcome to join the parade but neglecting to mention the event's date or the fact that President Chester Arthur and several state governors would be participating.

Two weeks later the Brooklyn Bridge opened. The *World* that day was dominated by a dramatic picture stretching across the first page and a story filling three columns describing the political, engineering, and human drama behind the making of this civic wonder. The page fairly demands to be read. One's eye is drawn by the heavily perspective line of the bridge's deck as it arcs across the page into Brooklyn in the distance at left. One's attention is piqued by the promise of a dramatic human story of tragedy and triumph behind the cutting-edge engineering achievement. One's interest is also attracted by the suggestion, implicit in the scale and emotional intensity of the page, that the bridge's opening and the newspaper's coverage added up to an experience most New Yorkers would now have in common to react to and talk about.

In short, Pulitzer was taking events out of their official context and framing them in stories with a sharp dramatic focus that suggested intense public interest. He achieved this effect by incorporating into journalism the elements of drama. What previously had been a sober eyewitness account of an institutionally defined event now acquired character, action, and plot. There were villains and heroes. Stories had beginnings, middles, turning points, endings. Not least, there was spectacle, thanks to the growing use of illustrations and dramatic graphic formats and the reporters' growing attention to colorful facts. In short, stories about constitutional events gave way to narratives of action directly reflecting the hopes and fears of the audience.

A story in the *World*, one of Pulitzer's editors remarked, involved "discovering some public good that can be accomplished and accomplishing it." When Pulitzer bought the *World* and discovered the Brooklyn Bridge about to open, for example, he quickly initiated a series of editorials to pressure the city fathers into backing down from a planned five-cent toll and letting both pedestrians and vehicles cross the East River gratis. Later, Pulitzer began a promotional campaign built around the Statue of Liberty, the eventual construction of which was paid for by donations from the *World*'s readers. Emma Lazarus's "Give me your tired, your poor, your huddled masses" was the first line of the winning entry in a contest the *World* sponsored to pick a dedicatory poem to be inscribed on the pedestal.

In sum, Pulitzer's strategy for attracting readers boiled down to creating materials that immediately interested a lot of people and that created the further suggestion that the whole world was watching—that there was something in the *World* for everyone and that by scanning the paper, a New Yorker wasn't merely accessing interesting information but doing what everyone else was doing and so connecting with others and the urban community.

Soon Pulitzer institutionalized these appeals in the brilliant, complex masterstroke of journalistic invention that is the front page.

Newspapers, of course, had always had a first page, but until the end of the nineteenth century it was not sharply differentiated from the other pages. All the pages, including the first, were locked into a rigid format in which column rules—the lines demarcating the vertical spaces in which the text is presented— ran the length of the page, separating columns from one another on the page and wedging all the lines tightly together in the bed of type to keep it from falling apart during printing. As a result, texts and heads were limited to one column in width, and the news assumed a largely epistolary form. Items began at the top of the leftmost column of the first page and, in early newspapers especially, continued—like a letter—item after item, separated in most cases by a simple head or horizontal rule, until they came to the end of the last item at the bottom of the rightmost column of the last page.

Newspapers acquired a front page in the modern sense as a result of the appearance of the stereotype rotary press after the Civil War. In this new technology, particularly suited to newspapers with large circulations, the actual bed of type is used only to create a mold from which a metal plate that duplicates the type is made. The plate is given a cylindrical shape and mounted on the press, where it prints a continuous sheet in a process that turns out some ten times more copies per hour than the older technology could. Since column rules aren't needed to give strength to the bed of type, lines can be more than one column wide and type can be used in any size, notably in heads. For the same reason illustrations could easily span more than one column.

As Pulitzer began exploiting this technology, the continuous, letterlike sequence of columns gave way to a hierarchically organized mosaic of freestanding graphic units. In real life events are events; their relative magnitude ("This is a big day," we say; "That's trivial," we argue) is in the eye of the beholder. But starting in the 1890s, Pulitzer's staff began attributing size and rank to stories by graphic means. By virtue of how they were laid out and where they ran, stories were made to appear big or small, sensationally exciting or utterly uninteresting.

Partly this was done by varying the dimensions of the story unit itself. The bigger and bolder the type a story's headline was set in, the more columns it stretched across, the more lines it contained, and the more subheads or decks that descended below it, the higher-ranking and bigger the story was. Further signaling a story's magnitude were the space it occupied, the illustrations that accompanied it, and the related stories ("sidebars") in its vicinity.

To specify the size and rank of stories even further, Pulitzer and his staff created a vocabulary of locations in the newspaper. At the top of the hierarchy stood the front page. The next highest-ranking address was the front page of an inside section; ranking a good deal below that were the back pages of sections; and at the bottom of the hierarchy were the inside pages of sections. Within the front page there was a further hierarchy of locations. The upper right-hand corner became the highest-ranking site, the upper left-hand corner the second highest, followed by all other sites "above the fold." The half of the page lying "below the fold" was the lowest-ranking front-page location.

This sizing and ranking of news involved making fine distinctions among events, and that in turn meant that events had to be brought into sharp dramatic focus. The emergence of the front page thus involved a reshaping of the news story itself. In particular, it led to the rise of the headline.

Before Pulitzer, stories usually ran under generic heads that broadly categorized the subject event, usually with a noun phrase. "Awful Event" was the head under which the *New York Herald* ran its story about the assassination of President Lincoln in 1865. Such heads, which kept to a low level the journalist's intrusion on and redefinition of the institutional event, were emblematic of the constitutionalist spirit of the old journalism.

In the 1890s Pulitzer began to substitute the modern headline, which consisted of a sentence with a subject, verb (usually active), and often an object. Rather than identifying a type of event, it tersely describes an action, with named people in a named place doing something specific.

Within stories, corresponding changes emerged. Previously, news stories had usually been written as chronological eyewitness accounts in which the narrator began at the beginning of the event and continued on to the end. Often what we today would consider the most newsworthy part of the story, or the lead, occurred in the middle or even toward the end of the story. An example is the *World*'s coverage of the speech made during the presidential campaign of 1884 by a New York minister who stigmatized the Democrats as the party of "rum, Romanism, and rebellion." The story reporting the speech described the campaign event as it happened, summarizing each of the speeches in the order in which they were made and finally getting around to quoting the inflammatory phrase in a late paragraph. The story's head: "Republican Rally"—hardly the way such an event would be covered today.

Pulitzer slowly phased out chronological narration in favor of the so-called inverted pyramid model for telling the news. News was now narrated as a list of facts in descending order of rank, with the highest-ranking fact being the lead paragraph that summarizes the event and brings it into sharp dramatic focus. Each subsequent sentence conveys more material in increasing fineness of detail and decreasing centrality to the event as defined in the lead paragraph.

The techniques of the front page reinforced the suggestion that the whole world is watching by applying the techniques of a type of speech classical rhetoricians called epideictic. Epideictic is the speech of the mass meeting and ceremonial occasion. Its purpose is to praise and blame, express shared values, and evoke a sense of community. The central method of such speech, Aristotle observed, is amplification. The speaker describes and dwells on those aspects of the person or action in question that he figures the audience will feel are praiseworthy or blameworthy. He doesn't attempt to reason about the nature of good and evil or weigh competing values or acknowledge alternative views; these are techniques suited to deliberative speech, the discourse of decision making and legislatures. He merely selects and amplifies according to his purpose and lets the audience's values and emotions do the rest.

Pulitzer's front page was a giant amplifier in all these senses. It turned news into a structure of crises, a standing epideictic cue that audience members have enough values in common to make a ranking meaningful and that the highest-ranking events hold very intense interest for all. It suggested that the newspaper has a special closeness to the people, one transcending the closeness of other institutions, including political institutions. It suggested that the values they shared were unproblematic, at least in the sense that their application to particular cases was clear and didn't require deliberation or the mediation of government or informal leadership.

The old, pre–Brooklyn Bridge journalism had also addressed social and political interests people had in common, but in a more reserved, less self-aggrandizing, more issue- and institution-oriented, more *constitutional* way. The old journalism had spoken to its readers as citizens, members of both a formal political society and (in many cases) an organized political party as well. It had embodied this sense of belonging on the part of its readers by covering public events in the terms and spirit of the institutions among which they occurred. The old journalism offered itself as a window on formal institutions. It engaged readers' sociability with information that reminded them they were citizens of a constitutional society and members of a political party and that enabled them to follow and participate in its formal affairs.

Pulitzer's new journalism, with its heavy overlay of communitarian story values, stood the old journalism on its head. It addressed, not the citizen and constitutionalist and partisan, but the private, prepolitical human being. Where the old journalism had invited its readers to step into, and renew their commitment to, constitutional and political processes, the new Pulitzerian journalism was inviting people to turn away from formal institutions and focus instead on the community evoked by the storytellers of the newsroom.

It was just the kind of communication the Founding Fathers had warned about. They had insisted that public opinion needed refining and that the job of leadership, formal institutions, and public education was to provide that vital service. History showed that in the absence of institutions that shape, inform, test, check, qualify, and validate popular views, public opinion degenerated into fleeting passions engendered by passing events and manipulated by unscrupulous demagogues, and self-government collapsed into tyranny. The founders meant to give the republic an immunity to this fate. They created varied institutions to connect officials with the most considered, most farsighted, stablest opinions of the public and to insulate them from momentary enthusiasms that would lead to the trampling of minority or individual rights and the sacrificing of future needs to present pleasures in a rush to do the impossible and please everyone always.

Everything the Constitution had done to make democracy safe for individual rights and prudent statecraft, Pulitzer's journalism was undoing. It took events out of their constitutional contexts. It focused on the near term. It stressed the emotional and the immediate rather than the rational and the considered. In was, in the new word people began applying to the *World*, sensational as opposed to constitutional.

The impact of Pulitzer's innovations is neatly illustrated by sociologist Michael Schudson's fascinating study of the evolution of news coverage of the constitutionally prescribed State of the Union Address during the nineteenth century. From 1801 through the Civil War, Schudson found, the leading newspapers simply reprinted the speech verbatim with little or no additional comment. The president, in effect, was allowed to speak for himself in the pages of the newspaper as he had been allowed to speak to the members of Congress.

After the Civil War, the pattern began to change. The war, the telegraph, and the railroad had made the reporter a much more important figure in the news business, and now he and his reportage began to have a higher profile in State of the Union coverage. The speech was still reprinted, but increasingly it was accompanied by a substantial news story in which the Washington correspondent reported the events of the first day of the new session of Congress, usually in a chronologically structured narrative. At the appropriate point in the chronicle, the story would note the way senators, representatives, and spectators in the gallery reacted to the president's message, which at that time the president conveyed to Congress in writing and which was read to the joint session by a clerk.

By 1910, reflecting Pulitzer's reforms, a radically different journalistic approach had taken hold. Gone were the verbatim reproduction of the president's speech and the meandering narrative of the first day of the congressional session. In its place was an inverted-pyramid news story, of the sort with which we are familiar today, about the State of the Union Address itself, representing the speech as a whole by means of what the journalists involved saw as its most newsworthy statement or theme. Thus, between the constitutional event in Washington and the reading public, there was now firmly interposed the reporter, the editor, and the news genre itself, which together defined a stage on which—and in terms of which—events now became visible and dramatically compelling to the American people and which focused intently on the words, deeds, and persona of the president.

Personally Pulitzer was no adversary of constitutional democracy. But like more and more Americans of the day, he had little attachment to century-old political ideas he had never studied in school. He believed, and not without reason, that the system created by the Founding Fathers had been profoundly corrupted by party politics and corporate bribery. As a result, Pulitzer believed, the old constitutional ways weren't something the country could simply carry on with. They had to be fought for and won back. That, Pulitzer insisted, was what his journalism was all about. The *World* would "fight for the people with earnest sincerity," the publisher promised. It would resist the "purse potentates," "expose all fraud and sham, fight all public evils and abuses," and be "truly democratic."

In fact, truly democratic and opposed to the power of purse potentates were the last things Pulitzer's journalism was. As the *World*'s ability to project powerful images of popular goods and evils grew and it found an ever bigger audience, Pulitzer's experiment began exerting an intensifying gravitational pull on, and itself started to come under the gravitational influence of, the other great emerging institutions of the age: the corporation and the state.

The modern corporation was invented in the final decades of the nineteenth century as an odd but effective marriage of the traditional business firm with modern technology and social science. At the core of this new institution was the revolutionary idea of management, or what the corporation's leading historian, Alfred D. Chandler, calls the "visible hand," the notion of bringing every element of the business enterprise under a rigorous centralized scientific scrutiny with a view toward creating new products, markets, methods, scales of operation, and efficiencies.

As the idea of management unfolded, there were major breakthroughs in fields from science to education as the founding fathers of the corporation invented mass production, modern budgeting and accounting, organized equity markets, and many other techniques and products we take for granted today. The corporation also achieved dominance, however, through a new, coolly manipulative, power-oriented approach to its relationships with the external political, economic, and social environment. What management's new efficiencies didn't accomplish by themselves, its aggressive way with people and popular institutions did.

From the outset, the corporation stood in a relationship to the larger society that was both easy and awkward. The easy part was that the corporation worked. The hard part was that the idea of a large, growing, centralized, capital-intensive, technology-based, scientifically managed enterprise clashed sharply with a key feature of the corporation's environment, which was characterized particularly by the rapid growth of often extremely competitive and highly unpredictable markets. The constitutional society that gave the corporation freedom to develop in ways of its own choosing also imposed on it the constraints and risks entailed by those markets.

From the beginning the new managers, emancipated from the

principled political economy of the Founding Fathers by the coolly rational social-science perspective of modern management, toiled ceaselessly to limit the uncertainty and danger of the market. Many of these efforts were bluntly traditional—cartels, threats and violence against competitors, mergers creating companies with dominant market shares, bribery of legislators and journalists. Other market-managing and -controlling ploys, however, were subtle and novel, particularly the two new strategies by which corporations worked to co-opt the news media's resources in support of their efforts: advertising and public relations.

Advertising had its origin in the rise of consumer product companies that developed efficient, high-volume manufacturing operations and suddenly found themselves eyeball to eyeball with the challenge of distributing and selling the torrents that came pouring off their production lines. The solution they came up with was the modern marketing operation, an imaginative blend of manpower, strategic savvy, and corporate communications. At the core of the exercise were brand names, corporate logos, trademarks, packaging, and advertising that positioned the product, created awareness of the producer, supported selling themes at the point of sale, reinforced customer satisfaction, sought to validate feelings of product loyalty, and attempt to erect barriers to entry by new competitors.

In the effort to put marketing information and images across, the new corporation faced two difficulties. One was the absence of a means of reaching people on the necessary vast scale and at efficient cost. The other was the mass audience's natural resistance to messages from large, distant, self-serving, obviously manipulative commercial organizations.

Pulitzer's journalism offered an excellent solution to both problems. It made vast numbers of people available on a daily basis. It reduced partisan segmentation of the market. Newspapers at the time were often overtly associated with, and sometimes covertly subsidized by, a political party, and though the *World* was a Democratic newspaper, Pulitzer's innovations were mainstays of the broader movement in American journalism toward nonpartisanship. Above all, its drama of crisis and community mobilization, suggesting that the whole world is watching, enabled advertising to persuade in a subtle new way.

The corporate marketers found that by presenting a seemingly descriptive message ("Ivory soap floats") in a medium perceived as being followed and accepted by the entire community, an advertiser could plant the suggestion that most people were seeing the ad, that most people cared about the product attributes it touted, that most people were feeling the tug of the ad's tacit offer to do business, that a lot of people may well be enjoying the product already. The advertiser relied on the individual's sociability—his inborn tendency to adopt perceived group norms, his innate human desire to fit in—to transform these neatly crafted images of community awareness and acceptance into behavioral realities. Pulitzer's journalism, in other words, enabled advertising to become a self-fulfilling prophecy, an image of community belief and activity that comes true because people believe that everyone in the community is following and responding to the medium in which the image appears.

The rapid growth of corporate product advertising around the turn of the century brought big changes to the news business Pulitzer was building. Newspapers had long carried classified ads and patent medicine pitches as a supplement to their core business of selling information to readers. Starting in the early 1880s, however, the traditional mix of revenues generated by advertising sales and revenues generated by reader sales shifted sharply. In 1880 about 65 percent of big-city newspaper revenues came from readers' purchases and 35 percent came from selling space to advertisers. By 1900 advertising revenues were 55 percent of the total, compared to 45 percent for reader-derived revenues. In 1920 the advertising share was more than 70 percent, and since then it has drifted above the 80 percent level.

There is no evidence that Pulitzer, when he first moved to New York and began creating the first modern American newspaper, anticipated this revolution in the structure of his business. He appears to have intended his sweeping innovations only as ways of strengthening the newspaper's appeal and increasing its audience. A dozen or fifteen years into his history-making experiment in Manhattan, however, Pulitzer had clearly become intensely advertising-conscious and was hard at work, not merely selling space, but making changes in his product for the purpose of boosting ad sales revenues. The appeal to Pulitzer wasn't only that the advertising market was large and growing but that it offered a way around the ferocious competition that characterized the New York newspaper market.

The entry in the 1890s of William Randolph Hearst into the New York media market, already crowded with over a dozen dailies, confronted Pulitzer for the first time not only with a competitor who used all of Pulitzer's own journalistic tricks but with one whose vast fortune and soaring political ambitions made him highly tolerant of the huge operating losses that flowed from his decision to cut newsstand prices to a penny a copy in search of bigger circulation. In 1898, for the first and only time in Pulitzer's experience as a newspaper proprietor, the *World* experienced a substantial loss. Creating and applying the devices of the front page was one of the central strategies by which Pulitzer sought to strengthen the *World*'s appeal to advertisers.

The transformation of newspapers from a reader-focused, reader-driven business into an advertiser-focused, advertising-driven business was a momentous event. Journalism slowly became less dependent on, and thus ultimately less responsive to, customer preferences expressed in the marketplace. Moreover, what connection with the audience news firms did retain shifted. Previously, in keeping with the nature of a consumer product business, they had focused on core news customers, the people strongly interested in news and willing to pay a high price for it. (In today's currency values, nineteenth-century newspapers charged a price in the range of fifty cents, a dollar, even two dollars a copy.) As they became more and more oriented to the special needs of advertisers for vast, distractible, suggestible audiences, the focus of the media shifted away from the core customer and a traditional product business, in which the quest for larger sales is subject to the constraint that the marginal transaction must be profitable. Now that the advertiser's presence freed the quest for circulation from that constraint, the media began to focus on the marginal customer, who, despite little interest in the news and little willingness to pay for it, was the building block of the ever-bigger audience sought—and paid for—by advertisers.

One result was a slow process of concentration and monopolization. Consumer product manufacturers and downtown department stores wanted to advertise to big audiences, the bigger the better. In search of their advertising patronage, newspapers lowered prices and spent heavily to build huge rate bases. As one newspaper emerged with the largest audience in its market category (morning or evening, upscale or mass), advertisers, seeking not only the largest audience but also the medium best able to sustain the illusion that the whole world was watching, converged on it. The runners-up in the competition for audience experienced a hemorrhage of market share, page sales, and cash flow until—often sooner rather than later—they were no longer able to stay alive. The fact that they might retain a substantial core of loyal readers wasn't enough to save them, since by now newspaper product prices had been driven by successful advertising-oriented media to a level far below that on which a reader-oriented newspaper could survive.

The demise of these otherwise often viable news media left the survivors to cope with the inherent volatility of retail advertising, new market segmentation patterns, and the rise of other media, notably television. Newspaper markets became more and more concentrated, and the media that survived became more and more disconnected from the reader.

Pulitzer's *World* itself succumbed to the process of concentration and attrition it had set in motion. After World War I the New York market divided into an upscale segment, dominated by the *Times* and the *Herald Tribune*, and a huge mass segment, dominated by the new *Daily News* and the Hearst papers. The *World*, which was positioned in the middle and suffered from weak leadership in the wake of the founder's death in 1911, slowly lost ground, finally collapsing in the depths of the Great Depression and being absorbed into a healthier newspaper, the *Telegram*.

The entente between the corporation and journalism also went forward on a second front: the corporation's efforts to script itself into a hero's role in the news genre's crisis-and-emergency-response scenario in the hope of making itself popular and winning the benefits and privileges emergency government could deliver. This second connection, initially known as publicity and now as public relations, was similar to advertising in its aims and strategy but different with respect to its means. Instead of putting the corporate message next to the news, the message was injected into the news.

As practiced by its earliest major exponent, a Princeton graduate and Progressive-era liberal named Ivy Ledbetter Lee, public relations began in the 1890s as an exercise in damage control. In a typical situation Lee would be retained by a railroad firm to handle the publicity involved in a train wreck. The railroads' instinct, then as now, was to minimize the bad news, keep journalists away from the accident site, and if possible, discourage any coverage. We are private business organizations with property and privacy rights, Lee's corporate clients wanted to say. Just now we don't choose to give the gentlemen of the press access to our private affairs. Today we would call this stonewalling.

Ivy Lee took the opposite tack. Contrary to the belief of some backward, self-serving business firms, he'd have his client say, we're a thoroughly modern social organization, and we acknowledge we're not just private property. We are invested with a public interest, and we are happy to own up to a public trust and social responsibility. In the case of this terrible accident, we're particularly anxious to make good on this obligation. It goes without saying that we'll do everything possible to enable the public and its representatives, the news media, to find out whatever they want to about the accident and to join us in satisfying themselves as to its causes and the steps needed to insure that such a thing never happens again.

Behind its defensive and reactive posture, public relations was an active, aggressive effort to gain positive advantages. It was, in effect, a political Trojan horse: Inside the seeming subordination of private rights to public needs, there was a concealed effort to turn the exercise of public authority to private advantage. In other words, the blurring of the distinction between public and private, superficially a source of benefit to the public, was intended as a means of extracting privilege from government.

In the case of the train wreck, for example, the advantage to be gained might be a public-private train safety investigation that would conclude that the railroad's procedures were up to snuff or that specified changes would eliminate any definable future risk. In other cases public relations efforts to co-opt the powers of the press and government to the sponsor's advantage achieved mind-boggling intricacy and scale. Consider, for example, the historic and today undeservedly obscure 1905 life insurance scandal, in which an inspired public relations campaign by the professional managers of the Equitable Life Assurance Company not only saved their power and jobs by diluting the voting power of the company's majority equity owner, who would have thrown them out if he could have, but induced government to protect the entire industry from ferocious competition by reorganizing it as a government-sanctioned, government-managed cartel.

It all began on a January night in 1905, when a tall, elegant, Harvard-educated Francophile millionaire and man about town named James Hazen Hyde threw a lavish costume ball in honor of his debutante niece. All New York society was present, Sherry's Hotel on Fifth Avenue was decorated to resemble the gardens at Versailles, the menu was sumptuous, and the festivities were an exercise in exuberant fin de siècle excess. At one point a celebrated French actress, borne into the room on a sedan chair by liveried footmen, stood to recite a poem about French-American amity and then performed a cancan on the table. The cost of the event was variously reported at $20,000 to $100,000, either way a lot of money.

The ball was a news story waiting to happen. The country was in the midst of a recession, wages were down, workers were being laid off, and a bank panic had recently cut many Americans off from their assets. Moreover, Hyde wasn't just any rich young dandy looking to throw a bash for his friends. He was a vice-president of the Equitable Life Assurance Society and a director of forty-eight companies the Equitable did business with. Later in the year, when he turned thirty, he was due to inherit a 51 percent controlling interest in the Equitable, which his late father had built into the second biggest life insurance company in America. When Sherry's presented Hyde with the bill, he in turn sent it to the Equitable to be paid as a business expense.

News of the party was leaked to the New York newspapers by James W. Alexander, president of the Equitable. Alexander was in the awkward position of being both Hyde's boss and soon-to-be subordinate. Rising to the bait, the press gave the party front-page coverage, lavishing attention on the wretched excess of it all and underscoring the irony that such indulgence should be taking place in an industry that prided itself on prudence, sobriety, and what the head of another big insurance company insisted were the industry's "missionary" responsibilities.

This self-made scandal gave Alexander the opening he sought. Moving with exemplary aggressiveness to deal with the crisis he'd created, Alexander promptly proposed to the Equitable's directors that Hyde be fired for "misconduct, incompetence, and misuse of funds." He also urged the board to preclude any possibility of Hyde's taking control of the company by enacting a new policy under which holders of life insurance policies would be entitled to vote for directors. The power of the equity owners would thereby be greatly diluted. Hyde would never take control of the company; Alexander, if all went well, could count on remaining at the helm for the rest of his career.

Journalists weren't the only people whose animal spirits were aroused by the *World*'s exposé. With the Equitable apparently in play and its management up for grabs, financiers such as Thomas F. Ryan and Jay Gould projected themselves into the picture, seeking alliances with the various factions and throwing their considerable weight behind the combatants' frantic efforts to get relevant parts of the government and other forces to intervene in their interest.

For most of the press, Hyde's French ball was a one- or two-day sensation. But for *World* reporter David Ferguson, who had independently been looking into rumors of corruption in the insurance industry, it was just the opening he'd been waiting for. The week after the story broke, Ferguson went to press with a shocking follow-up story describing for the first time the bitter inside struggle between Alexander and Hyde for control of the company. The Equitable denied the story and threatened legal action, but in vain. The *World* pressed on with its coverage, printing a copy of Alexander's charges against Hyde and demanding a full investigation by the state government. Several months later the New York State insurance superintendent gave the governor a secret report on the state of the industry, which the *World* got a copy of and printed verbatim.

The report was shocking by any standard. It showed a pattern of self-dealing, insider trading, conflict of interest, political bribery, and other abuses on a Brobdingnagian scale. Officers of the Equitable had routinely put personal funds into the same investments they were committing the company's millions to. Unaccounted millions were being spent to bribe legislatures and newspaper reporters across the country. The superintendent's report recommended a long list of reforms and seconded Equitable President Alexander's proposal that stock control of life insurance companies be abolished.

There followed the famous Anderson hearings of the New York State legislature, which, under the leadership of general counsel Charles Evans Hughes, put every significant figure in the life insurance industry on the stand and exposed in vivid detail the insensate aggressiveness with which this huge, fast-growing, highly profitable, blithely unprincipled industry had managed its affairs. The *World* and the rest of the press followed it avidly. By the time it was all over, Pulitzer's newspaper alone had run 128 separate editorials on the life insurance scandal.

The lives of nearly everyone involved were changed forever. All the top executives of all the existing life companies, including the Equitable's Alexander, resigned or were forced out in disgrace, many of them dying soon after and a few going to jail or living in exile. Hughes became the Sam Ervin of his day and with Pulitzer's enthusiastic support was speeded along the way to the state governorship and then to a seat on the U.S. Supreme Court. Least adversely affected was young Hyde, who resigned from the Equitable before the superintendent's report was completed and sold his stock position to Thomas F. Ryan at a healthy profit.

In the hearings' wake, the life insurance industry underwent a root-and-branch transformation. Previously it had been an innovative, fast-growing, lustily profitable collection of big, sophisticated companies that in a few decades had gone from being tiny enterprises to giants playing a major role in capital markets and expanding abroad as well. Suddenly this stellar aggregation of growth giants departed from the economic universe according to Adam Smith and became something almost unrecognizable. Equity ownership was eliminated in favor of the "mutual" idea, in which owners and profits don't exist and policyholders share in any operating surplus and vote for management. The companies, from having been decentralized, competitive, and innovative, became highly centralized bureaucracies whose products and prices were minutely controlled by state regulators. Growth continued, but at a reduced rate. Executive salaries and other benefits were cut back, reflecting the industry's new bureaucratic identity; security and stability became the great rewards for its employees. It became a model oligopoly, quiet, insulated from the customer, self-serving, stuffily respectable—a haven for graduates of the new business schools being established at Harvard and elsewhere.

The life insurance scandal of 1905, in short, showed how public relations and news management activities by private industry, amplified by the now-vigorous clout of the press, could turn constitutional society as a whole—not only the formal governmental process but the whole range of public policies and private behaviors that defined and maintained personal freedom, home rule, and the market economy—upside down to its special advantage. An opportune event, leaked to the press and publicized with energy, set in motion a process of revelation and investigation that ended in an exercise of emergency-style government that, despite the absence of a clear, coherently demonstrated, larger public purpose, established state control of entry, products, and pricing in a key industry, all in the name of business ethics and the public interest, and all in the actual benefit of the industry's professional management.

Meanwhile, across the Hudson River in Princeton, New Jersey, the uses and potentials of Pulitzer's front page were making an impression on a political scientist, university president, and wily liberal politician named Woodrow Wilson.

Wilson had built his career as a critic of the Constitution, particularly of Congress. His 1884 classic, *Congressional Government*, an excellent analysis that still deserves to be read, is a brilliant polemic against an institution he persuasively depicted as parochial, fragmented, meddlesome, leaderless, unanswerable, good at representing but bad at governing. The British Parliament, by contrast, Wilson believed, was good at both governing and representing because it unifies both power and responsibility in a government that can act but is answerable to backbenchers and, through them, to the people. The American system, Wilson argued, disperses governmental powers and renders government both ineffectual and out of touch. Wilson believed that the Constitution should be amended to give the United States a modified parliamentary system, which he hoped would be better able and more inclined to give the country the liberal social policies and state-assisted institution building that the ambitious reformer and social democrat favored.

As Wilson contemplated what Pulitzer's new journalism was making possible for the likes of the Equitable's cartel-minded managers, however, he began to reconsider his pessimism about the American system and his conviction that only fundamental, formal changes would do. Stimulated by the example of Theodore Roosevelt, whose career and strong presidency were in orbit at the time, Wilson began to conceive a way in which the country's traditional institutions might be given the powers and inclination to build the untraditional welfare state Wilson envisioned.

In 1908, twenty-four years after his first book, Wilson published a new volume on American democracy, *Constitutional Government*. A more radical change in attitude is hard to imagine. By now Pulitzer's new journalism had become the nation's standard, and the bright young political scientist had become the ambitious reform governor of New Jersey and the odds-on favorite to win the nation's top job in Washington, D.C. The new book celebrated a system in which the presidency had become a potent source of leadership and government had acquired a new ability to meet society's needs.

The disabilities created by the Constitution's dispersal of powers had been overcome, Wilson argued, by the recent evolution of the political parties and news media. With the support of the one and outreach of the other, Wilson argued, a president could create, within the Founders' framework, the equivalent of a prime-ministerial and parliamentary system. From his bully pulpit a president could mobilize the parties and public opinion, and through them the Congress, to take the actions a complex, fast-changing society required.

To a reader of Wilson's second book, the system it describes is easily recognizable as essentially the one that prevails today— just as a reader of the earlier book, while easily recognizing the Congress toward which we today have the same love-hate feelings as Wilson, doesn't recognize the ineffectual presidency Wilson describes.

At the heart of Wilson's new vision of constitutional politics was a radically altered presidency. As political scientist Jeffrey Tulis has explained in a fascinating recent study, the Wilsonian presidency—both the one Wilson wrote about in his second book and the one he conducted in the White House starting just four years after he published it—differed sharply from the office of Washington, Lincoln, McKinley, and Taft. It was, says Tulis, a *rhetorical* presidency in which Wilson routinely initiated and advocated new public policies, speaking over the heads of Congress to address the people as a whole.

Previously, as Tulis shows, presidents had avoided initiating and advocating policy proposals; their public speeches and statements dealt mostly with uncontroversial constitutional principles. By the same token they had avoided addressing the people directly or in person, or in a manner meant to stir them up, or on any matter involving a current issue of public policy. Traditionally presidents had communicated mainly with Congress and mainly through written messages. This practice had been inaugurated by George Washington in the conviction that the Constitution outlined a republican rather than democratic system of government and that under it an official's main allegiance was to the Constitution itself rather than to the people who elected him. Under the Constitution an official's job was to handle public business while respecting the coequality and independence of other officials and other branches of government. An official's job did not include mobilizing popular constituencies to manipulate other branches of the government.

The early republic's norm that officials were to speak decorously to one another, not demotically to the public, was so emphatic that when Congress drew up articles of impeachment against Andrew Johnson in 1868, one of the charges was that, by making a speaking tour of the country to advocate his program of reconstruction and attack its opponents, he had brought the presidency into "contempt, ridicule, and disgrace."

In this view of the Constitution, the press had the same standing as any member of the general public. It was entitled to observe the government's proceedings and report what public officials might say or do as part of the regular body of already public information it gathered together and made available to all and sundry. Just as officials refrained from speaking over their colleagues' heads to the general public, so did the press avoid giving public officials a special platform from which to make such pitches. In the era before Pulitzer invented the front page, the press presented information about recent events in a format that made no judgments about what the public thought.

Wilson's presidency was made possible by Pulitzer's journalism. With a press that emphasized political affairs and created a bully pulpit from which officials might address the masses over the heads of their constitutional colleagues, the rhetorical presidency became possible. The Wilsonian presidency and Pulitzerian journalism were mirror images of each other.

Thus, Wilson became reconciled to the Constitution once he understood that the press-assisted presidency would shift the American system to the emergency-power model. Superficially it would look like the constitutional system of yore, but under a patina of popular concerns, it would function in an autocratic manner by drawing attention to dangers warranting unilateral intervention by the president and a presidentially led Congress.

During his eight years as president, Wilson institutionalized his theory and explored what it meant in practical political terms. He built up the presidency by means of frequent policy-oriented speeches, a constant stream of special messages to Congress, an insistent quest for attention, an aggressive, self-serving idealism, a Manichean rhetoric dividing the world into a presidential party of light and an antipresidential force of darkness, and, of course, the war and presidential war leadership. During and just after the Wilson presidency, there were the formal institutional innovations that solidified presidential leadership of the legislative process, presidential control of the budget, and presidential management of the economy.

In policy terms Wilsonianism, true to the spirit of the progressive era as a whole, was ambivalence personified. There was a strong strain of social democracy and egalitarian reform. It was matched by a strong strain of self-promotion, militarism, authoritarianism, privilege, oligarchy, and oligopoly. Both elements of this politics have continued in a direct and unbroken line to our own time. Together they define the politics of news.

The new system of mobilizing journalism, manipulative advertising, monopoly-seeking public relations, and emergency-based presidential government worked because, behind the forms of an old-fashioned limited state based on rights and limits, it had created a mechanism for mobilizing the emergency powers of the state in support of a politics that used methods and served ends antithetical to those of the original constitutionalism. In effect Pulitzer & Company had engineered a hidden revolution that transformed the real politics of the nation while preserving an illusion of continuity. Into old constitutionalist forms had been poured a new, unconstitutionalist substance.

They were well aware of what they had wrought, excited by the notion of striking out on a course different from that set by the Founding Fathers, proud to be building a new kind of politics and economics for a new world of science, technology, and progress they were sure lay ahead. To Henry Adams, historian-intellectual and descendant of presidents, whose ironic autobiography, *The Education of Henry Adams*, is one of the monuments of American letters, the coming of a new age was a mock-glorious event that meant the passing of the world for which he felt fitted by his self-described nineteenth-century background. But for his best friend and neighbor on Lafayette Square, across from the White House, John Hay, a literary politician who had been an aide to Lincoln, married into a fortune, written Lincoln's biography, and built the American empire as a fin de siècle secretary of state, the coming of the new era evoked not a trace of irony or regret.

"Every young and growing people has to meet, at moments, the problem of its destiny," Hay declared in his eulogy for assassinated President William McKinley, which historian Martin J. Sklar describes as the Periclean oration of a new American society. The Americans, Hay asserted, had at last met up with their special destiny. "The 'debtor nation' has become the chief creditor nation. The financial center of the world, which required thousands of years to journey from the Euphrates to the Thames and the Seine, seems passing to the Hudson," he boasted. The first new nation was being born again. For Americans "the past is past, and experience vain."

> The fathers are dead; the prophets are silent; the questions are new, and have no answer but in time. . . . The past gives no clue to the future. The fathers, where are they? and the prophets, do

they live forever? We are ourselves the fathers! We are ourselves
the prophets!

As Pulitzer and his fellow titans prepared to make their exit, they
carefully finished off the new construction they had undertaken,
painted, and papered, brought the furniture back from storage,
policed the area, and painstakingly restored everything to its original appearance. For the new emergency state to work, for the
culture of lying to be believable, the nation had to be under the
impression that everything was working as it was meant to
and that the American system was in essence unchanged, albeit
updated in keeping with the needs of changing times. In the years
following Wilson's terms in the White House, Americans' awareness of the political meanings of the new journalism faded, and a
sense of the radical departure made by Pulitzer's generation was
stifled by a swelling drumbeat for the comforting myth that the
republic was returning to the ways of yore.

The theme of continuity was sounded aggressively by President Warren G. Harding when he coined the phrase "the Founding Fathers" and revived the malapropism "normalcy" itself.
(Harding, who rose to national office largely on the strength of the
"presidential" image he projected in the press, is considered by
many historians to be America's first pure media politician.) It
was echoed by the construction of the Lincoln and Jefferson
Memorials in Washington, D.C., in the 1920s and 1930s. It was
furthered when business leaders began evangelizing for free
enterprise even as their old and uninterrupted quest for antimarket subsidies and protections struck paydirt in Washington and in
many state capitals. To listen to both academic and popular inter-
preters of politics—from philosopher John Dewey or political scientist Arthur Bentley to journalist Walter Lippmann—the relationship prevailing among government, media, and the public was
just the same good old interest-group constitutionalism that the
Founding Fathers had put in place over a century earlier, updated
to reflect the faster pace and more advanced state of knowledge of
the twentieth century.

Within the journalistic sector this sense of normalcy was promoted by the notion that journalism is a profession, a notion
spread both in the self-descriptions of journalists and media firms

and, more importantly, in the rise of journalism schools and formal journalism education. In fact, it was and is and can be no such
thing, at least not in the important sense that there is a body of
proven expert scientific knowledge involved, as in medicine or
law. Journalism is inherently nonexpert, subjective, expressive,
personal, and contingent, like politics itself or like the novel. The
spread of the image of journalism as a profession was meant to
invest a newly powerful institution with the misleading but recon-
ciling and comforting aura that it is natural and that its practitioners are subject to a collective intellectual and ethical discipline.
The idea that journalism is a profession, in other words, was a
public relations flourish meant to conceal the true nature of the
enterprise, deflect criticism and attack, legitimate the industry,
and increase the new journalism managers' control over their
employees and subordinates.

Here, too, Joseph Pulitzer was the prime mover. But whereas
in creating news itself, he had been utterly sincere and engaged
to the limit of his awesome powers, in promoting the idea of a
professional journalism he tended to be cynical and hypocritical.
To Pulitzer the news was the product, journalism schools and the
accoutrements of professionalism just an exercise in public relations and media hype.

Pulitzer toyed with the idea of journalism education on and
off for two decades. Most of the time his interest was off. Ideologically Pulitzer was a liberal individualist. In his view, exemplified
by his own career, the journalist was essentially an amateur. He
observed and wrote about public affairs from the viewpoint and
with the powers and rights of a private citizen, no more and no
less. For such a person, Pulitzer and many others at the time
held, a broad liberal education was the correct training. The idea
that journalism should be viewed as a profession struck him as
grotesque. In 1879 in St. Louis, a Pulitzer editorial mocked the
idea of a professorship of journalism, which he considered "as
absurd . . . as . . . a professorship of matrimony, it being one of
those things of which nothing can be learned by those who have
never tried it."

Pulitzer's scorn for journalism education softened, however,
when his thoughts turned to celebrations to mark the anniver-
saries of his advent as a media mogul. He first took an interest in

the subject in 1892, when he was planning for the tenth anniversary of his purchase of the *World*. That year Pulitzer approached Seth Low, then the president of Columbia University, about the possibility of Pulitzer's endowing a college of journalism, which would have been the world's first. Low and his trustees weren't interested, and Pulitzer let the idea pass, though he did soon endow a modest annual lectureship to inform graduating seniors at Columbia about career opportunities in the news business.

A decade later, as Pulitzer made plans for his twentieth anniversary at the *World*, he approached Low's successor, Nicholas Murray Butler, with the same general notion of a Pulitzer-endowed school of journalism at Columbia. This time a deal was eventually consummated. But the nine years of often farcical contention between the two parties that preceded the completion of the two-million-dollar gift establishing the Columbia Graduate School of Journalism and a program of Pulitzer Prizes made it clear that Pulitzer was doing it for the personal fame and institutional legitimation and that he had little respect for the content or merits of the programs his money was bringing into being.

Soon after Pulitzer's benefaction was settled, the publisher in 1905 wrote an article attempting to define the purpose to be served by a special school of journalism. It wasn't to transmit technical journalism skills, Pulitzer argued; these, in his view, were best learned on the job. No, he said, the reason to have a journalism school is to instill in the fledgling journalist qualities of moral courage and devotion to the noncommercial duties of the news media. Journalism schools, Pulitzer argued, would do for prospective reporters and editors what military academies did for the physical courage of those destined for careers as military officers.

Pulitzer's advocacy of the Columbia journalism program as a school for moral courage was profoundly hypocritical. After all, if he felt the news media had become too commercial, he was in a perfect position to develop a strategy for making them less so, beginning with his own huge and highly commercial publication. By handing the task over to an academic institution that would have little of the power and knowledge needed to make changes, he was evading the problem under a pretense of addressing it. And as for strengthening journalists' moral courage and sense of social responsibility, Pulitzer's appreciation of these qualities was abstract at best. In real life he was a jealous, domineering boss, slow to delegate responsibility and quick to fire or otherwise punish employees who didn't do precisely what he told them to do. It is recorded that Pulitzer on a number of occasions came to blows with reporters in his employ.

When Pulitzer finally gave his money to Columbia for the journalism school, it was as a posthumous bequest, an act of resignation and despair on the part of a man who was profoundly alienated from the school he was endowing. After an initial and, as it turned out, premature announcement of Pulitzer's commitment to endow the school in 1903, the donor and his beneficiary fell into a bitter impasse that prevented the completion of the gift and the school's launch for eight years. Pulitzer believed passionately that journalism education needed a strong, continuing input from practitioners and that the school should be open to people of talent, whether they had gone to college or not. Columbia's academics, anxious, as a professor had said, to "escape the reproach of degrading the University," insisted that formal authority had to be in the hands of academics only. They conceded that there might be an advisory board of outside experts, but it would have to be limited to giving advice, its members would serve limited terms, and though Pulitzer would name half the initial members, their successors would be appointed by the university president.

One of the issues between donor and beneficiary concerned admissions. Pulitzer, keenly aware that he and most of his employees hadn't been college men, wanted the program to be open to able people without regard to previous educational credentials. Columbia resisted. In a compromise the Columbia side agreed that promising applicants without two years of college education might be admitted at the university's discretion. But, the academic side insisted, there'd be no guarantee that any such candidates would be admitted in a given year, and however well they might perform, they wouldn't be entitled to receive a Columbia degree. Degrees would be given only to journalism graduates with proper academic credentials. In other words, while it was theoretically possible that a Joseph Pulitzer would be admitted, there was no way he would be able to receive formal acknowledgment of his having completed a course of study.

With deep misgivings Pulitzer had swallowed all this, signed the agreement with the Columbia trustees, handed over his check for the first two hundred thousand dollars, and sent President Nicholas Murray Butler a list of the seven people that under the agreement he was authorized to name to the advisory board. Five were top names in the news industry, and two were distinguished academic leaders and friends of Pulitzer's who had taken an interest in journalism education—President Charles W. Eliot of Harvard and President Andrew Dickson White of Cornell. Butler and his trustees refused to appoint Eliot and White. "Understand jealousy," Pulitzer cabled back to his man on the Columbia project. "Telegraph Butler my insistence. Unalterable. Final."

Butler, thinking to pressure Pulitzer to go ahead with the project, issued a press release announcing Pulitzer's gift and omitting any mention of the members of the advisory board. If he thought this would overcome Pulitzer's resistance, he had misjudged his man. The prospective benefactor immediately trumped Butler's move, declaring that he wouldn't complete the remaining $1.8 million of the $2 million gift until the advisory board was completed. When Butler later tried to communicate with Pulitzer about the impasse, Pulitzer replied, "All further disagreeable cables forbidden."

There the matter rested for eight years.

Time, of course, was on Butler's side. Columbia had the name and authority to create a journalism school, and Pulitzer, his health fading, was resolved to create a suitably Pulitzerian, issue-oriented, public-spirited monument to himself. Unwilling to back down on the matter of his right to name half the members of the advisory board but insistent that eventually there would be a journalism school, Pulitzer relented. He declared that while he refused to subject himself to the anguish of further negotiations or the spectacle of the school going ahead with a system of governance he didn't control, he would nonetheless include the rest of the bequest in his will.

Butler was happy to wait. Pulitzer was in poor health, and when he died, quite possibly soon, Columbia would have the best of both worlds: all of Pulitzer's money and none of Pulitzer's values or advice.

When Columbia finally launched its journalism school in 1913, two years after Pulitzer's death, it was with an almost total lack of input from the man who had almost single-handedly remade American journalism. The project quickly came under the influence of people and ideas inimical to Pulitzer. The first dean, Philadelphia editor Talcott Williams, was a leader of the National Civic Federation, the elite, tripartite, progressive-era business-government-labor association that stood for a managed, cooperative approach to politics somewhat at odds with Pulitzer's reform-oriented Democratic politics, though of course entirely in harmony with the reality of the emergency-power politics Pulitzer's journalism enabled. The school soon fell into the orbit of the *New York Times* and its philosophy, espoused by Pulitzer's old rival, Adolph Ochs, of an objective, impersonal, centrist journalism quite different from the *World*'s. The Pulitzer Prizes, with their emphasis on long stories about subjects of social and political import, were more in keeping with the founder's values.

Aside from recruiting able young people to the news business and developing their technical skills, the important functions of the journalism schools and the professional idea they represented were to dignify journalism and, by suggesting that the field is properly a subject for academic study, undermine the idea of a journalism criticism by nonacademics, generalists, and ordinary citizens.

This new, protective, sheltered view of journalism was articulated most importantly in the postwar writings of Walter Lippmann, which, behind their veneer of genteel criticism, have been the principal legitimation of Pulitzerian journalism throughout the twentieth century.

In 1921 Lippmann, a founding editor of the *New Republic* and at thirty-two already a prominent social critic, coauthored with Charles Merz an analysis of the way the *New York Times* had covered the Bolshevik revolution from 1917 to 1920. Abysmally, Lippmann concluded. The *Times*'s news coverage was a pasticcio of anti-Bolshevik propaganda. Things that hadn't happened but served anti-Bolshevik purposes were covered, things that had happened but clashed with the anti-Bolshevik line were ignored. The *Times* was guilty of "seeing not what was, but what men wished to see," and this failure grew out of "hope and fear in the minds of reporters and editors." The gentlemen of the *Times* had been overcome by a "boundless credulity, an untiring readiness to be gulled, and on many occasions a downright lack of common sense."

If ever there was an occasion tailor-made for intelligent critical reflection on the nature of the press and politics in the era after Pulitzer, this was it. But in this work, and in *Liberty and the News*, the two that followed, *Public Opinion* and *The Phantom Public*, Lippmann turned his formidable intellect in a very different direction. For Walter Lippmann, the discovery that one of the nation's top newspapers had systematically misled the public about an important story by uncritically repeating the manipulative lies of interested parties was an occasion for meditating on the ignorance and unthoughtfulness of the public and the irremediable intellectual shortcomings of popular government. What the *Times*'s mishandling of the Russian Revolution showed, Lippmann argued, was not that journalism should be conducted differently, but that democratic institutions weren't capable of governing. The public, Lippmann held, lives in a world of crude mental images or stereotypes, all of them partly fictitious, and some of them entirely so. A nation's elites, no matter how well informed, cannot remedy or escape these mass limitations; the continuing growth of knowledge was bound to be negated, at least in part, by the intensifying political aggressiveness of the ignorant. Government in a modern society, then, was bound to be a disappointing and often dangerous affair.

Lippmann's oeuvre amounted to a fancy form of blaming the victim and denying the crime. Rather than lay bare the realities of a confusing new world, it sought to conceal and justify them. However valid in the abstract (and in the abstract Lippmann's point was perfectly valid: we *are* victims of stereotypes), the theory was a smokescreen. What had gone wrong with respect to the Russian Revolution was not that one hundred million Americans had simplified pictures of reality in their heads, it was that official sources had lied to journalists and that the journalists had accepted the lies and repeated and validated them. The news had been a manipulative fabrication.

To Walter Lippmann, however, then the foreign affairs editorial writer for the *New York World* and about to become its editor, that wasn't the issue. "News and truth are not the same thing," he wrote complacently. "The function of news is to signalize an event, the function of truth is to bring to light the hidden circumstances." Despite the exaggerated respect now accorded Lippmann as a public philosopher, his theory of news and democracy can only be described as professional propaganda. Its purpose was not to explain and criticize a complex new reality in which journalism, working in conjunction with oligopoly- and oligarchy-seeking institutions, had become a potent source of a routinized emergency power that was rapidly transforming the political economy of a less and less constitutionalist society. Lippmann's theory sought mainly to justify the new Pulitzerian journalism and to reconcile a still-constitutionalist public to the anticonstitutionalist politics it represented and engendered.

In the seventy-five years since Lippmann's apologia, the journalism and politics he was defending have flourished beyond anyone's wildest imagining. The novelty that Pulitzer, Wilson, et al. put on the map slowly but emphatically entrenched itself as a systemic reality in several ways.

First, the news industry became more concentrated, less diverse, and more mutually imitative, particularly following the advent of the nightly network news programs in 1963. For all the ways it differed from print journalism, television was a profoundly Pulitzerian medium. It used sound, moving pictures, live coverage, a national focus, and omniscient narrative to outdo even the front page in projecting the illusion that the whole world is watching. It relied on advertising sales, not for 80 percent of its revenues, as in the case of newspapers, but for the entire 100 percent. And amid enormous growth, television maintained itself as a tight-knit, government-protected oligopoly for many decades. In the 1960s television gave a nineteenth-century journalistic invention a greatly extended lease on life.

The second major change in the twentieth century has been the growth of big, interventionist government along the pragmatic, crisis-managing lines of the emergency-response news story. As the public sector became larger, especially after World War II, the relationship among the state, big private-sector institutions, and the press became more supportive and more consequential. The bigger government and private-sector institutions got, the more willing they were to enact the crisis-and-emergency-response pseudoevents that the press needed to do its job. The more the press responded to these efforts with dramatic front-page news stories, the bigger the government became and the more special benefit the private institutions derived, and so on in a mutually reinforcing spiral.

A similar dynamic of increasing mutual empowerment was set in motion by reforms of the national political process in the late 1960s and early 1970s. In Congress new rules extricated the legislative process from its long-standing domination by seniority-based committees and returned the lawmaking function to the control of the entire House or Senate. As a result, Congress became more reactive to and supportive of the news media, and vice versa. Much the same happened in the wake of the switch to presidential primary elections in the 1960s and the consequent displacement of the political party organization as the main source of presidential nominations.

The third line of evolution that took the news business from the age of the gaslight to that of the microchip was the growth of popular involvement in the emergency-power politics that Pulitzerian journalism routinizes. On one hand, news-based politics won substantial broad-based support as more and more groups learned to turn the new system to their benefit in the form of public subsidies, protections, recognitions, and other positive advantages. On the other, this widespread direct experience of the aggressiveness, manipulativeness, and dishonesty of media politics—and the spectacle of other groups using the same methods to gain advantage at the beholders' expense—have nurtured explosive public distaste. In a very real sense the popularity of Pulitzerian journalism is reflected in the vast majorities who, through public opinion polls and in other ways, express low regard for the moral character of the press and the political system it so profoundly shapes.

Toward the end of the Reagan presidency, the historical impact of that politics over the hundred or so years that have passed since it appeared on the American scene was weighed, in an indirect but dramatic way, by an economic historian named Robert Higgs in a study he entitled *Crisis and Leviathan*. The book was a fascinating quantitative and analytical retrospective on the growth of American government. Using a variety of measures, Higgs identified three basic dynamics.

One of these was a slow, steady, secular expansion of government associated with normal political processes and events—in effect, a gentle upward drift of the magnitude of the public sector.

A second dynamic, both more dramatic in itself and the source of the lion's share of the growth of the public sector during the twentieth century, was a crisis dynamic. During four short crisis episodes—World War I, the Great Depression, World War II, and the Vietnam War/Great Society period—government grew explosively. What expanded, Higgs found, wasn't merely the dollar volume of government activity, which would have been accounted for by the special effort to fight the war or remedy the depression. Equally important was a dramatic expansion of the range and type of government activities during the crisis period. It was as if, Higgs observed, organizations and groups with political agendas were standing in line awaiting a crisis that would provide an occasion for implementing their agendas.

A third dynamic identified by Higgs's research was what he called the ratchet effect. After a crisis the size and scope of the government would shrink, but not back to their precrisis level nor even back to the level implied by the slow, steady growth trend driven by normal politics. The government would shrink to a new, significantly higher base level from which future growth dynamics would proceed.

Higgs's study was interesting not only for what it found but also for what it didn't find. It demonstrated that a number of the explanations conventionally put forward to account for the growth of big government—modernization, changing ideology, growing economic inequality—don't fit the facts nearly as well as the theory that stresses the interaction of the crisis, ratchet effect, and normal drift dynamics.

At the end of his study, Higgs, ever the prudent scholar, notes that at least one unanswered question hangs like a potential millstone around the neck of his crisis theory of government growth: Why did crises vastly inflate the size of government in the twentieth century but not in the nineteenth century? Crises did happen during the 1800s in America—one need only mention the Civil War and the disastrous War of 1812. Yet they didn't unleash the growth dynamics that similar crises touched off in the twentieth century. Why not? Or, to put the same question the other way around, why did crises engender the ballooning of government in the environment of the twentieth century?

A substantial part of the answer, I would suggest, is that the emergence of modern journalism and the institutional adaptations to it by the corporation and the state created a coherent, self-sustaining, efficacious mechanism through which organizations seeking benefits from an expanded government could generate or co-opt crises, unleash the crisis power, and create both the reality and the appearance of popular support for institutional innovations jury-rigged during the crisis episodes. In other words, what Pulitzer & Company created around the turn of the century wasn't merely a new journalism, but a new and powerful permanent emergency mode of operation that constitutional government was routinely urged to resort to and routinely rewarded for doing so.

News in our time isn't merely a genre or mode of knowledge. It is also, in effect, a special type of political power. That is why, despite protestations of independence, the journalist and the official or "newsmaker" end up in such a tight embrace, one in which each depends on and enables the actions of the other, and both must maintain the fiction that they are merely telling it like it is when in fact they're putting on a dog and pony show to activate the extraordinary powers and immunities of the emergency state.

CHAPTER 3

How a News Story Lies

News is a genre, a form of writing, as distinct and predictable as the sonnet or the chase scene. The genre is the source of the culture of lying. The news story is a blueprint for mendacity. It is an invitation and license to lie, built around the Pulitzerian illusion that the whole world is watching. The process is illustrated by the following outstanding story. I reprint it here in full as it appeared on the front page of the *New York Times* on December 4, 1964.

796 Students Arrested as Police Break Up Sit-In at U. of California

by Wallace Turner

BERKELEY, CALIF., DEC. 3—The police arrested 796 University of California students in 12 hours today, dragging many on their backs down flights of stairs to end a sit-in demonstration.

The mass arrests were made in removing demonstrators who took possession of the administration building on the campus last night.

The Free Speech Movement, the protesting student group, retaliated by calling a student strike. Faculty members, at a special meeting, gave evidence of some support for the students. The dispute over students' political and protest activities has shaken the university for almost three months.

The strike was called after Gov. Edmund G. Brown ordered early this morning that sit-in demonstrators be removed by force from the corridors of Sproul Hall, the administration building. Mr. Brown said that the students' action constituted "anarchy."

Charges of police brutality were made as a result of the removals and arrests today.

In this 27,500-student university, the effectiveness of the strike was difficult to measure. In the morning pickets wheeled in front of the doors of all the classroom buildings and, although students continued to pass through the lines, there were reports that many classrooms were empty.

Clark Kerr, president of the university, issued a statement tonight declaring that the Free Speech Movement represented an "understandable concern" last September but that it "has now become an instrument of anarchy and of personal aggrandizement."

Representatives of about 75 of the 82 academic departments at the university, in a meeting this afternoon, found that about 20 departments were functioning normally in the face of the strike. Prof. Charles Hulten, chairman of the Journalism Department, said that individual faculty members would decide tomorrow whether to hold classes.

A meeting of 500 of the 1,200 members of the faculty voted a resolution this afternoon stating that the university faced a "desperate situation."

The faculty members favor new and liberalized campus rules for political activity and setting up a committee to which students could appeal administration decisions on penalties for violating university rules on political action.

Plan Telegram to Brown

The resolution also asked "that all pending campus action against students for acts occurring before the present date be dropped."

At the meeting, faculty members drafted a telegram to be sent to Governor Brown. It condemned the use of the California Highway Patrol on the campus and the exclusion of faculty members from Sproul Hall.

Last night about 1,000 sit-in demonstrators filled the corridors of Sproul Hall before the doors were locked at 7:00 P.M. They sat there, sleeping, singing, studying and talking until about 3:10 A.M., when Edward W. Strong, the chancellor for this campus of the multi-campus university, went to Sproul Hall.

Mr. Strong read a statement asking the students to leave. A few did, but most stayed. They had put up barricades at the stairways and were concentrated on the second, third, and fourth floors.

The police took an elevator to the fourth floor and began removing students there.

Capt. Larry Waldt of the Alameda County sheriff's office made the estimate of the number of students arrested.

By midday, the routine was standard, as illustrated by the arrest of Jean Golson.

When she found herself at the head of the line of demonstrators, Sgt. Don Smithson of the Berkeley police force told her, "You are under arrest for trespass and unlawful assembly."

Another Berkeley policeman held a microphone to record her answers and the sergeant's statements. A third made notes in a booking form.

"If you walk out, you will not be charged with resisting arrest, but if we are forced to carry you out, you will be charged with resisting arrest," the sergeant said.

'Female on Way'

Miss Golson said she would not walk out. A number was held to her chest and her photograph was taken. The Berkeley police pulled her by the arms for a few feet and then turned her over to two sheriff's deputies from Alameda County. They dragged her quickly down the corridor on her back, shouting "Female on the way."

At a booking desk, she was pulled erect and was fingerprinted. Then she was pulled into an office for searching by two matrons from the sheriff's office.

Then she was dragged back into the elevator, where other girls were being held. When the elevator was full, the girls were taken to the basement and were loaded into a van for transportation to the county jail.

The bail schedule was $75 each on the trespass and unlawful assembly charges and $100 for resisting arrest.

Total Bail Is $150,000

Booking officers at the Alameda County sheriff's office said that about 25 of the demonstrators posted bail soon after being booked. Meantime, lawyers, parents and others were meeting with a municipal judge attempting to obtain an order freeing the demonstrators on their own recognizance. The total bail involved will be more than $150,000.

For men, the handling was significantly different once they were turned over to the sheriff's deputies after arrest. Those men who would walk were dragged down four flights of steps to the basement. Those who remained limp were dragged by the arms down the steps, departing to the cries of "Good luck" from their friends.

There were about a score of sheriff's deputies whose job was to drag the men down the steps. As the day passed, their humor became more acid. Some bumped the buttocks of their male prisoners as they dragged them down the stairs.

"There'll be some sore rumps in jail tonight," one deputy said.

After the corridors of Sproul Hall were closed, a floor at a time, the litter of the sit-ins remained. There were empty fruit cartons, crushed soft-drink cans, a guitar, stacks of textbooks, sleeping bags and blankets and scores of notebooks with lecture notes in them.

Shouts 'This Is Wonderful'

When Mario Savio, a protest leader, was taken away by the police, he shouted, "This is wonderful—wonderful. We'll bring the university to our terms."

Another leader, Arthur Goldberg, said as he was led away, "Good. The kids have learned more about democracy here than they could in 40 years of classes. This is a perfect example of how the State of California plays the game."

Mr. Savio is a New Yorker who is the president of the Berkeley Chapter of Friends of S.N.C.C., the Student Nonviolent Coordinating Committee. He was involved last spring in recruiting demonstrators who slept in at the Sheraton Palace Hotel. He was arrested on a charge of disturbing the peace. He also worked in the S.N.C.C. program in Mississippi last summer.

Another leader of the Free Speech Movement is Bettina Aptheker. She is a member of the W.E.B. DuBois Club which has been described by Department of Justice sources as a front among college students for the Communist party.

The dispute that led to the arrests began last September when the university administration announced that it would no longer permit the use of a strip of campus property for soliciting political funds and recruiting protest demonstrators.

The students objected, and a series of demonstrations resulted. Eight students were suspended and the demonstrations were stepped up.

Last month, the university regents ordered that the students be permitted to recruit demonstrators and collect political contributions on campus. But the regents said the students must be held accountable for off-campus violations of the law in projects begun on campus.

They also said that discipline must be tightened.

Earlier this week, four students received letters from the administration indicating that they were to be disciplined, and perhaps expelled. Yesterday the newest demonstration began in protest.

Conservatives Quit Group

The Free Speech Movement was organized with an executive committee of about 60 members, each representing some campus organization. Initially, conservative groups belonged, including the Young Republicans, but these recently disassociated themselves.

The leadership is concentrated in an 11-member steering committee that appears to be dominated by representatives of campus chapters of the Congress for Racial Equality, the Young Socialist League, the Young Socialist Alliance, Slate (a student political organization) and the W.E.B. DuBois Club.

At a noon rally of about 5,000 students, Steven Weisman, a leader of the Free Speech Movement, called for an investigation of what he termed police brutality. He also demanded the removal of Mr. Kerr as president of the university.

In his statement tonight, Mr. Kerr denied that freedom of speech had ever been an issue and said, "The protest has been over organizing political action on campus."

Mr. Kerr accused the Free Speech Movement of violating the law, of intolerance, distortion of the truth, irrationality, indecency, and ill will.

In Sacramento, Governor Brown said, "We're not going to have anarchy in the state of California while I'm Governor, and that's anarchy. I did plan to go to Berkeley, but I have other things to do."

Opposition to the Free Speech Movement was in evidence here today. Some students standing at the noon rally held signs reading "Throw the Bums Out" and "Law Not Anarchy—The Majority of Students Do Not Support This Demonstration."

This is, of course, a magnificent piece of reporting and news-writing about an event that was as electrifying as it was consequential. Three decades later, the story still brings back memories (for those of us of a certain age), and reading it with the advantage of hindsight, one is struck by the prescience with which the story identifies the whole complex pattern of the campus protest and student radicalism of the sixties in its first major eruption. Nevertheless, this story perfectly exemplifies the way in which the Pulitzerian approach to the news business makes journalism an instrument of lying, manipulation, privilege, and oligarchy.

On the surface, to be sure, the story is a monument to facticity. This is a piece of writing that at all times is trying very hard to persuade the reader that it is a truthful, reliable, accurate report of what happened at Berkeley that fateful December day. Virtually every statement in the text is a statement of directly observable fact. With a handful of exceptions, every statement rests on a method of direct personal observation. Most of the factual statements apparently derive from the reporter's personal visual observation. The rest come from official texts put out by individuals or organizations or from earlier newspaper accounts.

The facts presented in this story are not only true, they are obviously true. Observation can be careful or cursory; it can detect small or gross distinctions; it can be in fine or rough focus; it may discern minute or broad characteristics. This story reflects a method of cursory observation in rough focus that seeks only the gross characteristics of visible physical particulars. These are statements of fact about matters that it's particularly easy to be right about and particularly hard to be mistaken about.

This may be seen most clearly in the vocabulary employed in the story. Nearly all the words used are in widespread popular usage; they are relatively few and recur fairly often; and most of them denote tangible things or qualities. Moreover, these words are not highly specific. Thus, people who are enrolled to study at the University of California are invariably described only as students, never as graduate students or undergraduates, juniors or seniors, premed students or electrical engineering students. Similarly, people who teach at the university are always faculty members and not scholars, researchers, teaching assistants, epidemiologists, or anything else. The crudeness of the reporter's lexicon makes the story particularly easy to accept as true, since an observer is less likely to err in identifying a student than he is in identifying a graduate student or nontenured associate professor or research scholar.

The story also invites us to accept as true and precise its account of the day's events at Berkeley by narrating them in a highly impersonal voice. Although the text was in fact reported and written by a human being, he never speaks in the first person or expresses his own feelings. The prose does not evaluate or qualify. By withholding the subjective aspect of the writer-event encounter, the story is telling us that it was written by a person with an intense commitment to factual reporting and the self-discipline to bring it off. It is inviting us to trust this man. It is also saying, somewhat inconsistently, that the events at Berkeley were so dramatic and unforgettable that they require no elaboration or rhetorical embroidery, no direct, in-person, writer-to-reader communications, for the entire episode to be intelligible and compelling to the reader.

A small indication of the impersonality of this authorial voice is to be found in the scarcity of adjectives in the story (some 10 percent of the words are adjectives). Moreover, almost all of the adjectives in this text denote number, sequence, location, or some other objective characteristic of the noun they modify.

A further element of impersonality is provided by the story's insistently chaotic structure. As one reads the story through, the subject changes no fewer than fifteen times; in only three instances are there five or more successive paragraphs treating the same subject without interruption, and the average number of successive paragraphs on the same subject is approximately three. The impression created is that the story is a more or less random list of facts about actions, with little or no interpretation or other input from the journalist.

It isn't so, of course. The news story's rhetoric of objectivity is just that, a rhetoric, a set of stylistic devices for creating an impression that, in the case of this news report, is sharply at odds with reality. This is no random bunch of facts. To the contrary, it's a story, an integrated narrative whole that possesses all the attributes classically identified in Aristotle's *Poetics* as fundamentals of drama.

There is action:

Last night about 1,000 sit-in demonstrators filled the corridors of Sproul Hall before the doors were locked at 7:00 P.M. They sat there, sleeping, singing, studying and talking until about 3:10 A.M., when Edward W. Strong, the chancellor for this campus of the multi-campus university, went to Sproul Hall.

Mr. Strong read a statement asking the students to leave. A few did, but most stayed. They had put up barricades at the stairways and were concentrated on the second, third, and fourth floors.

The action is illuminated by rhetoric:

There were about a score of sheriff's deputies whose job was to drag the men down the steps. As the day passed, their humor became more acid. Some bumped the buttocks of their male prisoners as they dragged them down the stairs.

"There'll be some sore rumps in jail tonight," one deputy said.

The action is also accompanied by spectacle:

After the corridors of Sproul Hall were closed, a floor at a time, the litter of the sit-ins remained. There were empty fruit cartons, crushed soft-drink cans, a guitar, stacks of textbooks, sleeping bags and blankets and scores of notebooks with lecture notes in them.

In this news story, as in all drama, one day's action is a development in a larger plot extending backward and forward in time and causality:

The dispute that led to the arrests began last September when the university administration announced that it would no longer permit the use of a strip of campus property for soliciting political funds and recruiting protest demonstrators.

The students objected, and a series of demonstrations resulted. Eight students were suspended and the demonstrations were stepped up.

The plot being acted out at Berkeley was characterized by reversals—a particularly desirable and thrilling feature of dramatic action, according to Aristotle's analysis:

Last month, the university regents ordered that the students be permitted to recruit demonstrators and collect political contributions on campus. But the regents ... also said that discipline must be tightened.

Earlier this week, four students received letters from the administration indicating that they were to be disciplined, and perhaps expelled. Yesterday the newest demonstration began in protest.

The action grows out of and reveals the personalities of the characters. For example, a key source of the events at Sproul Hall was the mercurial, controlling, vindictive, self-promoting personality the reporter saw in the university president:

Clark Kerr, president of the university, issued a statement tonight declaring that the Free Speech Movement represented an "understandable concern" last September but that it "has now

become an instrument of anarchy and of personal aggrandizement."

Mr. Kerr accused the Free Speech Movement of violating the
law, of intolerance, distortion of the truth, irrationality, indecency,
and ill will.

Equally noteworthy were the angry, manipulative personalities
the author saw in the young men leading the FSM:

When Mario Savio, a protest leader, was taken away by the
police, he shouted, "This is wonderful—wonderful! We'll bring
the university to our terms."

Another leader, Arthur Goldberg, said as he was led away,
"Good! The kids have learned more about democracy here than
they could in 40 years of classes. This is a perfect example of how
the State of California plays the game."

This was a story about a community in crisis. This feature of
the story is perhaps most importantly and obviously conveyed by
its graphic characteristics—the fact that it appeared on the front
page, was summarized by a banner headline spreading across four
columns, and was allowed to run to over two thousand words,
very long by the standards of a daily newspaper, even the *Times*.
The urgent, danger-laden, consequence-fraught nature of these
events is further evoked by the ironic sparseness and impersonality of the narrative voice—these events are so important they
speak for themselves, the story suggests.

The sense of emergency is also conveyed by the nature of the
events themselves, in particular by the fact that, again and again,
the institutionally defined aspects of events, though present, are
subordinated to some unnamed, superseding, larger concerns.
Thus, the second paragraph describes the arrests, the institutionally defined event, as a subordinate element of the larger, overarching enterprise of "removing demonstrators who took possession
of the administration building on the campus last night." By the
same token, the actual offenses for which the demonstrators were
put under arrest (trespass and unlawful assembly) are mentioned
in passing as a kind of afterthought, halfway through the story. By
contrast, the political issues raised by or over the arrests—the

FSM's charge that law enforcement officers had brutalized the demonstrators, the faculty's demand that police be removed from the campus, the governor's insistence that the demonstration had been an exercise in anarchy—are described explicitly and specifically in the opening paragraphs.

Notwithstanding all this, the story lies. It tells a lie, it is a lie.

The lie is the story's implication that the events are un-self-conscious and in that sense authentic, and that the journalist and reader are uninvolved observers whose presence and interest don't affect the newsmakers' behavior. Both of these implications are untrue.

The presence of the journalist, with his crisis-and-emergency-response concept of news and his big audience and his ability to activate the emergency power, greatly affects the newsmaker. The newsmaker is highly self-conscious, and his actions are carefully tailored to attract the media's attention and to advance the newsmaker's purposes in the emergency-powers arena. The journalist and the newsmaker both know all this. Yet both pretend not to. The newsmaker pretends to act without awareness of the observer's response. The journalist pretends that the newsmaker is being sincere. In short, the journalist and newsmaker more or less knowingly misrepresent both the event and their roles in the event.

Take the FSM. As the story explains, it was dominated by liberal and left activist groups recently energized by the civil rights struggle in the South. Returning to Berkeley after their Mississippi summer, some of the people who were soon to become leaders of the FSM began applying to the university perspectives and tactics they'd learned in the crusade for black equality. As the story reports, they began to confront the university administration over its restrictions on political activism.

These confrontations were both real and symbolic. They were meant to induce the university to relax or eliminate its prohibitions against on-campus activism. Alternatively, they were meant to elicit university resistance as an object lesson in the true nature of an institution that, like northern society as a whole, was widely viewed as decent, liberal, and enlightened but that the activists increasingly believed was actually illiberal, conservative, and repressive. Thus even if the confrontations didn't force the university to back down on the rules issue, they would, in the catchphrase of the day, raise the consciousness of the community, winning new converts to their cause and shifting the center of gravity of public opinion in their direction. For either of these outcomes to materialize, all the FSM needed to do was stage confrontations and get publicity. From such a combination they felt sure they would emerge big winners.

So when the FSM staged the sit-in in Sproul Hall or, after the bust, called for a student strike to shut down the university in protest over the arrests, they were engaged in a highly self-conscious strategy of political action and political manipulation. It was a strategy, in effect, of conceiving, staging, and arranging to derive political benefit from news stories. For it to work, all that was really needed was for the media to cover these actions on their own terms and thereby define them as real events. With the validation and outreach such coverage would provide, the FSM's program would move forward.

The FSM's strategies and tactics would fail, however, if they were ignored or if the news stories covering them decoded and deconstructed the actions as I've done in the paragraphs above. Stories reporting that the FSM was staging events designed to manipulate others in various ways were likely to harm the FSM's cause. Such stories would invalidate the ploys, draw attention to the manipulative intentions and approaches inspiring them, and discourage people from engaging in the reflexive responses the FSM was hoping its actions would stimulate them to engage in.

The *Times*'s dispatch from Berkeley covered the demonstration and student strike on the FSM's terms. Except for the statements by Mario Savio and Arthur Goldberg exulting in the authorities' repressive actions—which, as given, are bewildering and cry out in vain for further explanation along the lines of the analysis above—the story reports events in a way that strongly implies that they were un-self-conscious, unmanipulative, authentic. It thereby validates the FSM's made-for-media lie.

Since the reporter clearly knew a lot about this manipulative aspect of the day's events, it involved the *Times* in a lie of its own or, more precisely, two such lies. The first lie consisted of all the statements that presented the ostensible, public version of the FSM's actions without indicating the existence of the other dimension. The second lie was the *Times*'s implied assertion that it was being neutral and dispassionate in giving an objective report of the day's events, when in fact the reporter was well aware that the FSM was engaging in a made-for-media propaganda action that would achieve its effect by being covered by the news media as an un-self-conscious, authentic public event.

The same analysis applies to the other major actors at Berkeley. The *Times* was lying about their actions, too, in precisely the same way.

Pat Brown, the governor who ordered the law enforcement action to arrest and remove the demonstrators, was also engaging in actions that were intended to define a kind of dramatic propaganda against the activists of the FSM and in favor of centrists and establishmentarians whom the FSM was trying to discredit. A center-leaning liberal, Brown at the time was looking anxiously over his shoulder at a conservative movie star and actors' union leader named Ronald Reagan, who was then emerging as a right-wing challenger for the governor's office and who naturally took a very hard line against the FSM.

In ordering the police action against the sit-in, then, Brown was not only enforcing the law and seeking to reestablish order at the university, he was also trying to discredit the FSM and to forestall the potential criticism and challenge of Ronald Reagan. In other words, he was taking actions designed to manipulate public perceptions and actions in his favor merely by virtue of being covered as authentic actions. He was trying to demystify the left-wing adversaries of university-life-as-usual, who were pushing the FSM to confront and discredit the university as a symbol of the larger society. He was trying to raise *conservative* consciousness by his actions. By failing to cover this aspect of the governor's action, which of course was well known to the reporter, the *Times* knowingly misrepresented it, thereby validating the governor's manipulative pseudoactions as much as it was validating the FSM's actions.

The analysis could be carried over to other actors—the university administrators, the faculty, the police departments, and so on. The news story gave each a stage on which to enact a propaganda play designed to manipulate appearances and the public, secure in the knowledge that the story wouldn't decode, deconstruct, or otherwise undermine the performance. The news story thereby gave each an opportunity to turn public attention to private advantage by activating constitutional government's emergency powers in his own interest.

This subtle and complicated mendacity is a product, ultimately, of the ironic voice in which the news story is narrated. I use the word *irony* here in its classical sense of disguise and inversion, in which the narrator pretends to a point of view on the material under discussion different from the one he actually holds and in which he counts on the reader to make the correction and arrive at a correct understanding of his real meaning. A central purpose of irony is to create emphasis and, through the reader's active involvement in construing meaning, intensify the communion achieved by an act of communication. Irony is what is in play when one turns to a friend who has just come in drenched and miserable from an intolerably stormy day and asks, Nice weather, huh? The understatement and misdirection, in the context of the obvious fact that the weather isn't nice, are a way of conveying sympathy for his experience and distaste for the weather without being trite, formulaic, or overblown.

The news story tells its yarn in a voice that pretends not to be telling a yarn, merely reciting a list of facts. In fact, of course, what it tells *is* a story; the pose of objectivity is just a means of encouraging the reader to attend to and accept the story. The voice intensifies meaning, reinforces the particular story's construction of events, screens out discrepant, story-undercutting material, and invites the reader to get involved in the text.

That pose, however, has consequences that go far beyond those intended.

In real life, when we speak with others about events we have witnessed or experiences we have been through, we do not confine ourselves to facts or to objectively verifiable statements. We make whatever kinds of statements we think necessary to convey our experience as we understand it. Some of those statements may be objective and factual in nature. Others may not be. Often the facts are unclear or their significance is ambiguous, and in such cases we switch voices, as it were, drop any pretense to objectivity, and start talking about the uncertainties and ambiguities or broader meanings we're aware of, regardless of whether this means slipping out of our reportorial voice. In other words, we take responsibility for our meaning and (if any) our irony. If we come to a situation in which we can't be sure the reader will have the information he needs to decode and construe our ironies, we provide those cues. Stepping out of the ironic pose, we do what it takes to communicate experience and meaning successfully.

The news story can't or won't do this. It stays in its objective voice even when that becomes counterproductive from the point of view of successfully conveying information and understanding to the reader. There are several ways of thinking about why it does so, all of them arguably just different ways of saying the same thing. One could say that the news form is so rigid, and the news organization using and defining it so bureaucratized, that working journalists are denied the expository flexibility they need to insure that the meaning of the news story doesn't get out of sync with what they observed of and understood about the event. One could say that the working journalist is so desensitized to his intellectual responsibility to the reader, or so sensitized to the intellectual demands being made by the newsmaker, that he or she willingly tolerates a substantial discrepancy between what the story means and what actually took place as he or she understood it. Or one could say that the news organization is so intensely focused on the advertising sales-supporting effort to turn out a news product giving readers the impression that the whole world is watching, and so comparatively indifferent to the reader satisfaction-supporting effort to give its own best understanding of the event at hand, that it willingly sacrifices the latter to the former.

However one puts it, newsmakers know that the news story can almost always be counted on to stay in its ironically objective voice, and they aggressively take advantage of this fact. The news genre's refusal to shift voices implies that if a newsmaker pretends to an action and the media cover it, they'll cover the action more or less on the newsmaker's terms. They won't drop their accustomed posture of objectivity, accept responsibility for the meaning their words are conveying, and start telling a story that diverges substantially from the newsmaker's performance. Thus, the genre's objective voice turns news into a stage on which the newsmaker may strut his stuff, secure in the knowledge that backstage realities will stay backstage.

I remember, during my Washington days, an evening my then wife and I spent with a small party hosted by a senior White

House staff member and his wife. We began with drinks at the private bar in the president's box at the Kennedy Center, stayed to watch the play, then finished up with supper at a comfortable French restaurant on Pennsylvania Avenue. Around the table the conversation was dominated by the aide, who was full of amusing talk about this or that aspect of White House operations and the actual roles of various senior people. (This was early in the Reagan Administration, and Washingtonians were still doping out who was who and how the place worked.) The aide was a member of the nonconservative, centrist Baker-Deaver axis on the White House staff, and naturally his stories were favorable to the personalities and perspectives of his fellow nonconservatives.

Practically every observation he made and every vignette he told, it seemed, moved the White House correspondent of the *New York Times*, who was among our small number, to remark, in an enthusiastic, confidential tone, "That's a story." He must have said that half a dozen times, and he wasn't just being polite, it turned out. I was fascinated to note, during the ensuing weeks, that several of the matters the White House staff guy had talked about appeared as stories in the *Times* under our dinner companion's byline.

None of the stories made even the most veiled reference to the White House aide who had been their true originator. None described the aide's personal and political position in the White House staff at the time. None located themselves in the context of either the White House staff's overall communications goals or of the nonconservative wing's political situation. None took any note of the actual way in which the ideas came to the author.

The point here isn't that there was anything wrong with the way the *Times* ran these stories. To the contrary, this was a normal, up-to-standard exercise in Washington journalism. The genre's exclusion of reflexive and self-referential information about the origins of a story is a crucial element of the way the news story attracts attention and conveys meaning. How different the reader's impression would have been had any of the stories I saw pitched over dinner included, at the end, a little note reading as follows:

The subject of this story was suggested by a senior White House aide whom the *Times* has agreed not to identify as a condition of his assistance. The story idea was tendered during a theater-and-dinner party hosted by the aide and his wife; the aide is a non-Reagan loyalist and moderate who is aligned with the Baker-Deaver wing of the staff and who appeared to have been seeking to attract favorable publicity to his allies on the president's ideologically divided staff.

No such note is written because it would be inconsistent with the ironically objective voice of the news genre. As long as that narrative style prevails, the news story will be a standing invitation for newsmakers to invent events and fabricate postures.

CHAPTER 4

Wayward Heroes

Newsmakers almost always accept the news story's invitation to posture and lie. Theoretically, they could ignore the media and march to the beats of their own drummers. They know, however, that their prospects for continued success in their careers would in that case take a sharp turn for the worse. Moreover, the rewards of being in the news are practically irresistible. Thus, high officials almost invariably set private roles and institutional identities to one side and devote a nontrivial part of their work lives to the task of scripting and performing themselves into the world according to the news genre.

The media are highly responsive to these efforts. To a much greater extent than the public realizes, the news derives directly from newsmakers' initiatives and scripts. Consider the fourteen stories appearing on the front pages of the three sections of the National Edition of the *New York Times* for Tuesday, June 1, 1993. This was the first day after the three-day Memorial Day weekend, and not many hard news events had taken place in the preceding twenty-four hours. Thus, to an unusual extent the *Times* was free to impose its own journalistic standards and concepts in shaping its coverage. What's fascinating is how massively it opted for newsmaker scripts and institutional pseudoevents.

1. "Insurers Accused of Discrimination in AIDS Coverage" by Milt Freudenheim. The lead story, this was an interesting and troubling account of a series of lawsuits being brought by the national AIDS project of the American Civil Liberties Union against a number of health insurers that had limited or terminated benefits to AIDS patients. The ACLU was both the main subject and source, and though the story's reporting ranged across the entire legal and institutional terrain involved, the efficient event driving the story was the decision of program management to encourage and assist reporter Freudenheim in reporting a story about the progress of the ACLU's program.

2. "Four Years after Tiananmen, the Hard Line Is Cracking," by Nicholas D. Kristof, occupied the upper portion of the two left-hand columns. The report, run under the heading, "A Gentler China/A special report," was occasioned by two interrelated events. One was the decision by the Clinton administration, four days earlier, to extend trade benefits to China. That decision was made both in recognition of the Chinese government's recent human-rights progress and in the hope that a mutually reinforcing spiral of more liberalizing steps in Beijing, followed by more benefits from Washington, would pave the way to the U.S. government's decision to renew China's most-favored-nation trade status when it expired a year later. The other precipitating event was the decision of China's pro-freedom dissidents, amid continuing repression, to give interviews asserting that they were beginning to experience somewhat more freedom and more optimism about the future in their country—and a corresponding willingness by officials of the Chinese Communist Party to give interviews expressing a longing for acceptance in the West and a readiness to make the domestic changes required to win that acceptance, including political liberalization. Kristof's story did not ignore the continuing reality of repression in China. In a final section it even asserted that existing conditions such as inflation and corruption create a continuing or conceivably growing potential for another

Tiananmen-style crackdown. But these realities, while acknowledged, are overwhelmed by the concept of the event and story Kristof and his editors adopt from the tendentious events, declarations, and news strategies being put forward by self-interested, self-serving news-scripting principals in Beijing and Washington.

3. "Clinton Considers Tax on Hospitals" by Robert Pear. This was a classic instance of an official White House leak from, as the story described the source, "a senior White House official supervising the work of the President's Task Force on National Health Care Reform." Presumably the unnamed source was the president's wife, Hillary Rodham Clinton, the head of the task force. For the first fifteen of the story's twenty paragraphs, Pear described and validated Mrs. Clinton's trial balloon. The tax proposal "would be high on the agenda when Mr. Clinton meets this week with his advisers to review the design of his plan to guarantee health care for all Americans," the *Times* declared. The story reported no contrasting views of the agenda and didn't get around to naming a source or identifying a contrasting view of the hospital tax until the fifteenth paragraph.

4. "Clinton, in Vietnam War Tribute, Finds Old Wound Is Slow to Heal" by Thomas L. Friedman. The headline and text spread across the middle two columns, starting about one third of the way down the front page. Above it, running across three columns and occupying a large space approximately four inches by six inches, was a dramatic photograph of President Clinton kneeling, chin on hand in a pensive profile, in front of a portion of the Vietnam Memorial on which, the caption reported, the names of four high school classmates killed in Vietnam were inscribed. Both the story and photograph were the ultimate presidential pseudoevents, scripted and staged by the president's handlers and performed by the president for the sole purpose of inducing the *Times* and other media to cover it. The photograph, the dominant element on the *Times*'s front page that day, could not have been better from the president's viewpoint. Clinton looked like a movie star, his graying hair framed magnificently against the black of the name-covered wall. And in his Rodin's *Thinker*esque posture he looked humble and respectful, just as he and his handlers meant him to. The story, a hard-hitting account of both the cheers

and the jeers, declared in the fourth paragraph that Mr. Clinton "was greeted with a cacophony of enthusiastic applause, peppered by catcalls of 'Draft dodger!' 'Liar!' and 'Shut up, coward!' " It also held that despite the president's plea for unity, "Vietnam remained a national wound that would not heal." While these were hardly the specifics the president's people wanted to see covered, the underlying message and focus of the story was precisely the one they and their pseudoevent defined.

5. "Perot's Organization Shows Fissures and Sagging Morale" by Stephen Engelberg and B. Drummond Ayres, Jr. This aggressively anti-Perot story was sourced among and obviously inspired by some senior and middle-level officials who were quitting Perot's United We Stand America organization. Several of the sources were named, including Perot presidential campaign manager Orson Swindle, who was described as having recently quit the Perot organization to work for unannounced Republican presidential candidate Jack Kemp. Here, too, the story was the creature of the defecting Perotistas.

6. "New Haven's Task: Tying City to Region to Promote Growth" by George Judson. A long, interesting, intelligent story that was sourced in the New Haven Chamber of Commerce and focused on its effort to press state and federal officials to deal with deepening urban woes on a metropolitan-wide scale.

7. "African Ruler Finds Himself an Anachronism" by Bill Keller, reporting from Lilongwe, Malawi, no date. This was a very critical portrait of aging, isolated, authoritarian Malawi strongman Hastings Kamuzu Banda. While sourced mainly among critics and independent observers and notably lacking in direct input from Banda or his people, the story was occasioned by a public relations blitz put on by Banda to resuscitate his fading personality cult. In a pattern like that of the coverage of President Clinton's Vietnam Memorial speech, this story was accompanied by a wonderful photograph, almost as large as that of Clinton above it, showing Life President Banda in a dark suit appearing in the midst of dancers wearing colorful costumes decorated with portraits of the ruler. Even here, then, while the content of the cov-

erage went far afield of what the official source had in mind, the occasion of the story and the photo were precisely what Banda's handlers designed.

The first page of section B, The Living Arts, contained three stories, which very much continued the focus on newsmaker-scripted events.

1. The lead story, "The '93 Cliburn Competition: Pianissimo" by James R. Oestreich, was a report from Fort Worth, Texas, where the Van Cliburn International Piano Competition was under way. The story focused, not on the performances and talents that are the substance of the real event, but on the horse race, politicking, and journalistic imagery surrounding the event. Oestreich's theme was that the event's usual extra-musical furore was notably absent. The biggest news story thus far, he reported, had been an inexperienced page-turner's premature turning of pages of the score to Morton Gould's "Ghost Waltzes" from which a promising German semifinalist was playing. Although the performance hadn't been particularly affected, the young pianist was allowed to repeat the piece later in the day with a better page-turner, and he'd played spectacularly.

Continuing the no-news-on-the-Cliburn-front theme, Oestreich noted that the elimination of two highly regarded young players from Italy and the Republic of Georgia had caused not the traditional scandal and charges of unfairness and politicking, but merely chagrin on the part of the music critic of the *Dallas Morning News*, whose disapproving story was quoted. Briefly noting the music programs chosen by two promising American and one "soulful" Armenian, the story concludes with a discussion of the effort to de-emphasize the competitive aspects of the Cliburn event by permitting the contestants more opportunity to play music of their own choosing. This, however, Oestreich reported, had merely made the competition livelier. Besides, the story concluded, "There is still plenty of time and opportunity for some good old-fashioned mayhem and controversy."

Thus, of the story's 18 paragraphs, at most three dealt with pianists playing the piano, and the remaining fifteen focused on the representation of the contest to and by the press.

2. "To the Spider Woman, Broadway Is Home" by Glenn Collins was a profile of singer-actress Chita Rivera, in the midst of an extraordinary career comeback and awaiting, on the eve of the Tony Awards ceremony, the decision on her nomination for the Tony Award for best actress. The immediate occasion for the story was an interview in the star's dressing room at the Broadhurst Theater.

3. "Heedless of Scorners, A G-Rated Las Vegas Booms in the Ozarks" by Peter Applebome sketched the country music boom that's transformed Branson, Missouri. This story, based on the author's reporting trip to Branson, didn't indicate that it was invited or arranged by promoters. Still a promotional focus was clear. Author Applebome was "discovering" for the *Times*'s readers a place that has turned itself into a tourist destination and that might have a consumer interest for them in their roles as tourists and country music fans.

The front page of Section C, Business Day, contained four stories that with one exception continued the focus on newsmaker-defined and -controlled events.

1. "The Federal Reserve Prepares for a Rate War" by Steven Greenhouse, the lead story, was the ultimate inside-Washington, smoke-and-mirrors, newsmaker-defined story. It was based on an interview granted by Fed chairman Alan Greenspan and summarized by a photograph of a grimly determined Greenspan next to a bronze bust of Lincoln over a caption that declared that the Fed chairman "may be on a collision course with the White House." The story sketched Greenspan's self-described recent decision to conduct monetary policy with a view to reducing the inflation rate, 4 percent and rising, and his self-described willingness to take the heat he said he expected to be directed his way from the White House, which, he said, is committed to lowering interest rates as part of its strategy for bolstering the economic recovery.

How willing was Greenspan to take the heat? Well, maybe not all that willing. A later passage reported that at a recent meeting of the Fed's policymaking open market committee, Greenspan took the middle ground between the Fed's inflationary hawks and the Fed's inflationary doves and forged majority support for a compromise decision to raise interest rates, but not quite yet; the tightening would take place at a later date. No White House or Congressional economic policy source was quoted or appeared to have been interviewed for this story, which seemed to have been invited and dominated by the interview-giving, photo-op-seeking chairman.

Was any of this real? Was Greenspan really about to raise rates, or was he just signaling the White House that he'd be willing to do so on a future occasion in changed circumstances? Was Greenspan the leader of the tightening move or its pawn? Was he really at odds with the White House, or was this just a smoke-screen of mock combat to provide cover for a decision by policy-makers in the White House to back down on low interest rates? Or was Greenspan creating a diversion to draw attention away from *his* decision to back down on high inflation rates? Anything was possible, nothing was ruled out in this classic instance of a story that buys into, retails, and validates a newsmaker's script and doesn't take responsibility for the reality—or even try to define the issues concerning the reality or unreality—of the event.

2. "Seeking a Czech Version of the Chrysler Rebound" by Jane Perlez was a report filed from Koprivnice, Czech Republic, about the announcement by former Chrysler Corporation vice-chairman Gerald Greenwald that he was forming a group of investors and managers to turn around the once famous Tatra truck manufacturing company. Accompanying the text was a big photo of the hand-some, buoyantly smiling Greenwald against the backdrop of a Tatra truck cab. The story was a PR man's dream and may as well have been written by Tatra's or Greenwald's own staff.

3. "Mutual Banks Moving to Shareholder Owners" by Michael Quint was the only story on all three sectional front pages that not only wasn't about a newsmaker-defined, newsmaker-con-trolled event but showed how much real reporting about real events can accomplish. This was an excellent report of a broad trend in the banking industry; it referred to many specific cases, was based on a wide variety of sources, and focused on something real, interesting, and important. Since the trend wasn't linked to

an event that happened yesterday, this was the kind of story that could have abounded on the first day after a three-day weekend.

4. "American Airlines to Lay Off 350 of Its Pilots by August 31" by Dean Baquet reported the giant airline's plan to slowly lay off upwards of 3 percent of its pilots as part of a previously announced retrenchment. The event the story was built around was the *Times*'s receipt of, or the expiration of the embargo on, a press release from American Airlines describing a self-attributed intention to take a self-defined action at a self-chosen time in the future.

Again and again, on every page throughout the entire issue, the same pattern repeats itself. The news is occasioned by and focused on events conceived, scripted, staged, and performed by newsmakers. In most cases the story is in substance largely from the viewpoint and to the liking of the principal and source. In some cases, such as the stories about Clinton and Banda, they range afield of the official story and include independently sourced and negative material. This pattern is the reason why newsmakers work so hard to script the news—because, as the record shows, while not a sure thing, it's nevertheless possible to dominate and define the way the media cover them and their topics.

For all its theatricality the newsmaker's heroism has a curiously narrow, unsatisfying, somewhat perverse quality. At first glance, these people look wonderful in the news, like the picture of President Clinton in front of the Vietnam Memorial or, in a different vein, Orson Swindle's highly successful trashing of Ross Perot's political club. On closer inspection, however, they are easily decoded as the hypocrisies that they are. The newsmaker's heroism is of a strongly wayward sort.

For one thing, the activity of solving urgent public problems is basically a limited and unheroic exercise. Theoretically the emergency-response leader's part can win the kind of glory enjoyed by the general who wins the war. Most of the time, however, the newsmaker plays the role of social engineer and speaks the humdrum, recondite languages of economics, law, and bureaucracy. Thus, the characters who perform under journalism's melodramatic survivalist marquees are types for whom it's hard to muster much real feeling.

Most successful presidential candidates in recent decades have suffered as a result. During the campaign and in the opening phase of the first term, the disasters they resist and the solutions they implement seem compelling. But when quotidian reality reasserts itself, the mood passes, the president's approval ratings fall, his negatives mount, and his programs bog down in institutional gridlock. The media's heroes have little staying power. The newsmaker seems distant, mechanical, and manipulative, and our feeling for the people involved soon fades.

In the second place, the newsmaker's role has a strongly demagogic quality. It stands or falls on the emergency-response leader's ability to evade issues, blur choices, and avoid giving offense.

As political philosopher John Locke argued in his *Second Treatise* (which is still the most important discussion of the emergency power), acts of emergency government are legitimated by a quick and nebulous social toleration. With the usual methods of framing issues and eliciting consent suspended for the duration, what makes an act of emergency government right is the fact that the people—informally, en masse—believe it necessary, feel grateful it was undertaken, think it worked, and/or don't greatly object to its having happened. In other words, what the hero of the news story is seeking isn't the affirmative approval of the audience, only its acquiescence.

Gaining this easy acquiescence is a surprisingly sleazy activity. It means taking issues out of their true context, in which there are costs as well as benefits, outcomes are always uncertain, and values are in conflict. Instead, the emergency-response leader puts matters in a context that makes a quick, superficial judgment seem plausible. Typically he (or she) suggests that the emergency response being undertaken involves no major costs or uncertainties. Thus, the newsmaker is called on to misrepresent his best understanding of the matter at hand and his intentions and expectations with respect to the future course of events. His demagogic quest for the easy answer and the quick fix is the immediate source of many of the fabrications in our culture of lying.

A chilling example of this simplifying, falsifying impulse is the role played by Paul A. Volcker in the late 1970s and early 1980s, when as chairman of the Federal Reserve Board he ended the inflation of the 1970s. This was a desirable and overdue change in monetary policy that had the broad support of the American people, but it also exposed Volcker to substantial risks. Inflation's supporters would naturally resist the Fed's new policy. Moreover, reducing inflation was likely to raise interest rates, slow economic growth, and cause a recession. To get the support he needed and forestall the potentially ruinous opposition, Volcker had to cut a correct and irrefutable figure in the news.

On October 6, 1979, weeks after his appointment as chairman, Volcker called an unusual Saturday afternoon press conference at which he announced a sweeping new policy designed to bring inflation under control once and for all. The Fed, he said, was abandoning its old policy of short-term micromanagement of interest rates, which the research of pro-market economist Milton Friedman among others had shown tended to intensify business cycles and inflation itself. Instead, following Friedman's prescription, the Fed would stop worrying so much about interest rates and focus on setting and hitting long-term targets for the amount of money in circulation. It was neither intended nor expected that the new monetarist approach would cause a recession, Volcker said. When a reporter asked if the new policy would raise unemployment or slow economic growth, the chairman answered, "I don't think it will have important effects in that connection."

That was a lie. After a quarter in which the money supply had grown at a 9 percent rate, the attempt to meet the Fed's original 1.5–4.5 percent target for M-1 growth over the entire year was certain to send interest rates sky high and the economy into negative growth. "There wasn't any question that the board knew that recession would follow," Fed Governor Philip Coldwell told journalist William Greider later. "Others would say to me, 'Well, you know this will likely cause a recession.' I told them, 'Yes, I know that.' "

It was also a lie that the Fed was converting to monetarism. Neither Volcker nor the previously pro-inflationary liberal faction on the board of governors, which gave Volcker the votes he needed to put his policy across, were devotees of Milton Friedman. They meant to continue micromanaging the money supply in the traditional manner, only now what they meant to micromanage was a disinflationary recession rather than a pro-inflationary expansion. They saw in the announcement of a new monetarist policy a way to tighten the money supply, raise rates, and turn growth negative without admitting what they were really doing. A policy of targeting the monetary aggregates that had been announced for 1979 would, in the short run, have the effect of sharply restricting the money supply. In other words, monetarism and tightening came down to the same thing in the near term. By calling the Fed's new policy an effort to give the monetarist philosophy a try, Volcker et al. were trying to minimize opposition to their policy and setting up someone else to take the blame for the recession they were engineering.

Evidence that the monetarist strategy was more a cover story than a policy began to trickle in almost immediately. The Fed didn't meet its money-supply targets in the quarter or year of Volcker's announcement or in any subsequent quarter or year during Volcker's years in office. Monetarists, after savoring the pleasant rush of hearing their ideas acknowledged by a Fed chairman, were soon to be heard protesting that, whatever Volcker might be saying about his philosophy of monetary management, the approach he was actually following wasn't anything they recognized as their own.

In an absolute political sense there was no real need for Volcker's lie. The American people were fed up with inflation and ready to pay a high price to restore the dollar's stability. As things worked out, of course, they paid precisely such a price—the recession of 1979–1982—and they paid it with unusually good cheer for the entire three-year period. Moreover, Volcker himself was a man of intelligence, seriousness, and courage, who clearly intended to do the right thing with respect to inflation and economic growth. In other words, just as the people were ready to pay the price for disinflation, so was Volcker just the man to stand up and tell them what the Fed needed to do and why it was worth the price the people would have to pay.

Volcker lied because the news genre gave him no real alternative. He was a newsmaker, and his actions with respect to monetary policy would therefore be covered according to the crisis-and-emergency-response scenario. Had he told the truth and admitted he was engineering a recessionary tightening of the money supply, the headlines would have quickly destroyed the acquiescence his policy needed to succeed. The press would have told a story, not of a dramatic anti-inflation policy demarche, but of an infamous pro-recession policy. People on the Hill and in the White House and at the Fed would have immediately attacked the policy as itself constituting a financial emergency that required instant corrective action. By providing dramatic emergency leadership in behalf of such action, these critical voices would have displaced Volcker from the hero's role in the anti-inflation drama and redefined him as the enemy or goat. Volcker and his policy would quickly have been repudiated, and the inflation would have continued.

A third wayward aspect of the newsmaker's role grows out of the process through which his actions are fabricated. The public is aware that newsmakers sometimes issue formal statements or release prepared comments for the media. However, they are generally unaware of how massive the practice is and how profoundly it influences current events. Certainly I had no clear picture of how pervasive and consequential official self-scripting was until, temporarily as it turned out, I took leave of my journalistic career in 1978 to join the public affairs staff of the Ford Motor Company as a writer and editor participating in the process of creating company positions on public policy issues. Of all the things I witnessed at Ford, nothing was more striking than the massiveness and intensity of senior executives' efforts to script and perform the news.

During my two-year stint at Ford headquarters, I learned that when our executives testified before Congress or gave an interview to a journalist or paid a lobbying call on a Senator or even just picked up the phone to talk to a member of the board of directors, they were almost never speaking extemporaneously and personally or just saying what they thought. In the vast majority of cases, executives were using a prepared text. They were literally performing.

For formal occasions, like an appearance before a congressional subcommittee or a speech to students at the Harvard Business School, there was a full text for the executive to read, word for word, from beginning to end. Encounters with the press were guided by what we called Q and A, for question and answer. These were multipage catalogues of possible questions followed by suggested responses, often a paragraph or two in length. A journalist might think he was getting spontaneous answers to questions, but almost always the source was reading from or referring to the Q and A's casually tossed amid the seeming mess on his desk.

For a wide range of other circumstances, there were talking points. These were usually lists of sentences and phrases in outline or bullet-list format. They ran to a page or two in length (on rare occasions they were longer), and roughly or quite comprehensively they sketched the flow of a monologue the executive could inject, in whole or in part, into a conversation or deliver in the form of a short speech or offhand remarks. They were very popular with the top people at Ford. They embodied the preferred combination of formality and informality, and we toilers in the vineyards of public affairs, public relations, and government relations spent no small part of our time drafting them. Talking points were often prepared for a lobbying trip to Washington, an off-the-record appearance before the *New York Times* editorial board or the editors of Time, Inc., a dinner with local Ford or Lincoln-Mercury dealers, an interview visit from a professor at the Harvard Business School doing research for a book on the role of the board of directors or the future of the manufacturing sector, or even a phone call to a member of the board of directors. Often the talking points were off-the-shelf items, and a single conversational scenario would be adapted, with small changes, for a wide range of venues.

Executives liked being scripted. Usually only relatively senior people were given scripts, so having one was a status symbol inside the company. Moreover, scripting gave executives more control over what they said. In my experience, most Ford executives were intensely political people with great sensitivity to the nuances of relationships, and thinking every interaction through before undertaking it was a source of personal pleasure as well as comfort. Even top executives took scripting very seriously and routinely spent a lot of time worrying over what to say and how to say it.

Scripting sounds ridiculous and contemptible, like something out of a satirical Joseph Heller novel. But it was undertaken with great seriousness, and it reflected a serious intention. The scripts we turned out didn't just say what we thought about the merits of issues at hand. What Ford representatives said in public was almost never the same as what people inside the company thought. We wrote scripts in order to deliberate and create the performance we hoped the press would pick up on. Scripting was our way of inventing the views and persona we would project through the media. It was the newsmaker's main contribution to the larger process by which political events and news stories were rendered empty, meretricious, and manipulative.

The actions we scripted were almost always suggested by the general crisis-and-emergency-response scenario of the news story, together with some externally occurring event or trend. Typically the actions we took were responses to an initiative or driving event occurring elsewhere; our scripting efforts were nearly always reactive. Our efforts to get into the news consisted of thinking up, writing down, and acting out scenarios we calculated would attract the media's attention and endow us with a role in the news that would provide us some advantage—usually, make us look good to the general public or help us get something we wanted from the government, such as a subsidy or tax break or change in a troublesome regulation.

A typical script I remember working on was the text for the company's response to a speech by President Carter asking the four hundred biggest corporations to limit wages and prices in a voluntary private-sector program to reduce inflation. In fact, most executives at the company thought the president's program was a completely cynical gesture that would fail to reduce inflation and, by taking some of the pressure off the Fed, might make the inflation worse. It was decided, however, that we wouldn't say that. Saying what we thought, people figured, would only make us look callous, indifferent to an increasingly severe public problem, out of touch, self-absorbed, and selfish, yet it wouldn't defeat the policy or make it unnecessary for us to cooperate with it. A blistering attack from Dearborn on the emptiness and fraudulence of President Carter's ploy would change no minds and could provoke the administration into retaliating against us in some way.

So we took the opposite tack. Rather than say what we thought, we scripted a response that said what we imagined other people would like to hear us say and what, within their frame of reference, would push events in a direction from which we could reap some advantage. Our text warmly welcomed the president's initiative, enthusiastically endorsed its goal, and in spite of the fact that our plans implied that in the program's second year we were going to be raising our car prices by more than the president's guidelines, we promised Ford's active support and cooperation with the program.

In other words, we were trying to associate ourselves with what we saw as an unstoppable political juggernaut and to derive some special advantage from it. We hoped to curry favor with the president and win some chits at the White House that we could turn to our advantage on some other issue. To a minor extent we hoped that consumers and customers would feel reassured and pleased by our promise to restrain price increases. And to a major extent we hoped that by getting on board the president's program, we would be helping to build pressures on our suppliers, including the United Auto Workers union, to restrain the increase in their prices to the company.

The scripting process has two important effects.

First, it makes the newsmaker's role manipulative. The scripting process subjects every aspect of every news performance to a more or less systematic calculation of the newsmaker's advantage. The newsmaker does what he does from the head, not the heart, and with a view to bettering himself at the expense of the audience. Even when his news performance expresses authentic feelings, their entry into the script is regulated by the prior calculus of opportunity and personal advantage.

Second, the roles and personae produced by the scripting process tend to be unstable and inconsistent over time. Circumstances, opportunities, and dangers are always changing, and as a result, so are the views expressed and personae projected by newsmakers. Seen from the perspective of the time frame in which they're offered, newsmaker performances often have the ring of truth and reality the newsmaker intends. Over time, however, they often prove to be changeable and inconsistent as well.

Consider Lee Iacocca. Seldom has so seemingly attractive and convincing a public figure been on as many sides of as many issues as the former Ford president and Chrysler chairman. As this book was in preparation, Iacocca came out of retirement to take a leading role in the political offensive mounted by the Clinton administration to persuade an extremely reluctant

Congress to ratify the North American Free Trade Agreement. There, suddenly, was Iacocca articulating the president's free trade message in press conferences and on TV spots. Unmentioned—and unmentionable—was the fact that Iacocca had spent much of the preceding fifteen years, first at Ford, then at Chrysler, urging policymakers in Washington to impose stringent quotas and tariffs on Japanese automotive imports and otherwise curb foreign manufacturers' access to the United States.

To introduce Chrysler's 1992 product line, Iacocca made a series of public statements and commercials touting the air bags with which Chrysler's minivans were now being equipped and making much of the fact that its foreign competitors' products had no air bags. Unmentioned—and unmentionable—was the fact that Iacocca for almost two decades had been point man in a concerted lobbying campaign by Detroit's Big Three to block the auto-safety movement's ongoing effort to pressure the federal government to mandate the installation of air bags.

In Iacocca's second autobiography, *Talking Straight*, the Chrysler chairman, in the course of extolling the efficiencies made possible by the modern executive jet, laments the thoughtless, self-serving executives who abuse company jets for personal purposes and warns that such misbehavior could lead boards to restrict executives' access to this useful management tool. Unmentioned—and unmentionable—were two awkward facts: first, that at the time the book was published, Chrysler owned Gulfstream Corporation, the premier manufacturer of executive jets in the United States; and second, that in 1981, the U.S. Treasury Department, while overseeing the $1.2 billion federal loan guarantee for Chrysler, had required the company to sell off its one remaining corporate jet, reserved mainly for Iacocca's personal use, after it was observed parked in an airport near a baseball spring-training site in Florida.

Sooner or later, virtually everyone whose job brings him into routine contact with the media as a newsmaker becomes similarly compromised. Changing circumstances and shifting career interests, refracted through the scripting process, lead newsmakers to take positions and adopt personae that are at least different from, and often substantially contradictory to, the actions and personae of previous performances.

Nowhere is this state of affairs more strikingly visible than in Washington, D.C. When I moved to Washington in 1981 to reorganize *Fortune*'s bureau there, I was profoundly excited to be living in the city I'd dreamed of so often as a teenage worshiper of JFK and studied for so long as a political scientist. This feeling quickly passed. Up close and personal the capital community was phony beyond belief or toleration. The Washington I got to know as a resident was a city of intense hypocrisy, a Mecca of hypocrisy, a Vatican of hypocrisy. The hypocrisy of the place impoverished conversation, undermined friendship, stupefied the mind, saddened the heart. Washington, I learned, was to hypocrisy what Mexico City is to smog, what France is to ethnocentrism, what Chernobyl is to nuclear risk, what Newcastle was to coals.

The vast majority of Washingtonians made their livings by turning society's pursuit of the common good to private advantage. Yet they never presented themselves in this light. They spoke of themselves as neutral, expert, beneficent providers of needed services to society. They were students of policy problems, gatherers of information, managers of trends, doctors of the body politic, mediators of conflict, experts on the future in a changing world, architects of global survival, security engineers. They talked like professors, think tank staffers, public health doctors, theologians, ethicists. The one thing they didn't admit to was what they were. In Washington people practiced a politics of self-interest in which no one owned up to an interested self.

The clients and constituents in behalf of whose selfish interests they toiled were invariably highly deserving. Due to no fault of their own, an exogenous event over which they had no control was harming them. A natural disaster had just overwhelmed them. A mindless bureaucracy was about to deprive them of life, liberty, or property. In short, bad things were happening to good people, and there ought to be a law against it. Government help was urgently needed.

And their opponents were evil incarnate. The capital city was abuzz with alarums about malefactors and villains; the place was a snake pit of character assassination. When the Arab oil embargo sent petroleum prices skyrocketing in 1973 and 1974, Washingtonians rushed to define as villains, not the Arab politicians who were responsible (with them we were going to deal), but the oil company executives who, in keeping with principles of market economics, raised prices to clear petroleum markets thrown into turmoil by the sudden, political shortages. When liberals ginned up a campaign to reject the nomination of Robert Bork to the Supreme Court, they projected onto a serious, talented conservative jurist, with whom they had a legitimate disagreement and whom they were right to oppose, a grotesque, made-up media identity as a kind of juridical mugger who would rob women and minorities of their rights.

Congress passed laws regulating pollution, workplace safety, employment discrimination by race and sex, pension-fund finance and management, the minimum wage, and noise levels, yet exempted itself from all. Officials routinely campaigned as critics of the system in Washington who, in office, would clean house; once safely elected or reelected, however, they coolly voted for the very programs and system they'd run against. The president had presented himself to the voters as an advocate of traditional morality, yet he'd been divorced, had married highly successful career women both times around, was estranged from some of his children, and didn't go to church. Liberals preached racial integration and egalitarianism yet lived in all-white, upscale neighborhoods and sent their children to unintegrated private schools. Conservatives preached globalist foreign policy and favored military action in defense of American interests, yet none of their sons and daughters served in the armed forces. Business organizations advocated free enterprise but lobbied to gain business advantage from big, interventionist government. Naderites preached deregulation of oligopolistic industries but urged laws strengthening the power of unions to monopolize the representation of workers.

There was a lunatic, out-in-the-open, through-the-looking-glass quality to the media-oriented dishonesty I became familiar with in Washington. The lies on everyone's lips were the obvious, classic lies of the demagogue. They were the lies that promised good news only and no bad news, the lies of the free lunch, the lies of the public figure who seeks to curry favor and avoid all criticism. Anyone could, and everyone routinely did, decode them. Yet for the most part people did this in the privacy of their own unspoken thoughts. In public or private conversation, Washingtonians rarely unmasked the lies or the people behind them. The dishonesty of the lies going about at any given time was an open secret. People were aware of it but didn't acknowledge it.

In Washington people were so strongly attuned to the world of outward appearances and political performances that if something was in the news, it was real; their inner, private selves rarely had a strong, independent, divergent response. When a president talked about family values, people took it seriously and didn't readily contrast the performance with the unstated, unperformed, unjournalized, contradictory reality. This insensitivity to the inner reality of people and events and issues was reinforced by a social norm that, in polite company, you were welcome to talk about anything, including quite technical subjects, except what, behind the public performances, you and your conversational partner were really up to. If you broke the taboo and talked about the secret reality underlying the artificial surfaces of people's pitches and poses, you could expect to be ignored or subtly punished.

It worked. The lies and postures often got officials the coverage they sought, and the coverage in turn usually pushed public opinion and government action in desired directions. A news story is, in effect, an element or phase of a bandwagon, and media-led bandwagons, it turns out, are a highly effective way of persuading people and getting things done. That is the conclusion of a celebrated series of experiments at Yale University by political scientists Shanto Iyengar and Donald R. Kinder in the late 1970s and early 1980s.

In Iyengar and Kinder's study, small groups of Yale students and other New Haven residents were brought together every night for a week to watch videotapes of network TV newscasts that had been expertly doctored to include or omit stories on such topics as inflation and defense policy. Massive before-and-after questionnaires were administered to identify changes in attitude. The findings were startlingly clear-cut: Watching even a single story substantially increased the importance the viewer attributed to the topic the story was about, and even modest increases in an issue's perceived importance were associated with changes in a person's attitude toward presidents and toward preferences among candidates for Congress.

The reason for this phenomenon was illustrated, in another context, by Gioacchino Rossini, the great early nineteenth-century composer of comic operas, who is celebrated for, among other things, the so-called Rossini crescendo. Rossini loved to write passages that began pianissimo with just two or three instruments playing a deft, pointillist, staccato theme and slowly built to a climax as new instruments joined in to repeat the theme over and over and everyone played louder and louder. Opera is a mimetic art, and Rossini's crescendos are representations of sociability. They imitate the way individuals come together to do things in swelling, compelling, ever-chattering social wholes. It's a mindless process, as the mechanical repetition suggests. But it's also an emotionally affecting process that catches up even the most resistant. Rossini crescendos, for all their dumb predictability, are deeply rousing and curiously refreshing.

What Rossini knew—it was the point that Tocqueville was to make in his epochal *Democracy in America* a few years after Rossini retired at 38 and the same truth on which Pulitzer & Company rebuilt the news business in the decades following Rossini's death—was that the modern individual is an intensely social being. Lurking behind the proud, independent, rational, individualist face he pretends to show the world, there lies a heart of pure social schmaltz. If you orchestrate a proper crescendo of news, events, and other invocations of social sentiment and social authority, there's practically nothing you can't get this person to do or believe, no matter how silly or imprudent or evil. The crescendo becomes doubly powerful when it also includes cues indicating urgent danger, thereby activating constitutional government's emergency powers and suspending normal deliberative skepticism about drastic and hasty action.

Newsmakers, while cultivating and benefiting from the press, quietly loathe it, too. They experience journalists as powerful and themselves as weak when it comes to determining the content and spin of the story. Scripting and staging news performances take a great deal of time, yet the chances of putting one's version of reality over are often modest. Dreaming up pseudoevents makes newsmakers anxious, since they're committing themselves to lies and misrepresentations that may have to be denied or covered up or contradicted later. And journalism is based on an idea of public accountability that many people at the newsmaker level resist as a matter of principle and self-concept.

Above all, newsmakers dislike the institution that empowers them because the effort to dominate the news requires that they translate themselves and their institutional purposes into the crude and distorting language of crisis and emergency response. The chief executive of a big company or the chairman of a Senate subcommittee or the leader of a Marine platoon or the coach of a track team or the music director of an opera company or the chief resident for pediatric surgery isn't merely more comfortable talking the language of his profession or organization. Typically he has devoted his adult life to that vocation and believes in it. In any case it, far more than the news, is the medium in which he primarily works, and succeeds or fails, on a daily basis. Cooperating with the media represents not just a risk but a betrayal.

CHAPTER 5

Editocracy

In a liberal society with a decent respect for the opinions of mankind, in a news industry based on providing an honest information service to the reader, the lies of news and the betrayals of newsmakers would be acknowledged and discussed and dealt with. Things would not be allowed to continue on their current course. Changes would be made. The news story might be reconstituted. The business strategy it is based on might be redirected. People would agree that the situation was intolerable and that something had to be done to ameliorate it.

In the society and news industry that prevail in America today, these problems are rarely acknowledged and little is done about them. While many factors contribute to this unhappy state of affairs, unquestionably the most formidable is the structure, culture, and especially the management of the news organization.

We are used to viewing the reporter as the key figure in the news business; in deference to his visibility, we attribute the virtues and vices of journalism to the personal strengths and weaknesses of the news worker in the trenches. This is a great mistake. It is the editor, not the reporter, who is the key figure in modern journalism. It is the editor, not the reporter or even the newsmaker, who is the principal villain of the culture-of-lying story.

The news organization is, by nature, highly centralized. Contrary to the conventional view of journalists as collegial professionals who largely manage themselves and are guided by a shared concept of news, what the news organization does is actually done at the express direction, or with the detailed approval, of the senior editorial executive and his immediate deputies. The senior editorial executive stands in much the same relation to his staff's daily editorial output as a conductor does to the output of the opera company or symphony orchestra whose performances he conceives and directs. The actual writing and editing and laying out, like the actual singing and playing and staging, are done by others, but these activities go forward under the minute scrutiny and at the detailed direction of the boss.

The editor is the central figure in the news business. He and his television counterpart, the executive producer, exercise an absolute right to assign stories and to run, kill, edit, package, and place the texts that result. He hires and fires, assigns and promotes, approves pay raises and bonuses, and says yes or no to expense items and reimbursements. He decides if a story warrants a reporting trip to Palermo or Peoria and what event will lead the issue or broadcast.

This, in short, is no mere theoretical or ceremonial role. The editor is the one actually in charge. He and his deputies are the bosses, and they dominate the news organization through intellectual firepower and strength of character as well as by formal authority. Their control is reinforced by two crucial circumstances. One is that there is usually an abundance of stories and a scarcity of time or space in which to run them. The other is that most editors got their jobs by being outstanding reporters and have the skills to take over the story and rewrite it by themselves at any time.

The dominance of the editor is demonstrated by a simple but highly revealing study of front-page coverage by David Shaw, who was at the time the media reporter for the *Los Angeles Times*. For the first 155 days of 1977, Shaw compared the stories appearing on the front pages of the *New York Times, Washington Post,* and *Los Angeles Times*. He found that, contrary to the conventional wisdom, the three newspapers had very few stories in common.

On a third of the days studied, each had a different lead story. On a fifth of the days, the three front pages didn't have even a single story in common. On half the days studied, the three front pages had only one or two of their eight or ten stories in common. A fourth of the stories occupying the lead position in one of the papers didn't appear anywhere, not even as a condensed filler item on an inside page, in either of the other two.

In other words, there is no shared understanding of news. Deciding what events are and are not news on a given day is a mostly personal, mostly idiosyncratic activity, and these decisions, and the assertions of personality, politics, and preference they rest on, are made by the boss. News as a sampling of a day's events is whatever the boss decides it is.

Editocracy—the priority and preeminence of the editor—is also visible in the uncanny similarity between the personality of the top editorial executive and the character of the publication or program he runs. Outsiders often want to know why a news medium covers a topic in a particular way, as if there were some complicated explanation known only to those on the inside. There almost never is. The "explanation" of news is almost always the obvious one: What the media run is whatever the boss thinks or says the story is, period. Put a different person in the top spot, and you get a different pattern of coverage reflecting, in part, a different personal view of the world.

The boss almost always has a view of what the story is and isn't. Sometimes he preemptively imposes his view on the news process. More often he buys into a subordinate's view of the story. In my experience it is extremely rare for a top editor to go along with a subordinate's view of the story without testing and owning it.

I'll never forget the reaction when, as a young editor at *Fortune*, I sent a story in for the managing editor's sign-off with a note that the piece was now acceptable "if still unprepossessing." What I meant was that the story was now OK to run, but it wasn't anything to take pride in and never could be. I'd worked hard to improve it and fulfill the marching orders the ME had given me, but now I'd come to the end of the line. I'd exhausted the reporting, thinking, and writing skill that lay behind the manuscript. It had become all that it could be, short of turning into my article. If the ME didn't like it, I was saying, it was because the piece just didn't have the makings of the excellent article he'd hoped for. No amount of editorial intervention on my part was going to change this fact. I was inviting my boss to accept the piece for what it was and no more.

The little note was a big mistake.

Summoned peremptorily to the boss's office, I was made to understand that this was not the spirit in which he was prepared to receive and run edited articles. He had no intention of running material that he and his editors considered mediocre or dumb or second-rate. He expected that everything he ran would be excellent journalism in which he could have pride and confidence. I would now go back to my office and resume work on the manuscript and stay at it until the story was right.

Shaken, I did so, imposing more of my words and thoughts than is desirable but succeeding in making the text read a bit better even though it remained the essentially unprepossessing piece it had been all along. This time, however, I subjected the ME to no off-putting, self-aggrandizing talk about how *Fortune*, by running this piece, would be committing itself to anything less than the ideal. This time the boss could tell himself he was running precisely the right piece.

When the editocracy is working properly, the editor's job is to have lunch and define reality. That's oversimplifying a bit, but only about the lunch part. Editors also have to have dinner, meet people for drinks, send out for pizza or sandwiches or tandoori while working nonstop to supervise and close a story, and in general talk and eat and eat and talk in an endless, peripatetic process of close personal interaction with writers, bosses, art department people, copy editors, copy processors, fact checkers, and anyone else whose contributions may be necessary to the creation and completion of the story.

The late Michael Oakeshott defined politics as the conversation of society. And conversation is the politics of journalism. The editor's job is to make an issue of a newspaper or magazine or a news broadcast, and he must elicit and coordinate tens or scores of contributions by scores or hundreds of contributors. It's done mostly by talk, and expense account meals make appropriately warm, personal, informal occasions for the kind of conversation editors and reporters need to do their jobs. They aren't the only or even the statistically most frequent place for editorial conversation, but they are the quintessential venue, the one in which the participants and actions are most at home.

What they're trying to do is figure out what the story is. The editor is the boss, and he knows what he wants and doesn't want. The reporter is the one who knows what's happening—who has interviewed the principals, observed the events, read the clips, picked up on the subtexts, and educated his intuition as to what is and isn't to be said about the subject.

The reporter talks about what is going on in the area in question. The editor compares this to the picture of the world he has in his head. If what he hears is identical with an element already present in the picture, it isn't a story. If it fits with the picture but adds something fresh, it's a story. If it's new but contradicts the picture, editors resist and cross-examine until they believe it's true and accept the changes in their picture of the world it implies. That's saying a lot. Editors, in my experience, are worldly, intelligent, demanding people. When a story is scrutinized by an editor, it's no small matter.

Often these transactions are effortless. The reporter anticipates the editor's wishes and, as it were, assigns and edits himself. The editor, drawing on her experience as a reporter, figures out what the story is and how the lead paragraph goes. The business between them is dealt with in minutes. When discussion is needed, they go to lunch.

In the end the editor decides; the story is always covered the way he chooses. When the editor listens to the reporter, and defers to him as appropriate, the news is covered well. When the editor doesn't listen or defer appropriately, the news is covered badly.

The Pulitzerian approach to the news business distorts the vital process of discussion between reporters and editors. For this conversation to create genuinely shared understandings of what is and isn't news and why, bosses and subordinates, deskmen and legmen, must be able to talk about who they are, who their audience is, and what point of view they will take in covering, or not covering, this or that story. News is a text, told from a viewpoint, meant for an audience, created by a subordinate, supervised by a boss. It reflects and furthers shared understandings when the participants can clearly discuss who they are, what viewpoint they're adopting, and who their audience is. It reflects and creates intellectual chaos when editor and reporter can't honestly and clearly discuss who they are and what they think and what they're up to.

What's on the editor's mind? What interests and perspectives drive his decisions? They vary from medium to medium, person to person, case to case, time to time. Still, some generalizations are possible.

There is almost always an important element of business strategy at work driving editorial decision making. Editors are appointed by owners or top corporate management, and in the dynamic media markets of recent decades, those in charge have generally given the people they appoint to edit the product a number of substantial and often difficult business-strategy objectives to accomplish. At the *New York Times* in the 1970s, for instance, executive editor Abe Rosenthal was given the assignment to enable the *Times* to follow its upscale, increasingly out-of-city, out-of-the-metropolitan-area audience and to develop new categories of advertisers, as the old ones—for example, the downtown department stores—became less and less productive. At the *Washington Post* starting in the 1960s, executive editor Benjamin Bradlee was given the daunting task of building a great newspaper worthy, and supportive, of its monopoly position in the capital city of the Free World. Such business-strategic goals occupy much of senior editors' time and attention and have a significant impact on the way they handle day-to-day news stories.

A second consideration that always weighs heavy on senior editors' minds is hanging on to their jobs, a task that entails satisfying those who hire and fire senior editors. A characteristic of these transeditorial powers is that the non-business-related demands they make of the editorial product are occasional, unpredictable, arbitrary, and often whimsical. The senior editorial people often have a hard time anticipating what their bosses really want and how much they want it. Thus, editors are in a permanent state of anxiety and often keep themselves uncommitted on key editorial decisions, since they never know when they'll have to reverse course in response to a phone call from the publisher or a frown on the face of the CEO. This is also a reason why editors place high value on personal loyalty in a staff editor or reporter, since they never know what they'll need to ask their subordinates to do on short notice. This is also why edit staffs are notoriously plagued with personality politics.

Third, editors often have a lengthy technical agenda—a way of writing, a style of illustration, an approach to layout, a list of pet peeves and special preferences they are introducing.

Finally there's politics. Editors and editors' bosses are always coming from somewhere, politically speaking, and these preferences have an impact on the news. This fact is always concealed and routinely denied, to be sure. But it's there—in decisions about whom to hire and whom to promote, which reporter to give this story to or to keep that story from, and so on. At *Fortune* it was clear to me that my neoconservative political views and my personal ties with neoconservative figures such as editor Irving Kristol and political scientist James Q. Wilson and Senator Daniel P. Moynihan were important bases of my career there. When, in the early 1980s, I stopped being a neoconservative and broke with my neocon friends and mentors, my standing in the world of *Fortune* and Time, Inc., was clearly renegotiated downward.

Except for their technical journalistic concerns, editors in the Pulitzerian tradition can't openly discuss much of what's on their minds. In the media business according to Pulitzer, there's supposed to be a rigid separation of editorial church and economic state, and media-firm business-strategy objectives aren't legitimate editor's concerns. Neither is the need to satisfy the personal demands and preferences of owners and corporate executives. As for an editor's ideological and political motives, these are, if anything, even more verboten: Pulitzerian journalism is supposed to be objective and nonpolitical. Thus, the editocracy can't publicly or articulately come to grips with many of the real issues framed by decisions concerning what to cover, how to shape the story, whom to assign, and so on. Editors have little choice but to resort to an arbitrary, imperial style of management—unilateral, preemptive, manipulative, heavy-handed, and often abusive.

An instance of imperial management I'll never forget took place in the twilight of the Carter presidency, when Henry Anatole Grunwald, the top editorial executive of Time, Inc., decreed that each of the company's magazines would publish a number of articles outlining an agenda for the eighties in the magazine's special area. The series would run under the title "American Renewal." At *Fortune* several American Renewal pieces were mapped out, and a friend of mine, Walter Guzzardi, Jr., was assigned to do the one on poverty and race.

Walter, a charming, brilliant, high-spirited sixty-year-old, was one of the two or three most talented people at *Fortune*. A pro-market sort-of conservative who had written memorably about regulation, law, and economics, Walter also had a sympathetic interest in social problems and social policy. His stories were lively, serious, unexpected—and so well written that they had a curious, Teflon-like ability to repel editorial interventions. Walter was no ivory-tower scribbler, either. In earlier phases of a varied career, he had been an assistant managing editor, a personal assistant to Time, Inc., founder Henry Luce, Rome bureau chief for *Time* magazine, and vice-president for public affairs of Merrill Lynch, where under longtime chief executive Donald Regan he played a leading role in lobbying for deregulation of the securities brokerage industry. Walter was the worldliest of journalists.

As Walter's American Renewal piece entered the editing process, a problem began to emerge. The story naturally devoted some space to affirmative action efforts to deal with racial discrimination. While conceding that no one appeared to have any compellingly good ideas about how to handle issues of race, Walter's piece argued that the experience of the 1970s had made it clear that there was one thing the Reagan Administration should do right away: terminate affirmative action and other such racialist color-preference policies.

The problem was that Henry Grunwald disagreed. The editor-in-chief was taking a special interest in the American Renewal pieces—the whole series was his brainchild, after all—and while he, too, felt that no one had any compellingly good ideas about how to handle issues of race, he felt strongly there was one thing the Reagan Administration should not do: terminate affirmative action programs. It should make a special point of continuing them as an earnest of the nation's commitment to racial justice.

There was never any question as to who would prevail. The editor-in-chief is responsible for everything that appears in *Fortune*, he is expected to involve himself actively in deciding how the magazines under his supervision deal with delicate topics like race, and thanks to the company's official view of objectivity in journalism as a myth, no one had to be coy about joining the issue. If Henry Grunwald wanted *Fortune* to print an American Renewal piece endorsing affirmative action, that's what was going to happen.

Walter understood and accepted that. But he pressed his views in the hope that Henry might change his mind or else back off and let *Fortune* print a viewpoint he himself didn't share—a not-unusual outcome at Time, Inc. Walter also cooperated with his story editor and the managing editor in searching for a way of dealing with the subject that everyone could live with. But he didn't back down. One way or another, he meant the story to say that affirmative action should go, and fast. If Henry couldn't live with that, Walter would take his name off the article. In that case, Walter said, Henry would be in his rights to rewrite the piece to his own liking and run it without a byline. Or Henry could kill the piece. Either way, there'd be no hard feelings as far as Walter was concerned. Couldn't a compromise be worked out?

The answer was no. Henry wanted it all—the story in the American Renewal section, the endorsement of affirmative action, and Walter's byline as well. The editor-in-chief simply started making changes in the story and sending them down to Walter to get his assent, and he kept on making changes until he had satisfied himself. Normally at *Fortune*, the draft the managing editor approves for publication is designated ME-1. Thereafter, only very modest changes are made to deal with remaining or late-breaking checkpoints and to fit the story to the layout; most stories go to the printer around ME-5 or ME-6. Henry was still rewriting and pressuring Walter when the manuscript was a virtually unheard-of ME-15. And when everything seemed settled and the story was at the printer's, Henry still didn't stop. He kept on fiddling with the manuscript, holding up the printing of a part of the issue at a cost of untold thousands of dollars.

From afar the episode may seem comic. Up close and personal it wasn't. A writer closing a story is anxious and vulnerable. An editor's real job is to support the writer and gently help him deal with the problems standing between the manuscript as it is and the ideal story as it exists in the writer's mind's eye. Henry was doing the reverse: using Walter's vulnerability to make him betray the story that was not only in his heart but pretty well perfected on paper, too. Soon the story editor and managing editor were cut out of the action, leaving the writer to face the editor-in-chief in a brutal exchange of thrusts and responses, with Henry on the thirty-fourth floor of the Time-Life Building injecting his words and thoughts into Walter's story, then sending the manuscript to the eighteenth floor for Walter to answer.

Walter, conceding minor points, defended his turf, and Henry pressed his attack day after day, draft after draft. Walter and I joked over the stream of drafts and calls issuing from Henry's office, but the laughter we shared was hollow. What was happening wasn't funny. Walter was being abused. Beneath the jovial banter, my friend was feeling shock, disbelief, resentment, guilt, denial, passivity, confusion—the classic jumbled symptoms of a victim of abuse. The editocracy of Time, Inc., had stopped working to perfect the story in the writer's heart and mind and had begun to function as its adversary.

In the end the story ran under Walter's byline and continued to take the view that affirmative action ought to go. But it was hedged about with clunky qualifications and asides, and together with the rest of the American Renewal pieces in *Time, Life, Fortune, Sports Illustrated*, and *People*, it quickly vanished without a trace the moment it was published—the fate of all writing that settles for saying the usual things to the usual people. A few years later Walter Guzzardi took early retirement. *Fortune* wasn't fun any more, he said. While still accepting occasional assignments for the magazine, he spent most of his time in the years that followed teaching journalism at Princeton and Yale and pursuing book projects.

At the core of the management style that prevails in the Pulitzerian news business is a combination of aggression and silence. When an editor wants something done, he simply orders it done and neither seeks nor responds to others' views. When he is dissatisfied with a story or an idea, he simply overrules the reporter or middle editor involved. If he senses a reporter or editor is unresponsive to his wishes, he tends to raise the issue directly with the person in question only for a short time, if at all. After that he can be expected to avoid direct contact and to preemptively reassign or otherwise punish the offending journalist.

Most reporters experience their bosses as rough customers who tend to be domineering at best, paranoid at worst. I remember running into an old student of mine at a party in New York in 1980. After savoring the glories of the Harvard *Crimson*, he had gone on to a fast-track career as a reporter at the *New York Times*. I hadn't seen him since he'd taken my course in journalism and politics, and soon I found myself asking him about the regime of A. M. Rosenthal, then the *Times*'s executive editor and for almost two decades a highly influential, and controversial, star in the *Times*'s managerial galaxy. I'm sorry, said my ex-student, and it was evident that he really was sorry, but I can't possibly talk about Abe. I know you won't say anything to anyone, but somehow, sometime, what I say will get back to Abe, and I've seen him blight too many reporters' careers to take a chance on that happening to me.

To a journalism outsider the comment might seem paranoid. I knew it wasn't, and my ex-student knew I knew. My doctoral dissertation had focused in no small part on the Rosenthal saga, in which a brilliant, mercurial, forty-year-old foreign correspondent was brought home from Tokyo to overhaul the *Times*'s coverage of one of the few places he'd never been sent to—New York City. The city staff was a journalistic monstrosity, with overvalued hacks and underused geniuses chafing cheek by jowl under layers of bureaucracy and routine. Rosenthal, the most unbureaucratic of journalists, took the place on tooth and nail, pushing aggressively for the kind of unformulaic reporting and writing that had been his trademark in New Delhi and Turtle Bay and Warsaw and ridiculing those who resisted in the name of objectivity. He'd made enemies by the dozen and shown a knack for infighting that had become legendary. He'd also assembled a growing cadre of talented loyalists whose careers flourished as his ascent proceeded.

Rosenthal is not an isolated example. Most news executives do their job more or less the way Rosenthal did his, and most end up being feared by their staffs.

Editors tell themselves—as someone who has spent years pushing a blue pencil, I have told myself—that there isn't time to talk. They say that ferocious office politics makes discussion suicidal and consensus a pipe dream. They point to the hopelessness of dealing rationally with reporters who have gone off the reservation to become allies of a given political viewpoint. Above all, they experience reporters as a source of trouble that they have to deal with under murderous time pressures.

I remember once at *Fortune*, when a story I was in charge of wasn't going well, the managing editor, in an effort to make me feel better about a tense situation, reminded me that this was the sort of thing that came with the territory—what else can you expect of a fucking writer, he asked? To editors, in their hearts, all writers are "fucking writers"—perverse people who spend their lives creating problems that editors have to struggle to solve in impossible circumstances.

In reality, of course, office politics, malingering, and time pressure are reasons for deliberating more, not less—for putting more emphasis on establishing clear, shared prior understanding of what the news organization is trying to do. The editors' self-justifications are actually thinly veiled rationalizations.

The editocracy employs a number of methods to keep the upper hand. One is the imposition of a norm of cursory reporting.

Editors maintain tight control, on a daily or even hourly basis, of the reporting that reporters do. In a daily news operation, reporters are usually assigned to stories on a daily basis or, in the case of a reporter assigned to a standing beat, monitored at least once a day. The general expectation in most news organizations is that reporters will produce a story a day—or more or less, depending on the circumstances of the case.

We think of news as being based on a reporter's thorough immersion in and familiarity with the fact of the event in question as gathered from and validated by a multitude of sources. In fact, such immersion and familiarity are unusual. Most news stories are based on a cursory exposure—typically an extremely cursory exposure—to the events, people, and issues involved. Just how cursory is suggested by Stephen Hess's study of the Washington press corps.

In 1978 Hess persuaded some 237 reporters to keep a detailed diary of their work for a week. When he tallied the results, he found that they wrote an average of seven stories, some of them major stories, the rest short items. In reporting longer stories, they conducted, by average, between four and five interviews per story. Most of these contacts were by telephone, and the diaries indicated that over three-quarters of them lasted ten minutes or less. In total the typical full-length story was based on less than an hour of actual interviewing.

For those not personally familiar with news work, it should be said that these statistics are evidence of no small industriousness. One and a half stories a day is a lot of stories to report and write, even when one of them is a short item rehashing a press release. And conducting four to five interviews per long story reflects a fair amount of enterprise. Reporting is a time-consuming, labor-intensive, nerve-wracking business of making phone calls, leaving messages, waiting for callbacks, and juggling simultaneous calls and callbacks while writing a story on deadline. For every telephone interview completed, a reporter has often made or received three or four unsuccessful calls and callbacks.

Thirty or forty or fifty minutes of real-time interviewing with four or five sources is, then, both a lot and a little. It is actually a fair amount for one person to pull off in the course of a hectic day, and it represents a substantial exposure to the subject if the test is whether the reporter is in a position to write a story that covers the basic facts about an event as these are assembled and put out by an organization, plus a few quick inputs and reactions from independent sources. But thirty or forty minutes of interviews with four or five sources is an absurdly small and inadequate amount of reporting if the test is whether the reporter is in a position to write a story based on his own independently validated information about and interpretation of events.

The cursoriness of the reporting behind most stories is partly the result of economic pressures. Reporting is expensive. Other things being equal, an effort to make a significant improvement in the reportorial foundations of news stories could easily involve a doubling or tripling of a news organization's single largest edit-side expense item.

Cursory reporting is also partly a reflection of the nature of the news product, which is a complex daily account of daily events in which many different elements—assignment, reporter travel, picture, headline, copyediting, and layout—must be produced in a matter of hours and brought together on an extremely tight and inflexible schedule. More or less by definition, the news organization's time horizon often locks it into a pattern of coverage in which there is time for the reporter to get a press release, ask a PR representative some follow-up questions, get comments from a few other sources, dash off a formulaic story—and for nothing more.

But the main reason why so much reporting is so cursory is that editors, in effect, demand that it be cursory. The subject and overall content of most news stories are decided on by an editor at the time the reporter is assigned to cover the story. In practice, the making of the assignment always involves the making of a tentative decision about what the story is. The tentative decision leaves the reporter with the job of filling in the details and validating the editor's original guesses. For this job cursory reporting is fully adequate.

To be sure, the editor's initial definition of the story can be changed. If the reporter finds the premises of his assignment are invalid, persuades his editor of that judgment, and can make clear to the editor what the story should be, his alternative version will likely prevail. But these conditions often add up to Catch-22— meeting them all can easily take more time than the reporter has been given. So the reporter often ends up ignoring any subversive, antistory vibes and confining his energy to the cursory reporting routines that validate the assignment and produce copy by press time.

Cursory reporting tends to blunt journalists' awareness of sources' deceptions. It gives journalists a spurious impression that the stories they tell are authentic and truthful. It protects the prejudgments of the editocracy from empirical inquiry.

A second technique of imperial management is the news organization's long-standing habit of stonewalling criticism. There are grounds for criticism, God knows. Pulitzerian journalists turn out a lot of tendentious news. Moreover, a high proportion of news stories contain errors of fact, as is to be expected of reportage produced in a few hours. Most of these mistakes are small: a misrendering of a name or title, an error in number or rank. But small or not, the myriad acts of journalistic slovenliness and partisanship call forth a torrent of public and private complaint.

Media respond to this feedback with fear and loathing. Whether at broadcast news outlets, where virtually no airtime is available for feedback, or at newspapers and magazines that run letters to the editor, a corrections department, and an ombudsman's column, journalists act defensively. They react as if the criticism were largely without merit, or the mistake were insignificant, or the person complaining were without standing to do so. They do whatever they can to ignore the issue and hope that by doing so they will make it go away.

A letter or phone call from a reader or viewer with a factual correction, substantive objection, or alternative viewpoint usually goes unanswered. If there is an answer, it is apt to be an acknowledgment of receipt, not a substantive response. If the reader or viewer persists or is someone whose position in the community is such that he or she can't be ignored, there may be a brief reply to the point's substance. The medium will usually refuse to print or air the complaint.

In the relatively rare case in which the news outlet concedes that there may be something to the complaint, it often offers to print an edited-down letter to the editor, usually without an editor's comment or concession as to the complaint's validity. (Television news programs can make no such offer because they have no such format, of course.) Alternatively, the outlet will offer to print or air a correction, but in that case it will do so in a very brief item told in its own voice—the complainer won't have a chance to tell his story in his own words. Thus, even when they're successful, people who pursue grievances against news media generally end up feeling like skunks at a garden party.

When criticism comes, not from the principal of a story seeking a correction or retraction in his particular case, but from an independent journalist, scholar, or critic, the range of response is narrower and the level of hostility higher. Press criticism, no matter how well founded, is usually ignored. When media do respond to their critics, it is usually as part of an active public relations campaign to discredit both the criticism and the critic.

Under the regime of the late William S. Paley, CBS News was long the most bloody-minded in dealing with critics. When journalist Edith Efron wrote her path-breaking book on the anti-Nixon bias of network news in covering the 1968 presidential campaign, CBS News went to extraordinary lengths, not just to deny the undeniable, but to discredit the author's qualifications, fairness of mind, and motives as well. It hired social scientists to write a hostile evaluation of Efron's methodology, ridiculed her content analysis by using extreme and unrepresentative examples, tried to pressure her publisher into reversing its decision to reissue the book in paperback, and otherwise attempted to blacken the name of a talented and serious journalist then working for *TV Guide* and previously employed at the *New York Times*. It wasn't, of course, simply a matter of disagreeing with Efron's critique or wanting to preserve the network's prestige. The study documented a massive violation of the fairness doctrine that opened the door to severe regulatory retribution. Efron knew it, CBS knew it; the stakes were high, CBS was desperate. Efron's next book was called *How CBS Tried to Kill a Book*.

Efron's experience, though extreme, is not an isolated case. I remember, in the fall of 1976, receiving a phone call from a man who identified himself as the president of a media research firm in New Jersey. We've never met, the voice on the line said, but I just wanted to call to congratulate you on the accuracy of your piece last summer in the *New York Times Magazine*. He was referring to an article I'd written on the networks' coverage of the presidential primaries, which had quoted at length, and critically, from the stories themselves, including a number that had aired on the *CBS Evening News with Walter Cronkite*. The voice on the line explained that CBS News had hired his firm to check all my quotations and he was happy to report that, to his surprise, he'd found every one of them to be 100 percent accurate. Once again, he said, congratulations, and rang off. I wasn't surprised he'd found no errors—knowing what had happened to Efron, I'd been fanatically careful to get all the quotes and facts right—but I found myself feeling shaken that I'd apparently been the target of an official, paid-for CBS News Division probe to evaluate the extent of my vulnerability to a counterattack.

When media organizations do admit error, usually under duress, they tend to put the blame on an individual reporter, who is often dealt with severely, by suspension or dismissal. To admit the responsibility of the editors, copyeditors, cameramen, and others involved in producing the story in question would be to admit that news isn't a mirror but a text told from a viewpoint under the direction of a boss.

Third, the dysfunctional management style of the editocracy rests on the notions that journalism is a profession and that the news worker's basic job is that of compiling an objective account of the day's events. These sound, and are meant to sound, idealistic and benign, as when journalists declare that while perfect objectivity may not be possible, they try anyway. Actually, however, these notions are pernicious. In practice, they blight discussion inside the news organization.

As I said earlier, journalists, though they practice an important and demanding craft, are not professionals in the full sense of the word as it applies to doctors or lawyers. Unlike real professionals, journalists need not have formal specialized training, aren't licensed under the state's aegis, exercise no special body of expert knowledge, are subject to no peer review or sanctions, and except for a limited exemption from the duty to give evidence in court proceedings in many states, have no special authorities or immunities. Yet newsmen, reflecting their strong identification with their calling and the value they attach to journalism's role in society, have long thought of themselves as members of a profession. The field today fairly swarms with the institutional accoutrements of a real profession—university degree programs, professional societies, awards, journals, and so on ad nauseam.

The import of journalistic pseudoprofessionalism (to call a spade a spade) is that it enables news executives to deploy the epithets *professional* and *unprofessional* as justifications for preempting discussion and as tools of managerial control.

The idea that journalism is a profession suggests that news is an objective thing out there in the real world for the professional to operate on and study, like the healthy body that is the object of medicine or the lawful society or individual that attorneys work toward. Thus the job of a journalist, the rhetoric of professionalism implies, must be to gather this naturally occurring substance, more or less as a Piedmontese farmer goes out to harvest truffles with his sow or the original forty-niners panned for gold in the Sierra Nevada.

In fact, of course, news isn't a thing—it's a text about materials created by officials and told by a journalist from a viewpoint under the direction of a boss. As such, there may be more than one legitimate way to make news, and deciding what news to produce may warrant discussion. But the rhetoric of professionalism suggests that this isn't so, that an editor's directions are legitimate, that disagreement is illegitimate.

A friend of mine once worked as an editor of one of the big newspaper Sunday book review sections, and of all his comments about life and work there, the most striking concerned the way the rhetoric of professionalism had been deployed. A book review is, of course, partly a report of the book's contents and partly an evaluation and assessment by the reviewer. But if journalism is a profession and news a thing, the subjective, evaluative aspect of a review doesn't or shouldn't exist.

My friend, a conservative of sorts, had been hired in part to add some ideological diversity to an overwhelmingly liberal staff and to get conservative reviewers and books into the review more often. However, in his job interviews with the newspaper's top editorial executives, this intention was never put that way. Instead, my friend's prospective bosses declared that the purpose of hiring him was to increase the review's fairness and balance. It was a curious and confusing way of defining the job, my friend observed. After all, he'd made his career writing and editing from a conservative point of view in publications with a conservative slant. There was no question they expected him to go on doing what he'd always done and being what he'd always been. Yet that wasn't what his marching orders said.

This discrepancy, it quickly developed, was no mere curiosity. Naturally my friend soon began articulating his conservative point of view in planning meetings and in decisions to review books, assign reviewers, and accept, reject, and edit manuscripts. And just as quickly he began running into opposition from his fellow editors. Conservative writers whom my friend suggested as potential reviewers, or conservatively inclined reviews by conservative writers whom my friend had commissioned pieces from, were attacked as unprofessional. The reviewer or review wasn't the objective report it was supposed to be, my friend's liberal opponents would say. The reviewer wasn't a professional, wasn't objective.

Book reviews were just supposed to be the news of books and nothing more, they admonished when my friend reminded them of his mission. Rejoinders that liberal reviewers were allowed to write liberal reviews in the review's pages were turned aside. Those weren't liberal pieces, my friend's colleagues would say, they were just the good, objective reports we're in business to publish.

It was, my friend observed ruefully, an extremely powerful way to press the argument. Not only did it rule out an honest discussion of the merits and demerits of a writer or review, but it put my friend on the defensive. Had anyone said, "Let's not use that guy (or draft) because he (or it) is too conservative," or "Let's do this book from a liberal or left viewpoint," that would have been fine, my friend pointed out. The issues would have been out on the table, and the critic would have been taking responsibility for his own proliberal or anticonservative position. But when my friend's colleagues used the rhetoric of professionalism, they defined their position as a neutral or objective one and his as unprofessional and illegitimate. They redefined their disagreement with him as his failure to do his job properly as a good journalist. It was, my friend remembered, a very unpleasant and— behind the self-serving pretense to self-effacing virtue—a very aggressive way to do journalistic business, one he found extremely difficult to deal with.

One of the things I liked most about working at *Fortune* was that Henry Luce hadn't accepted the myths of objectivity and professionalism. He had unapologetically embraced the truth that journalism must have a point of view, and he was perfectly willing to be held answerable for the viewpoints expressed (usually often, vigorously, and openly) in his publications. The Lucean heritage, though retreating fast, was still largely intact at *Fortune* when I worked there, and it was a source of institutional strength. At *Fortune* we could speak honestly, extensively, and civilly about point of view. I felt free, as an editor, to say that I didn't want to do this story or take that angle or feature that source because I'd be damned if my Washington section was going to make propaganda for Lee Iacocca's neoprotectionist campaigns or the Business Roundtable's weird opposition to the Reagan business tax cuts. That left my journalists free to take other views without dishonor or to find a way to deal with my objection that maybe I hadn't thought of. It also clearly defined the issues for my boss, the managing editor. If he disagreed with me, he could say so, override my preferences, and tell me to start covering this or stop attacking that.

I remember an ongoing discussion with one of my writers about the political point of view of our Washington coverage and of the magazine as a whole. I, still a neocon, took the position that *Fortune* had, and should have, a broadly conservative perspective, while he, a neoliberal of sorts, argued for centrism or eclecticism. We remained on good terms and had an excellent working relationship despite this disagreement because we didn't have to preach a professional rhetoric that would have put us at each other's throats. We were free just to be journalists who happened to have different political points of view. What a comfort it was! How awful for journalists who are forced to pretend otherwise!

A final technique for dominating the newsroom is a rhetoric of bluster, menace, humiliation, and obfuscation with which, in the manner of Don Giovanni, editors evade answerability, deflect attack, and aggrandize themselves.

I plead guilty to having done some of this myself on occasion. I remember, as a newly minted assistant managing editor at *Fortune*, being the target of an angry memo to the managing editor from a writer who was offended by my editorial manners. This was soon after I'd returned to *Fortune* from Ford, and the story in question was a controversial (in retrospect, prescient) piece about how the Japanese car companies were in the process of abandoning their old policy of manufacturing in Japan and exporting to the United States and beginning to build plants in the United States and the other markets where they were selling more and more of their products. Skeptical, fascinated, wanting (I now understand) to lay claim to expertise in the subject matter, I scribbled comments all over the draft. While some were appropriate editor's queries and comments, most were just personal reactions by someone steeped in the topic and highly reactive to the issues involved.

My marginalia constituted a serious breach of editorial ethics. A draft belongs to the writer, not the editor, who is supposed to intervene in a measured and respectful way with specific issues and necessary suggestions. The writer, a Time, Inc., veteran who knew his rights, understandably took umbrage and sent my boss the angry memo.

Summoned to the ME's office to explain myself, I declared breezily, "I wish he'd written his first draft as well as he wrote this memo." It was a completely unfair comment—demeaning, irrelevant, obfuscatory. And it worked perfectly. The managing editor was greatly amused, we shared an unjust laugh at the writer's expense, and I never heard another word about the episode. My use of an issue-confusing, responsibility-deflecting rhetoric of condescension had protected me.

Editors are men and women in the middle, continually squeezed in the vise of Pulitzer's big lie. They experience an often threatening and painful discrepancy between what they really do and what they're supposed to do. They routinely resort to this rhetoric of abuse and self-aggrandizement as a means of resolving the contradiction. This way of talking and interacting verbalizes a view of the world that defines the many people who impinge on the editor's work life as objects to be manipulated, not subjects to be connected with.

No major editorial executive in our time has exemplified this style better than Benjamin C. Bradlee, the former *Newsweek* Paris correspondent and Washington bureau chief who in 1966 was put in charge of news operations at the *Washington Post* and over the ensuing quarter century built the newspaper up into one of the world's great publications. Bradlee, now retired, was the mastermind of the *Post*'s cutting-edge coverage of the Watergate story (he was played by Jason Robards in the movie *All the President's Men*). He was also in charge during the infamous Janet Cook affair, in which the *Post* printed an exposé about an eight-year-old ghetto crack addict named Jimmy, then was forced to repudiate the story as a hoax, fire its author, a staff writer named Janet Cook, and return the Pulitzer Prize she had won for the series. In the ups and downs of a tumultuous and important career, Bradlee demonstrated many strengths, but candor and a sense of answerability in the face of criticism weren't prominent among them. To the contrary, when the conversation took a turn that might not be to his advantage, he often responded in an aggressive, obfuscatory, defensive, self-aggrandizing way.

I witnessed a memorable performance at a Reagan-era debate pitting Bradlee against media mogul Rupert Murdoch on the question of whether the national press has a liberal bias. Naturally Bradlee argued the negative. He admitted nothing and denied everything. What was liberalism, anyway, Bradlee sneered? There was no such thing any more, if there ever had been. The proposition made no sense to start with.

Bradlee then went on to attack the competence and intellectual honesty of researchers Robert and Linda Lichter and Stanley Rothman, whose careful, professional survey of press attitudes had concluded that a large majority of reporters and editors are liberals. The survey was a lie, Bradlee blustered. The researchers couldn't possibly have interviewed the staff members of the *Post* they claimed to have interviewed. Bradlee knew these people intimately, and they weren't the liberals and elitists the Lichters and Rothman said they were. The centerpiece of Bradlee's talk, which he read from a prepared text, was a lengthy rehearsal of the biographies of key *Post* reporters and editors who came from small towns or went to nonelite colleges—as if only Harvard grads or native New Yorkers could be liberals.

But the leading case of self-aggrandizing Bradlee smoke-blowing is the one that unfolds in his 1975 book, *Conversations with Kennedy*, completed in the year the *Post*'s Watergate coverage forced Nixon to quit the presidency. This record of a warm friendship and productive journalistic relationship with John F. Kennedy is a bravura editorial performance on several levels. It is, among other things, a heartfelt memoir of a departed friend and golden life experience; a preemptive refutation of any notion Nixon loyalists might have entertained of accusing the man in charge of the Watergate story of holding a grudge against presidents as such; and a pre–Jason Robards bid for personal celebrity. The book is also, however, an occasion for journalists to reflect on relationships between presidents and reporters and on the ethical standards that should guide them.

The relationship Bradlee describes, while coolly affectionate in the ironic fifties manner, was primarily professional—and exploitative. The journalist and the president were enmeshed in a bustling barter of journalistically and politically useful information. When the president had a message to put out, he'd whisper it into Bradlee's ear, and *Newsweek* in turn would pass it along to its millions of readers. When Bradlee needed information for a story or to satisfy his bosses' interest in such matters as what *Time* was going to put on its cover the following week, he asked JFK, and the president or one of his aides would quickly provide an answer.

Both at the time and in retrospect, Bradlee was in awe of the glamour of it all. "It happens to very few of us that some neighbor, some family friend, someone whose children play with your children (however reluctantly), becomes president of the United States," he gloats in the introduction. "It now seems clear that when it happened to me, that friendship dominated my life, as Walter Lippmann had warned me it could."

Yet what lay beneath the glittering surface was a coldly mercenary relationship in which the president was on top and the journalist in a distinctly inferior position. Thus, when Bradlee was quoted in a 1962 magazine article as saying that the Kennedys were obsessively jealous and controlling as newsmakers, the president, as if to prove the point, brusquely retaliated by terminating all contact with his pal from *Newsweek* for three months. To this haughty move—utterly out of keeping with the friendship Bradlee's book insists they had but perfectly fitting the context of a collaboration to make and sell self-aggrandizing presidential images and journalistic lies—Bradlee responded as an increasingly abject supplicant.

At one point during this exile, Bradlee sought and was given access to FBI investigative materials on extremist political groups that were putting out a story that before his marriage to Jacqueline the president had had a secret marriage that had been quickly annulled. This information was provided on two conditions: that no copies of the FBI materials be made and that

Bradlee submit his finished story for the president's personal approval. Bradlee tells his readers how he took the typescript to a vacationing JFK in Newport, Rhode Island, waited while it was read and OK'd, then heard his presidential Pythias cruelly tell the British ambassador as he arrived for the next appointment that the newsie wouldn't be joining them later to watch the America's Cup race.

In the post–Pentagon papers, post-Watergate, adversary-journalism world in which Bradlee was writing and we still live, this relationship cries out for critical evaluation. Does Bradlee still think it acceptable that a journalist, acting on his own, should formally agree to submit to a newsmaker's personal censorship stories about a subject of great political and personal sensitivity to him? Does he think that one of his reporters at the *Post* would be justified in entering into such a relationship at a time when the newsmaker was punishing the reporter by refusing all contact with him?

My own view is that Bradlee's conduct was ill advised and that he should have recanted and repented in this book, written a decade and more after the events in question. However, I can imagine a serious argument for taking the view that, given proper management by *Newsweek*'s top editors, the journalistic benefit was worth the compromise of the reporter's independence and self-respect. But Bradlee doesn't offer such an argument. He tries to blow past all these difficult issues with his standard editor's blustering, obfuscating, self-aggrandizing patter. He seeks to exculpate himself on the uncompelling ground that he isn't likely to have such a relationship again. The one implied apology he issues is for the "sin"—of which no one accused him—of failing to keep complete notes of his conversations.

> I never wrote less than I knew about him, filing the good with the bad. But obviously, the information Kennedy gave me tended to put him and his policies in a favorable light, even though all such information was passed through special filters, in the first instance by me, and to a greater extent by *Newsweek*'s editors. If I was had, so be it; I doubt I will ever be so close to a political figure again. If I should get that close again, there will be nothing missing from my record of conversations.

Seven years later, Bradlee reaped as he had sown when he and his institution were victimized by the hoax about an eight-year-old crack addict fabricated by a staff reporter who practiced the journalistic ethics her boss espoused in this unintentionally revealing book.

There is room—not a lot, but room—for diversity, disagreement, and independence in an editocracy, even a very repressive one. But at the margin the tendency is almost always away from freedom and diversity and toward control and uniformity. The higher you rise in a news organization, and particularly as you go from writer/reporter up into editorial management, the less independence you have and the more pressure there is to toe the line. You might think it would be the other way around, that the top editors would have the most freedom and the youngest new reporters the least, but it isn't. The editocracy is about control, not freedom, as can be seen from the different experiences I had with two professional crises that came my way at different stages of my career at *Fortune*.

Crisis No. 1, similar to Walter Guzzardi's encounter with Henry Grunwald over affirmative action, occurred, when I was a fairly new member of the writing staff, in connection with a story I wrote for another Time, Inc., inventory of the state of U.S. institutions, this one a celebration of the bicentennial. My subject was the press, and the problem was that Hedley Donovan, Grunwald's predecessor as editor-in-chief, wanted to remove some material from my text that I thought should stay in the text.

At issue were some quotations by four very prominent figures in American journalism who, in my interviews with them, had expressed qualified agreement—*heavily* qualified, but still agreement—with the substance of Vice President Spiro Agnew's attack on the "nattering nabobs of negativism" in the national press. (Drafted by then–Nixon White House speechwriter Pat Buchanan, the statement anticipated by two decades Vice President Dan Quayle's attack on Murphy Brown for the social agenda implied by her decision to become a single mother.) The quotes reflected the intense discomfort many senior newspeople and media executives had felt about hounding a sitting president out of office, however much he may have deserved it. The names attached to the statements were impeccable: Katharine Graham, CEO of the Washington Post Company; John Chancellor, then anchorman of the *NBC Nightly News*; Howard K. Smith, the ABC on-camera commentator; and Richard Clurman, former chief of correspondents at *Time*. All said what most journalists had therefore denied, namely, that while they disliked the man and opposed the political intentions of what he'd said, they reluctantly had to concede that Agnew's critique had some merit.

Hedley wanted the quotes out of the story. This wasn't because he'd decided against allowing *Fortune* to print a story making the substantive point I was marshaling the quotes to bolster (the point stayed in). And it wasn't because Hedley thought the quotes weren't authentic (I'd taken the unusual step of having the fact checker call each of the people to confirm the quote, in effect allowing them to recant; none of them did). Hedley wanted the quotes out, apparently, because he just didn't want us to embarrass one or more of these particular press grandees.

I refused to go along for the obvious reasons—the quotes were both newsworthy in themselves and integral to the story. Hedley insisted, so I took my name off the story and that was the end of it. Though I was allowed a more honorable form of defeat than Walter Guzzardi was five years later, the experience was nonetheless awful and for the same reason Walter's experience was awful: When I was at my most vulnerable, my editors were attacking my article for its merits and were trying to make the piece say something other than what I believed. Moreover, by defying the man in charge of all Time, Inc., magazines and a powerful member of the company's board of directors, I was taking a career risk.

Actually, things worked out surprisingly well. My editors at *Fortune* were sympathetic to the substance of my position. The issue was so simple that there wasn't much to argue about, so no one said anything in the heat of debate that he later came to regret. When the managing editor called me in to ask me to reconsider, I said that it was his magazine but my name, and thanks, but I couldn't put my name to this. He replied, gracefully, that as far as he was concerned, it was partly my magazine, too, and he hoped that I'd come to share that feeling. The only really lasting negative consequence of the episode was a chill between me and the story editor, a writer and editor of great intelligence and technical skills and mostly sympathetic views, who had been a mentor of sorts and from whom I'd learned a lot. He and I rarely spoke after that. We never worked on a story together again.

A couple of years later, as a newly minted story editor determinedly shinnying my way up the greasy pole, I found myself doing to other writers' work what Hedley and my story editor had done to mine. An experience I'll never forget is editing a troubled piece about airline deregulation by a talented staff member who was something of a specialist in transportation companies.

Like many in the airline industry, this writer was scornful of the idea that airlines should be deprived of their government license to operate as an official cartel and forced to start competing in a newly freed-up marketplace. His article was an attack on airline deregulation in the guise of sketching a strategy by which airlines could renew their business without having to endure the radical surgery being planned by the newly influential pro-market forces in Washington.

Not long before, I'd written a piece about deregulation myself, in which I'd strongly supported the cause of remarketizing the airline business. Naturally I hated the writer's story when I read it in first draft, which appeared to have lots of editorial problems as well as the political problem of saying something that I hated and that was contrary to the position *Fortune* had taken on the issue previously. Seeing that the writer and I were going to be at each others' throats over the substance of the piece, I went to the managing editor and asked him to kill the story or assign it to another editor who could be more sympathetic to the thesis.

The ME listened carefully, but he didn't have a suitable substitute ready to run in place of this one, and the other editors had a lot on their plates just then, and anyway, I was the member of his staff with the special background in regulatory issues that would be needed to do the thorough rethinking and potential rewriting that would be required to get the piece in shape for the coming issue. If that meant rewriting the piece myself, well, he knew I could do it.

I outlined my editorial points with the writer and halfheartedly sent him back to his typewriter for a fresh draft. As I'd anticipated, however, his heart wasn't in the changes I'd sketched, the piece didn't get better, and with time running out, I took it over and rewrote it myself. The result was barely publishable; a rewrite man coming into the picture at the last minute to rescue a sick article never makes it really well, least of all when he hates the point the piece is trying to make. And naturally the revised version ended up saying roughly the opposite of what the writer believed.

Soon thereafter the writer went on leave to take up a position in Jimmy Carter's Office of Management and Budget. He never returned to the magazine.

Looking back, I believe I should have stuck to my guns. When the ME rejected my advice to kill the piece or give it to another editor, I should have done what, as a writer, I'd insisted be done with respect to my article on the press. I should have refused the editing assignment. An editor should never attempt to make a writer betray the story in his heart and mind.

The fact that I didn't do the right thing says something about the nature of editocracy. A writer can take his name off an article at little cost to his career—top editors can accept such behavior, some of them may even admire it on occasion. But an editor who refuses an assignment has to expect to be fired. When I went along with the ME's request and butchered the antideregulation writer's piece, it never occurred to me to say no. It wasn't just that I was ambitious, that I liked and identified with the managing editor, that I thought he had a right to make his own decision after listening to all claims and viewpoints. It was that the whole point of being a magazine editor was to be in charge. As long as I wanted to be an editor, it made no sense to refuse a legitimate editing assignment, and if by some strange stroke of fate I had been seized by an uncontrollable impulse to do the right thing by this airline writer, it would have been the same as deciding I didn't want to be a *Fortune* editor after all.

The analysis in this chapter has been based primarily on my personal experience as a reporter and editor. There is plenty of external confirmation of this perspective, however. Most popular and historical writing about particular news organizations and executives—Gay Talese's *The Kingdom and the Power*, for example, or the spate of books in the late 1980s and early 1990s about the collapse of CBS News—take a similar view of the journalistic community, emphasizing the swirling interpersonal politics and domineering bosses. Perhaps the most striking reinforcement of the view I've taken of the news organization, however, is to be found in the widely ignored yet absolutely extraordinary research Chris Argyris conducted at the *New York Times* in the late 1960s and early 1970s.

Argyris, a Harvard management professor who has made a specialty of applying psychological and psychiatric perspectives to the study of organizational behavior, sought and received permission to study and improve the decision-making process of top editorial and corporate management at the *Times*. For three years, with the support of president and publisher Arthur Ochs Sulzberger, he had wide-ranging access to observe, record, and intervene in senior management meetings, in effect functioning as a kind of organizational and management therapist. After three years the relationship was terminated, and Argyris returned to Cambridge to write up his findings in what I take to be a deliberately unapproachable tome, *Behind the Front Page: Organizational Self-Renewal in a Metropolitan Newspaper*. The nation's newspaper of record was given the pseudonym *The Daily Planet*, and the names of the various editorial and corporate luminaries were represented by letters. But for a reader who takes the trouble to look past the social-sciency diction and to figure out that P was Sulzberger, R executive editor A. M. Rosenthal, and T editorial page editor John B. Oakes, the book is a profoundly fascinating— and shocking—look at the way the world's most important journalistic organization is, or was, managed.

Argyris describes what he calls a living system of informal norms and actual management behavior. The system was characterized by the following traits:

• In meetings, the most frequently observed behavior was the assertion of a personal point of view. The next most common, which occurred much less often, was the expression of openness to new ideas or others' views. The least frequently observed behavior—in fact, Argyris never observed it in scores of hours of sessions—was the expression of an executive's feelings or of openness to another executive's feelings.

• Competitiveness, conformity, and low trust were the norm. People related to others as objects to be manipulated rather than subjects to be connected with. Interactions were approached as if they were a win-lose game.

• Comments tended to be more judgmental than diagnostic, control-oriented rather than innovation-seeking, and incoherent in the aggregate—everyone talked, but no one seemed to be listening to or affected by the comments of others.

• Conflict was avoided or covered up and threatening information was withheld. Such consensus as emerged in meetings was often an illusion that would disappear as soon as people got back to their desks. The meetings themselves were viewed as a waste of time.

• Actual decisions were made at the top and in secrecy. The *Times*'s executives believed that real leadership was controlling and directive and focused on specific tasks and objectives. It did not, in their view, pay attention to feelings and emotions. There were two main leadership styles, one overbearing and dominating, the other withdrawn and passive.

Argyris was witness to the deliberations surrounding a number of important decisions taken by the *Times*. One was the 1970 decision—in retrospect an exceptionally successful one—to create the paper's now-famous and widely imitated op-ed page. It had been under increasingly active consideration for four years, but action had been blocked because the two topmost editorial executives—Abe Rosenthal representing the news department and John Oakes representing the editorial page staff—were at each other's throats over the question of who would control the new page. Finally, Argyris reports, president and publisher Punch Sulzberger simply made the decision by himself and presented it to his management team as a fait accompli, with Oakes getting control and Rosenthal losing out.

This was not, however, because Sulzberger was particularly on Oakes's side. Quite the contrary, Argyris found substantial ongoing disagreement between Oakes and Sulzberger on the political viewpoints and style expressed on the *Times*'s extremely influential editorial page. Argyris quotes a typical expression of the talk-ing-past-one-another relationship the two had (in this passage, T is Oakes, X is Argyris, R is executive editor Abe Rosenthal, and P is Sulzberger):

> T: The paper for years had a reputation of being a great paper except for its editorial page. I think maybe what I consider to be vigorous and definitive is what you would call angry, and what R considers shrill, which is a word I don't appreciate but use because he did so.

> X [to P]: Do you believe there is shrillness and striden-cy in the editorials?

> P: Yes, sometimes, and that concerns me.

> T: I don't think they're shrill at all.

> P: I think they are, on occasion, and my associates feel it more than I do.

> T: I really reject totally the criticism that we run a shrill editorial page. I really do not believe this is justified. I would say that occasionally a phrase gets by that gives some basis for that remark, but it is rare.

A few years later a still vigorous, still-heedless Oakes was pushed into retirement.

Argyris brought no particular scholarly background in journal-ism to his work, which is confined rigorously to the framework of organizational psychology. At the end of his book, however, the otherwise scrupulously scientific author allows himself this reflection on the larger implications of the organizational and interpersonal behaviors he encountered at the *Times*. His com-ment is occasioned by a remark made by one of the participants when the *Times* abruptly canceled Argyris's study.

"You launched us on an important trip," the *Times* man observed. "We just began. . . . I wonder if it was enough to make us want to move forward, or are we frightened by the vision of an open society?"

To which Argyris responds in a comment that makes a fitting conclusion for this discussion of the editocracy and the culture of lying:

I would agree that these men are frightened. But I believe that what they fear is not so much their vision of an open society but the ways in which they would be required to live and work if the vision were to become a reality. It seems to me that these people manage to maintain their sense of integrity by living with visions. When they make requirements for actual behavior, they make them for everyone except themselves, and for institutions other than their own.

Individuals of high intellectual ability can live with this paradox by doing to society at large what they have learned to do within their own living system—project their difficulties and problems onto others. Thus they attack local and state governments, national political institutions, business, labor, education, and so on, with impressive vigor, thus fulfilling their role as watchdogs of society. The irony is that newspapers may be performing these valuable services by systematic processes that could eventually distort the validity of their reporting, interpreting, and editorializing.

If this is the case, one could predict that newspapers will vigorously resist the behavior they would require of others. For example, newspapers may demand that institutions of government be open to the press, but they will nevertheless argue that they themselves should be closed to examination. They may insist upon being the artillery of the press, but they will see no reason why outsiders should take aim at their methods of operation. And newspaper officials will be quick to condemn their critics not only because they represent a threat to the freedom of the press, but because an investigation of the internal workings of the press might reveal that newspapers are managed by a system whose characteristics are the very ones they so often denounce.

CHAPTER 6

Traitors to Their Experience

A rugged process of selection and self-selection controls entry
into the news business. Non–team players are ruthlessly weeded
out, and those who make the cut generally follow the rules of the
news genre and cooperate with the editocracy. They tend to
behave like the reporters who attended a May 10, 1971, press
conference in Washington, D.C. at which Father Theodore M.
Hesburgh, the president of Notre Dame University and President
Nixon's Civil Rights Commission chairman, released the annual
report of the commission and called on the nation to redouble its
commitment to civil rights and racial progress while avoiding divi-
sive rhetoric of confrontation and blame.

The reporters weren't buying Hesburgh's seemingly complacent summons to civic virtue. His theme sounded suspiciously
like the administration's proposals for "benign neglect" of racial
issues, a position that had been trashed by liberals and civil rights
activists as a cover for neosegregationism. Since Hesburgh was a
liberal Republican who truly believed in civil rights and not a

Nixonite, the reporters began pushing him to disavow what they took to be a disingenuous civility and own up to the contempt he really felt for the administration's record on racial issues:

Q. Father Hesburgh, how would you now at this point assess the commitment and personal leadership of President Nixon?

A. I think he has spoken to the problem of civil rights a good deal in the past six months. We as a commission have disagreed with a number of his stands, as we have stated publicly. I think this is a problem which is going to require increased commitment and increased leadership over the years to come, especially over the months to come.

Q. Father Hesburgh, how can you expect [the Department of Housing and Urban Development] and the other federal agencies to follow a vigorous program of civil rights enforcement when the president . . . has indicated very definitely that he is against the idea of mixing economic and racial questions into the whole problem of residential desegregation?

A. All I can say is that we think the two questions are very much connected and that they have to be pursued concurrently.

Q. Well, are you criticizing the president for failing to do that?

A. We are certainly disagreeing with his stand, although I would have to say his stand is completely legal in his judgment I would guess. . . .

Q. Father Hesburgh, I'm still a little unclear as to how you assess Mr. Nixon's aggressiveness or lack of aggressiveness in the civil rights field.

A. Let me take a long shot at it. I think that what we have said in this report is that the whole bureaucracy has to move, and I assume that means it has to move from the top down to the very bottom. As one of our commissioners said last night in discussion on the matter, what our report really amounts to is that the dinosaur finally opened one eye. But that is hardly a complete move forward. We have said in the past, and we say it again today, that the whole government needs to be more committed to this. It needs to speak more forcefully about it and act more forcefully, give more leadership from top to bottom.

Q. Well, are you—

A. I can't make it any more clear than that.

Q. Well, are you dissatisfied with the leadership from the president?

A while later they were still hard at it.

Q. Mr. Chairman, when it takes the Justice Department six months to come to a decision, which it hasn't yet reached, on Blackjack [a Missouri town where racial integration in federally subsidized housing was at issue], and it takes them two years to decide what to do about tenant and site selection, do you feel there is any particular locus in the federal government for delay in civil rights?

A. I think it runs throughout the federal government. I think if you read this report carefully you will find very little that is cheering in any part of it. Now, you see little places where you're making small advances. You see a lot of promises. But I think I'd have to say that there are very few civil rights heroes through the government today or in the last three administrations with the possible exception of Lyndon Johnson.

Q. Why is there a very evident reluctance on the part of the commission as a whole, with the exception of a few isolated statements here and there, to pinpoint leadership and to blame particular officials who are in the policy-making position? ... I sense here you want to blame everybody without pinpointing the leadership of the nation.

A. I think it's easier to get headlines though if you say the president is a bum or something like this, but that doesn't really answer the question. What we're saying here

is we need a systemic change. You're not going to solve it—
one man isn't going to solve anything. You could put the
good Lord in as President of the United States and He
wouldn't solve this problem if everyone wouldn't cooperate.

Q. Don't you agree, Father Hesburgh, it's been shown
over and over again in civil rights cases that whether it's
the mayor of a town or a police chief out on the street or a
President of the United States, when you have the word
passed, when you have leadership, that you find the rest of
the troops falling into line whether they like it or not?

A. Yes, I grant you, strong leadership across the board
gets it. It has to start from the top and it has to go to the
bottom. . . . I think it's easy to say, "This guy is to blame,"
and the rest of us go home and relax. I think you're to
blame. I think I'm to blame. I think the American people are
to blame. And I think we need more commitment and more
leadership from top to bottom.
Now if you say, "Does this mean there isn't enough on the
top?" Of course it means that. Does it mean there isn't enough on
the bottom? It means that, too.
All I say is I don't want to take a simple way out of this and say
the only answer to this is one man doing something or ten men
doing something. I think it's going to take a commitment of many,
many men, and the higher you are the more you have to be committed. I'll say that.

On that note of unchanging dissonance, Act I of the Hesburgh
press conference came to a close, and the reporters retired to
newsrooms, bureaus, and broadcast studios across Washington. In
Act II, which opened immediately thereafter, the reporters transformed their encounter with Hesburgh's report into news stories.
A sharper contrast is hard to imagine. Forgotten as if it had never
happened was the aggressive rudeness of the press conference;
now all was sweetness and light. That evening and the next day,
the media calmly played the story Hesburgh's way.
"WASHINGTON, May 10" began the story in the upper left-hand
corner of the front page of the *New York Times*.

The United States Commission on Civil Rights, which reported
seven months ago that the Government had virtually abdicated its
responsibility in rights enforcement, said today that there had
since been some progress in enforcement by the Nixon Administration.

"The dinosaur finally opened one eye," said the Rev. Theodore M. Hesburgh, chairman of the commission, at a news conference in which he summarized the findings of a new Government-
wide survey.

But the commission also found substantial "regression" in
civil rights activities in some agencies. . . .

In the rest of the press and on the TV networks, the story was
much the same—that the Civil Rights Commission's annual
report had sounded a mostly positive note in calling for a renewal
of America's commitment to civil rights. The stories did not
report, as their authors had obviously wanted to, that Hesburgh
had attacked Nixon or viewed the president's record on civil
rights invidiously. Neither did they report, as in all honesty they
should have, that journalists had pressed Hesburgh to attack
Nixon and that the good father had determinedly refused to do so,
to the point of misrepresenting his own critical views of Nixon's
record rather than give the newsies the ammunition they wanted.

In other words, despite their relish for a story about the liberal
appointee of a conservative president attacking the man who
appointed him, the reporters went along with the newsmaker's
version of reality. When the good father stood his ground, spurned
the reporters' invitation to speak frankly about his views of the
administration's civil rights strategy, and persisted in giving the
report a disingenuous pro-Nixon spin, the reporters, once they
saw their pressure tactics weren't going to work, caved in. They
stopped fighting for the truth as they understood it and wrote the
story Hesburgh's way even though this meant saying things and
giving an impression they thought was untrue.

The reporters could, after all, have told the truth about what
happened. They could have written that Hesburgh had given a
disingenuous, pro-Nixon version of the event, that he had rejected the reporters' aggressive invitations to own up to his real sen-

timents about the president's record, and that he'd refused to say clearly what he thought about Nixon's strategy in an apparent effort to avoid embarrassing that strategy. Telling the story this way, however, would have required the reporters to make statements about Hesburgh's meaning that would be inconsistent with what Hesburgh said he meant, and this in turn would have required the reporter to take intellectual responsibility for the story. This the reporters in this drama evidently weren't prepared to do. They hid their lights under the bushel of their habit of evading narrative responsibility. They handed over to the principals of their stories carte blanche to control what would and wouldn't be in the news.

Knowing or finding out the truth about a situation, then writing a story that slights one's big discovery and misrepresents one's understanding of the event—this is the core experience of Pulitzerian journalism. It happens at every publication, it happens on almost every story, it happens to every reporter. Knowing one thing and writing something else is to daily journalism what blocking and tackling are to football, what olive oil is to Italian cuisine, what Shakespeare is to English literature. It isn't always like that, to be sure; there are occasions in which things work out more happily. But much of the time the working reporter ends up a traitor to his experience of the topic at hand.

Sometimes this happens with stark explicitness. Edith Efron recalls the time in 1945 when, as a recent graduate of Columbia Journalism School and a newly hired staff writer for the *New York Times Magazine*, she was assigned to cover a convention of the National Association of Manufacturers in New York. With the war winding down and thoughts increasingly fixated on the issue of integrating millions of servicemen into the postwar civilian economy, the Committee on Economic Development had formulated a joint government-business pledge that every returning GI would have a job waiting for him when he got out of uniform. Efron's task was to report and write a story about the plans America's industrialists were making to implement this pledge.

The inquiring reporter quickly discovered that there were no such plans. There was no program by the federal government to encourage or help pay for the returning veterans' employment, and in the absence of such a program, the members of the NAM were despairing. What are we supposed to do, they asked, fire our existing workers to make room for the veterans? A promise had been made that couldn't be delivered on, and the business people were scared and upset about what was about to unfold.

This was obviously very big news, and Efron quickly wrote the story and handed it in to her boss, Lester Markel, the newspaper's legendary Sunday editor. Next thing she knew, Markel was discussing the piece with the *Times*'s publisher, Arthur Hays Sulzberger, and with high officials in the CED and the federal government itself. Soon Markel passed word along to Efron that the story had been killed. With the war still underway, he explained, it would be demoralizing to the troops in the trenches as well as to the American people as a whole to be told that there were no jobs waiting for the returning soldiers after all. Efron recalls her sense of shock and astonishment at the spectacle of big journalism, big government, and big business coolly and explicitly collaborating to validate a lie and withhold important information from the public.

Usually the lies of news aren't explicit or visible. The editocracy's close control of the reporter's time and agenda guarantees that reporters rarely encounter and get involved in big stories that their bosses haven't already sanctioned and the newsmakers haven't already scripted and enacted, stories like Efron's discovery that there were no jobs plans. As a result, journalists are usually only dimly aware of the made-up, manipulative, collaborative quality of news events and stories. Thus, they are rarely very conscious of being parties to a lie. What they *are* aware of is doing their jobs under murderous time pressures and amid ferocious cross-cutting demands and, when the story is done, possessing a certain amount of unused material that didn't seem to fit in with the story but that is still important and interesting.

These leftovers are a measure of the dishonesty and manipulativeness of the culture of lying. They are not, however, evidence of conscious lying, at least not often, on the part of the reporters. The culture of lying grows out of reporters' innocence and submissiveness, not their cynical dishonesty. Editors, whose work puts them in a position in which the choices they're making are often sharply defined, are indeed often cynical and unscrupulous. But to the reporter working in the tightly controlled environment of the news business, the choices aren't so sharply apparent and the level of personal responsibility is lower. As they see it, they're simply covering the news and discovering that, when the day is done, some important, contrary information somehow seems to have stayed in their notebooks and minds. They don't mean anything by it. Indeed, they vaguely regret it and frequently tell themselves they'll have to do something with it sooner or later.

Why do reporters accommodate themselves so comfortably to the requirements of the genre and the pressures of bosses and newsmakers? The answer is straightforward: Because they have a weak sense of self and a correspondingly strong need for the validation of others, especially powerful others. In other words, we are courtiers, people strongly oriented to vertical social relationships, avid for the approval of those above us in the social hierarchy and the deference of those below, quick to reflect those who relate to us with approval and to reject any who manifest criticism or withhold approval, deeply enmeshed in a personal as well as societal politics of privilege and advantage.

The reporter is able to embrace lies and contradictions when these are validated by the people whose approval and deference he or she needs. To put the same idea the other way around, the reporter's need for approval and deference is often so strong that he or she is able to embrace contradictions and lies with little difficulty.

Working at *Fortune* was a feast for a courtier's appetites. It exposed me on a friendly footing to the topmost members of the American hierarchy—to senators, CEOs, leading experts of every kind. A reporter's career is unmatched for the vertical and horizontal reach of the affiliational satisfactions it offers. Below are the hundreds of thousands who are the journalist's readers or audience. And just above and below are the members of the news organization and the other politically relevant reference groups of which the journalist may be a member, as I was a member of the neoconservative circle.

People who go into journalism are typically people with a strong attraction to politics, sports, business, or some other arena in organized society but people who stop short of actually becoming a politician or executive and choose to stand on the sidelines as an observer instead. A bestselling author who had been a reporter for the *New York Times* before going on to write widely acclaimed books about journalism and other topics once told me in a not-for-attribution interview:

> Like me, the typical reporter didn't make it on the football or basketball teams when he was in high school. But he still wanted to identify and associate with sports and athletes. So he became a sportswriter for the school paper. That way you get to ride on the team bus and sit next to the coach. You can get into the locker room any time you want, and you have more status than the team manager. So you can get along as the school's sports reporter, and you find that journalism provides access to all arenas of life.
>
> Reporters are politicians manqué or athletes manqué. If they have any influence, they love to swing it around and tell people about it. Reporters are always bragging to one another about how they can fix parking tickets and things like that.

The journalist, then, is torn in two directions. On the one hand, he's pulled by a powerful impulse, natural to the human species, to participate in public affairs—to collaborate with officials and fellow citizens, to develop viewpoints, to assert himself in their behalf, to lend his voice to the conversation of society. On the other hand, he's in the grips of an impulse to hold himself aloof. It's the posture of the adolescent, torn between a lingering attachment to the security of childhood and a blooming attraction to the adventure of adulthood. It's also the stance of many writers and artists down through the ages.

This is a tension to which there's no solution or end within the framework of journalism. While it waxes and wanes according to the person and story, it's never completely absent. The two motives that create it are both highly fruitful. The participatory impulse engages the journalist's heart and mind in the topics at hand. The disengaging impulse opens up a space between him and the officials he covers and links him with the perspective of the audience. The notion that the participatory urge is a vice in a journalist and the disengaging impulse is his only virtue is silly. Journalists have and need both traits, each tempering the other and both together placing the journalist in that middle ground between self-assertion and self-denial in which writing about public affairs so often takes place.

The news form and the editocracy sharply skew the balance between these vital impulses. They intensify the disengaging, self-effacing, responsibility-denying, immature impulse and weaken the participatory, self-assertive, responsibility-taking impulse. In the journalistic tradition started by Pulitzer, the reporter is a person selected and rewarded for acceptance of the editocracy's primacy. He is a person who is or becomes comfortable hiding his own light under a bushel and subordinating himself to powerful and abusive others. He is a person who is or becomes used to the concealment, conspiracy, opportunism, and displacement of life when it is lived amid oppression.

The journalist's identity as a person whose motives and commitments are disowned and displaced is clearly visible in the matter of the journalist's politics.

As professionals journalists profess to be politically neutral, and within the frame of reference of the story, they often are. But the frame of reference of the story is not politically neutral, and neither are most journalists as a personal matter. Most news people, particularly in the national press, are Democrats and liberals. By ratios of two to one and three to one, depending on the survey, they indicate that they are registered as Democrats or have voted for Democratic candidates for president. This is roughly the same proportion of Democrats and liberals that surveys find among professors. Moreover, many newspeople are members of the Newspaper Guild or some other union and thus often hold union-oriented perspectives on economic issues particularly.

These affiliations are visible in the news from time to time. In my opinion, journalistic liberalism was especially powerful in the late 1960s and early 1970s, reaching a high-water mark beginning from the Tet offensive in early 1968 and coming to a pinnacle in the Watergate affair in 1973 and 1974. Thereafter it faded as liberalism itself weakened. Today liberal bias, though still in evidence, is a shadow of what it was back in the days when, as Edith Efron's pathbreaking study showed, the negative material on network news concerning Richard Nixon's 1968 presidential campaign exceeded the positive material by a factor of ten. And while it certainly hasn't happened yet, it seems conceivable that, at some point in the future, members of the working press would exhibit a conservative bias.

Most journalists indignantly deny that they're liberals or that their views affect their work. In this they're about as believable as university professors who make similar denials. Any doubts I may have had about the liberalism of members of the national press were laid to rest by my experience, as a member of *Fortune*'s Washington bureau in the early 1980s, of viewing Ronald Reagan's televised press conferences in the offices we shared with *Time* magazine's large Washington staff and hearing the guffaws and groans from the assembled *Time* correspondents and researchers. They were the signature guffaws and groans of a liberal audience.

As far as I'm concerned, there's nothing wrong with these liberal biases. They happen not to be my own just now, but this is a free country, and journalists have a right to lean where they're inclined to. Moreover, I believe a journalist *should* have political views; to me, there's something profoundly unnatural and undesirable about the idea of a person who spends his days observing, talking to, pondering, and writing about public figures yet brings away from these pursuits no attachments, preferences, or opinions of any kind.

The responsibility-evading trait is also visible in the theatricality exhibited by many reporters. Most journalists disavow such qualities and see themselves as practical, fact-oriented people. Print-news workers badmouth TV journalists as show-biz types devoid of substance, implying that they themselves are serious men and women admirably indifferent to tinsel and hullabaloo. For their own part, TV newspeople admit they work in what they often call an entertainment medium, but they insist that within the framework of the medium—which, they imply, they didn't choose and don't particularly like or respect—they do their best to inform the public in the serious spirit it deserves.

In fact, the journalists I've known, especially the best ones, are theatrical personalities at heart. TV newspeople, of course, are flagrantly theatrical, that being one of the main qualities they're selected for. As for the rest, many may not seem notably flamboyant and more than a few look positively nerdy. But beneath the surface, journalists are performers who are happiest when they have an audience and are telling a story.

Put a notepad and felt tip in their hands, or a keyboard under their fingers, or a camera crew in their faces, or copy and a blue pencil on their laps, and they turn into magicians of the spoken or written word. Events a nonjournalist would dismiss as trivial or miss entirely take on for them an unsuspected reality and importance. What a nonjournalist would render in a clumsy sentence or phrase becomes, in a matter of minutes, a perfect story, with a pithy beginning, engrossing middle, and satisfying end. Touches of heroism, drama, color, and pathos sparkle in the narrative. Under the alchemy of the newsperson's passion to perform and the journalistic techniques that have developed over the years to make journalistic performances credible, real-world events that are intrinsically vague, confusing, and hard-to-define become clear, crisp, meaningful, interesting, amusing, sympathy- or indignation-evoking, sometimes awe-inspiring. That is to say, they become news.

Coming to journalism relatively late in life, I was delighted to find in the field all the opportunity I could ever use to perform and be on stage. I particularly loved the technical aspects of the business, which one deals with in endless hours of private drudgery but which lead to wonderfully theatrical effects in very public places. I could spend hours utterly absorbed in the drafting of a head (or "hed," in the useful Time, Inc., convention that kept typesetters from mistaking the word as text) or lead paragraph ("lede," we wrote) to achieve just the right effect. I could and did spend days editing stories to get the right pace, mood, and seamless coherence and stylishness. I loved working with designers and picture editors to create arresting graphics. As an academic I'd considered myself a good writer, but I was surprised by how much I learned from editors about the tricks of the trade, such as (to take a typical, mundane example) how neatly the unconversational word *amid* works to link (or juxtapose) a focal action with a set of circumstances in a way that is economical and chatty but that draws attention both to the linkage (or juxtaposition) and to the subordinate status of the circumstantial element.

Many of the people I worked with were also caught up in the technical and theatrical aspects of the business. The higher-ranking a person was at *Fortune*, the more likely he or she was to think about journalism in technical terms. When I became an edi-

tor, I discovered that the discussions I had with the managing editor about the stories I was editing usually touched only lightly on
issues of substance. Most of the talk concerned technical matters.
Editing, as we discussed it, consisted mainly of finding the theatrical touches that would make a piece seem finished and pol-
ished. One rarely had to mess around much with the substance of
a piece even when there were problems with the substance.
During my years at *Fortune*, we went through three complete
redesigns of the magazine, changes that took up a large amount of
editorial time and attention. By contrast, we essentially never sat
down to rethink the substance of our coverage.

When I started my own tiny magazine, an illustrated newsmagazine about politics, policy, and personalities at the Federal
Reserve System, I too relied heavily on technical ideas. What was
original about my *Fed Fortnightly* was mainly technical. The magazine was in effect a high-quality newsletter dressed up to look like
a newsmagazine. That's no small transformation, and it entailed
big consequences for the content. But the truth about my entre-
preneurial experience is that it was a lot like what I'd observed at
Time, Inc. I paid lots of attention to format, graphics, illustrations,
letterheads, logos, media sales kits, and the like, and though my
reporters and I certainly talked plenty about financial policy and
politics, such substantive matters ended up in second place in
terms of how I spent my time and where I focused my creative
energy.

The journalist's fascination with display, rhetoric, and the theatrical aspect of the business was independently identified by the
widely discussed personality-structure research conducted over a
decade ago by political scientists Robert Lichter, Linda Lichter,
and Stanley Rothman. In the late 1970s and early 1980s the
Lichters and Rothman administered thematic apperception tests
to hundreds of reporters employed by the national press and
compared the results to the test scores of a sample of corporate
executives. They found that, compared with the executives, the
journalists scored high on the "narcissism" and "power need"
personality dimensions, while executives scored high on "utilitar-
ianism," that is, an orientation to getting things done.

The Rothman-Lichter work was furiously rejected by many in
the world of journalism. *Washington Post* executive editor

Benjamin Bradlee was so antagonistic to the findings and so insistent on discrediting them that, as mentioned in the preceding chapter, he not only accused the authors of making up the data but even ridiculed the random-sample research methodology used, not merely by these researchers, but by all the public opinion polls commissioned and covered by the *Post* itself. But all this was in fact storm and fury signifying the accuracy of the findings and the closeted, responsibility-denying nature of the journalistic personality. Narcissism (in the nonclinical sense) and theatricality are about as familiar in the world of journalism as photosynthesis and the color green are in the world of plant life.

The in-the-closet, disowned aspect of the reporter's personality is most fully expressed in his submissiveness toward powerful people. In the mythology of the profession, the journalist is an aggressive advocate of the little guy, a thorn in the side of the pompous and powerful, a professional rebel. In reality, however, reporters are basically submissive toward and dependent on people they perceive as powerful. They are selected for this quality at entry into the news business—news organizations don't hire or promote many people who aren't fundamentally comfortable with tight, domineering, often abusive editorial control. And inevitably this quality carries over into the journalist's dealings with the people he covers. People accustomed to disowning their judgments and points of view have no real choice but to acquiesce in the views and actions of the principals of their stories.

Journalists resemble Zelig, Woody Allen's hilarious other-directed bourgeois hero who takes on the physical and psychological traits of the person he's in the company of. Journalists who lack a Zelig-like tendency to mirror powerful and important people are rarities. Though it's possible to do journalism without taking on the characteristics of one's sources, it's harder that way.

I remember one member of *Fortune*'s Washington staff, back in the days when I was in charge of the bureau, whose Zelig coefficient was below par. He was an outstanding journalist in every important respect—a tireless reporter, strong writer, clever finder of stories, and a man ambitious to experience everything the journalism business had to offer from bottom to top. He was well educated and had unusually broad interests, and when I resigned from the magazine, he became bureau chief on my recommendation, then went on to meteoric success as a newsmagazine editor.

His problem was that he wasn't good at kowtowing to sources. It wasn't that he was offensive. He liked and took a genuine interest in the people he covered, he was unfailingly polite, and he was suitably deferential. But he had a somewhat cool, withdrawn, defensive manner and robust inner ambition that prevented him from making people he interviewed feel warm, happy, admired, reinforced, seduced. Combined with his knack for asking good questions and not settling easily for nonsense, this quality, in close quarters, tended to make people anxious. Sometimes it made me anxious, too. Was he challenging my authority? I'd wonder when he quietly and coolly queried me on some idea I'd expressed in a story conference or one-on-one editing session.

From time to time I got sidewise comments about "that green-eyed reporter" from people around town he had interviewed and who had found the experience upsetting, invasive. I didn't mind his questions, one person the journalist had interviewed remarked to me, but he seemed so . . . so . . . challenging! The man, a prominent figure in business and government who was familiar with the news game, was saying that when he gave an interview, he was used to receiving a stream of strokes indicating identification and submissiveness. When he didn't get them from my reporter, alarm bells had gone off. Why was this *Fortune* guy withholding the usual fix of positive reinforcements, he'd apparently begun wondering? Might this newsie be out to do a hatchet job? In fact, the green-eyed reporter was no assassin, and his story was mostly favorable, as almost anyone could have anticipated.

I was no exception. I, too, identified with the rich and powerful. I, too, had more than a little Zelig in my personality profile.

What I liked best about being a journalist was meeting, talking with, thinking myself into the shoes of, and generally identifying with people at the top of government agencies, companies, and other important institutions. I loved being able to see virtually anyone I wanted to short of the president himself. It was delicious to be received cordially when I arrived at their offices for the interview. When asking questions, I tried to be inviting and encouraging, and not only because I wanted to inveigle the news-maker into a self-revelatory response but also because I genuine-ly liked these people, I wanted to make them feel happy in my presence, I wanted to be as close to them as I could. As I said, I identified with these people.

I experienced a recurrent fantasy after an interview. The per-son I'd just spoken with, I'd imagine, would take a liking to me and offer me a job as his special assistant. I would work closely and happily with him, helping to put affairs in his company or agency aright, then, with his backing, go on to glory, power, and wealth in my own right as a high-ranking principal in affairs of state, corporate business, or publishing.

I remember, in reporting a story about the press, I interviewed Mike Wallace, then as now the premier adversary journalist on CBS's *60 Minutes* show. He was an intelligent, candid, interesting source and gave me a very useful interview. At one point I opened a line of questioning about CBS's habit of stonewalling its crit-ics—this was in the immediate aftermath of Watergate, which had occasioned any number of tough Mike Wallace investigative pieces on Watergate perpetrators. I found myself, without having previously intended to, asking the question the way Wallace him-self would have. At least that's how it seemed to me at the time. I wasn't nervous, I didn't stumble, I just put the question to him, cogently, a bit rhetorically, with the easy, aggressive intimacy that's Wallace's trademark. It felt wonderful to imitate this famous man in his presence and turn his own tricks on himself.

And, most wonderful of all, it worked! Wallace, apparently torn between his intellectual honesty and his desire to be loyal to CBS, stammered and spewed, making false starts on an answer and discovering, to his consternation, that what was coming to his mind wasn't anything he wanted to be quoted on. Pen poised over notebook, I watched coolly, triumphantly, as I imagined it, letting the man stew in his own juices as I'd seen Wallace himself do with his own victims on any number of Sunday evenings. Alas, a camera crew wasn't present to record the event, and since Wallace never did say anything much, the exercise produced no quotation I could use in my story. The experience came down to a private thrill in which I lived out a quintessentially journalistic fantasy of identification and imitation.

Not many of the hundreds of interviews I've conducted have been as satisfying as that one, of course, but most of them have given me the feeling that I was, in a small and unofficial but still quite real way, a junior member in good standing of the American ruling class.

With so much psychologically at stake for me in my interviews, I usually had a queasy feeling in my stomach and a tremble in my hands as I put in the phone calls to introduce myself and set up appointments. What if they said no? a small voice worried inside my head. What if they said, Who the hell are you? Why should I bother to see and talk to the likes of you?

One time my worst fear was realized. I was reporting a story on the Environmental Protection Agency's regulation of sulfur emissions—what is now referred to as the acid rain problem—and I made an appointment to see Frank Zarb, the associate director of the Office of Management and Budget in charge of EPA-related matters. The day the interview took place, the *Washington Post* reported that Zarb had been named director of the Federal Energy Administration, so I arrived at his office with high hopes of an extra productive and personally elevating session.

Zarb had a different program in mind. He began by keeping me waiting in his outer office for twenty or thirty minutes, then had me ushered into the inner sanctum and said we could now go ahead with the interview. But as I started in on my list of questions, he responded curtly to each by saying that for obvious reasons he couldn't talk about that topic just now. If he was trying to make me squirm, he certainly succeeded. Within minutes, I was blushing in confusion and humiliation. Soon, not sure of what to do but painfully aware I wasn't wanted, I closed my notebook, mumbled something about having no further questions, picked up my briefcase and raincoat, wished him well in his new job, and stumbled out of the room.

Afterwards I tried to get mad at Zarb. He could have canceled or apologized, I told myself. He'd behaved like a shit, I told myself. But I was never able to feel really angry at the man. Anger presupposes a degree of autonomy I didn't possess when dealing with newsmakers like Zarb. Whenever I thought about this moment, it conjured up feelings, not of anger, but of rejection, humiliation, and worthlessness.

When I was with Mike Wallace and was allowed to identify with him, I felt like him. You can be sure that Mike, or Paul Weaver playing Mike, would have had the last word with the likes of a Frank Zarb, who somehow would have been made to emerge from his attempted psychological mugging much the worse for wear. But when Mike wasn't around to lend a hand and I was all by myself with a powerful man who gave me permission only to play the part of his victim, my obsessive identification with the people who were the sources and principals of my stories led me to become that victim.

This psychology of identification and dependency leaves its telltale imprint on the news. While reporters may not be the people newsmakers wish they were, by and large they write the stories newsmakers enable and invite them to write. The news, as a result, is massively and minutely faithful to the newsmaker's version of reality. The reporter labors to bring forth a story that makes him a traitor to his experience.

Every time a courtier-reporter in the Pulitzer tradition covers a story, he or she enacts a fascinating, often excruciating drama of discovery and repression. The newsmakers' lies and poses rarely fool the news worker entirely. While the reporter may not use this knowledge in writing the story, he or she nevertheless does usually sense what is really going on.

Like many Americans and most academics, I once viewed journalists as glib and superficial people condemned by their lack of theoretical sophistication and rigorous intellectual purpose to skate forever on the deceptive surface of life. Nothing surprised me more, when I left the ivory tower to become a journalist, than the intellectual depth of the journalistic enterprise. Doing journalism is a learning experience of great power, and journalists are or easily become profoundly knowledgeable, often much more so than they themselves realize. If social science professors could break out of their cloister and get on more intimate terms with the real world, they'd be shocked to discover how little reason they have to condescend to reporters and how much journalists know that they, the supposed experts, have hardly an inkling of.

The reporter's desire to be on intimate terms with very important people is a powerful motive whose objective is often fulfilled.

For reporting is, by its very nature, a highly effective means of gathering information and developing personal understanding.

Reporting consists of asking questions, mainly by phone, recording answers, and making stories with the materials gathered. It's a method that establishes public facts fast, often accurately, and responsibly when officials cooperate. When they don't, reporting still suffices to get the facts of what happened—given enough time. Sooner or later, the reporter will always get the story.

If the principals won't cooperate, other people with experience of the events in question will. Any organization or person important enough to be seriously interesting to a journalist is known to many other organizations and people, and sooner or later you'll find one who'll talk to you. Except for stories involving acts punishable by law, there's practically nothing that can't be found out by reporting. It may take months or years to do it, but old-fashioned shoe-leather reporting almost always will do the job.

I remember, at my little newsmagazine about the Fed, wanting to do a story about the efforts the Fed was making in the fall of 1986 to sell American banks on the Mexican loan bailout the Fed and Treasury had cooked up. I asked my senior Fed reporter to query his sources, and he returned with the thought that nothing much was happening and that this was a story the Fed didn't want to see reported. On the theory that, if people at the Fed thought nothing was happening but didn't want to see it written up, it must be a story, I told my most junior staff member to start phoning every conceivable potential recipient and observer of the Fed's loan-marketing, bank-lobbying activities. He had no connections, no sources, no special background at this kind of thing, but for this kind of reporting, you don't need those resources. All you need to get the story, or to confirm that there is no story, is energy, talent, and the assignment to start reporting and to keep on reporting for as long as it takes.

A week later the kid had the story, courtesy of a number of more or less hostile sources. Some Japanese financial institutions had been helpful, but the sources who'd really broken the story were the senior people at a few banks in South Texas who'd been burned by loans made to Mexican parties as part of their regular local lending business. Having followed the rules and written their bad Mexican loans down as they became nonperforming, they had no intention of making the same mistake twice, and they were delighted to tell my reporter all about the things Paul Volcker's boys were doing to push American lenders to throw good money after bad south of the border.

Most of the time, a journalist acquires a sense of the situation, not by digging, which is expensive and thus is rarely authorized by the boss, but by osmosis. Over time, normal cursory reporting gives the reporter not only the basic story but a large fund of contextual information about newsmakers' state of mind, previous behavior, and the like. Newsmakers may think that their well-crafted lies are impenetrable to reporters, but that's rarely the case. The reporter almost always sees through the newsmaker's scam. It's practically impossible to fool a reporter.

Sources often explicitly signal that they're lying by requesting to go off the record. Sometimes the material they restrict is the lie, sometimes it's the truth they don't want attributed, but either way, going off the record is a clear sign that the newsmaker is making up some of what he's saying or concocting part of the persona he's presenting to the audience.

When there isn't an explicit signal, reporters often become aware of sources' lies as a result of unstated contextual indications, the most common of which grows out of the fact that the lies involved are gross and obvious.

For a 1975 story I wrote for *Fortune* about the United Nations, my researcher and I interviewed then-Secretary General Kurt Waldheim, his deputy Brian Urquhart, and other top UN bureaucrats. We naturally asked a lot of questions about the growing disenchantment with the UN, which had become a circus barge of patronage, socialism, and anti-Westernism. They responded by denying everything. They blithely insisted that the organization was in great shape, and as evidence they pointed to and took credit for just about every good thing that had happened on the planet since 1945—I think they missed Teflon and Mother Teresa and the low-drag, fuel-efficient car, but not much else.

It was evident that they were lying grotesquely and counting on the fact that they were giving me an interview to induce me to quote their statements respectfully, thereby giving my imprimatur to their flights from reality. In this case things worked out differently. Because Waldheim's lies illustrated the fact that the UN system had become mired in intellectual dishonesty and a destructive sense of unreality, I quoted Waldheim at length—after noting that the unreal, Tower-of-Babel aspects of the organization were nowhere more evident than in the Secretary General's unreal view of the UN's role in the world.

Of course, it was easy for me to do that. I was never going to write about the UN again, and Waldheim was never going to have the satisfaction, on a future story, of refusing my request for an interview or directing his press relations people not to return my calls or answer my questions. Had I been a daily press reporter covering the UN beat, I could have expected such retaliation, at least for a while, unless I was affiliated with a major wire service or one of the handful of top publications that a Secretary General of the United Nations would feel he has to keep in full touch with regardless of the amount of humble pie he might have to eat.

In addition to disclosing gross lies, reporting gives journalists a front-row seat from which to observe the many cues, sometimes subtle, sometimes not, that sources give when they withhold the truth.

As *Fortune*'s senior person in Washington, I once attended a dinner and press briefing that General Motors put on for selected journalists to meet Roger Smith, then GM's new CEO. After dinner Smith stood at a podium and read from a text. He was evidently so indifferent to the audience or so out of sympathy with the message that had been prepared that, instead of just reading it in his dull, mechanical voice, he began prefacing new paragraphs with the words, "It says here. . . ." In other words, he was parodying the scripted message and himself.

Not only was Smith acting out his sense of alienation from his message, but he was giving what turned out to be an eerily accurate omen of his ten-year reign at the giant auto company. In his first year as CEO, Smith had made it clear that, in the context of the GM system, he was an iconoclast and reformer. On the other hand, it was unclear whether, having torn GM loose from some of the old ways, which were inadequate to a newly competitive marketplace, Smith would be able to create and inculcate throughout the company a workable new approach to its business. On this score the chairman's speech raised doubts. If the man couldn't deal appropriately with his sense of discomfort at a briefing for some Washington journalists, what reason was there to think he'd be able to handle the bigger challenges of his giant but starting-to-be-deeply-troubled car company? I filed all this away in the back of my mind for future reference. A decade later, when GM's market share was off by a third and the company began downsizing itself in a panic, I told myself I'd seen an early portent of the process in a new CEO's bizarre after-dinner remarks to a few Washington journalists.

The in-depth learning that reporting engenders was brought home to me one weekend about three years into my career as a journalist. I'd recently run into a political scientist friend who was a coauthor of one of the best-selling college-level introductory political science textbooks, and during our conversation it developed that he was in the throes of preparing a new edition. Would I be willing to take a look at the sections on government regulation of business, he wanted to know, considering that I'd been covering that subject for *Fortune*? Sure, I said, and after a while the chapters had been forthcoming. Now I was taking a weekend to read the material and write up my comments as asked.

The sections weren't very good, as I saw it, and I had a lot of suggestions for improving them, but what really struck me about the experience was how much my work as a reporter had taught me. I'd never given regulatory programs or issues any special study while a political science student or professor; more or less everything I brought to my reading of these textbook passages had come from the reporting I'd done for my stories for *Fortune*. That turned out to be a lot. I found I knew a great deal about regulatory issues and politics that I hadn't known I knew.

Whenever I've turned from reporting a story or subject to reviewing the social science literature on the same topic, I've always had the same feeling of being intellectually in command of the issues to an extent that often (but not always) outstrips the author's. I'm almost always aware of cases that don't fit, or flatly contradict, the empirical and theoretical generalizations offered. I'm often acutely aware of a lack of familiarity on the social scientist's part with the people and pitches and ploys that explains why his generalizations are so full of obvious holes. It isn't that I don't learn from the social science work. It's just that I usually find it shallow, unpersuasive, naive, unworldly.

The reporter's experientially grounded way of doing research—meeting and hanging around with and going back and forth with the principals of his stories—has the crucial advantage of exposing him to both backstage and onstage behaviors. Thus, over time, the journalist acquires the experience and contextual knowledge with which to decode the ploys and postures his subjects are concocting for public consumption. The social scientist, with his standardized questionnaires and his limited personal offstage interaction with the principal, isn't anywhere near as able to discern where the performances leave off and the authentic behavior begins. At Ford I drafted suggested Q and As for use by top executives being interviewed by distinguished professors of business administration and economics from Harvard and other such places. I remember realizing I was thereby poisoning the intellectual well to a far greater extent than by a similar scripting of a press interview.

Seeking and coming to know the truth about the subjects of one's stories, yet routinely withholding significant elements of what one discovers, in consequence enabling the subjects to lie, and failing to make good on one's implied responsibility to audience and self—these add up to an intrinsically uncomfortable experience for the journalist. They mean that the journalist is involved in injustices partly of his own making, day in and day out. Injustice is an attack on the human self, an experience no one undergoes casually. Newspeople, subjected to its pains and tensions on a virtually daily or hourly basis, respond in a variety of ways.

Not the least of these is denial. The intense pace of news work, which cycles from anxiety to manic exertion to emotional exhaustion as often as once or twice a day, frequently leaves journalists too tired and distracted to even acknowledge, let alone resolve, the larger issues and problems limned by their experience. That journalists think of themselves as professionals and that many affect a personal style of breezy high spirits further desensitizes them to the injustices lurking in their work. So does the use of tobacco, alcohol, and other drugs, which in my day at least were not uncommon in the business.

The most potent means of denial is the reporter's sense of professionalism, the idea that news is a thing out there in the real world and that the reporter's job is to find it—implying that realities that don't get included in the story aren't news and thus don't raise any issues. In a recent documentary essay on Washington journalism in the PBS *Frontline* series, Bob Woodward, the *Washington Post*'s Pulitzer Prize–winning, best-selling journalist-author, who with Carl Bernstein broke the Watergate story, was asked by host William Greider why the news so often cooperates with official stories and official lies. Woodward, his discomfort with the exchange apparent in an unusually tight close-up, took the position that, practically speaking, there was little a journalist could do about the problem. After all, he declared in a classic expression of journalistic professionalism, "If the president says it, you have to report it."

Cynicism is another means by which reporters deal with the contradictions of their work. Making an elaborate show of rejecting ideals, of expecting the worst, of perversely resisting good news and positive experiences is a way of defusing, at least somewhat, the troubling reality of their work and behavior by overstating and exaggerating it, thereby creating room in their hearts and minds for positive experiences and true ideals without feeling obliged to do anything about them.

A further strategy by which journalists handle their guilty experience is that of getting out of journalism, either partially or altogether. Some newspeople identify with sources so much that they realize what they really want, give up the pretense of being a journalist, and go to work for sources directly, taking jobs in public relations, advertising, lobbying, politics, law, or business. Quite a number of journalists seek an outlet for the learning and talent that the news business doesn't have room for by shifting, part-time or full-time, into other genres, including novels, screenplays, ghostwriting, academic research, biographies, and the like.

It also happens that, rather than sidestep the abuses of their daily work, journalists address them directly, rejecting newsmakers' lies and their own codependent complicity in those lies and seeking to put out a more truthful version of the story.

While working on an assignment, the journalist, as we've noted, runs into a lot of information that's tangential to or subversive of the story. If domineering newsmakers and editors had their way, these fugitive facts would deposit themselves dutifully in the dustbin of history and vanish forever from the mind of man. But sometimes they don't. After the story is closed, the outlaw information sometimes keeps itself alive in the back of the journalist's mind. There it mills around, raising a ruckus, calling attention to the weaknesses of existing news stories, slowly constituting a counterimage of the journalistic universe, and creating an increasingly specific desire to tell the true new story and to discredit the false old one.

Eventually something clicks or snaps in the journalist's mind, and he switches sides. He loses interest in the old definition of the story, becomes its critic and adversary, stops covering it, and starts writing a new story that in important respects is the opposite of the old one. The old story is redefined as a lie, and journalists focus their energy on exposing and debunking it.

News and the culture of lying are characterized by many such sudden reversals of posture, role, and perspective.

In 1968, the first year in which the three network news programs reported the primary and general elections in the basic current format, presidential election coverage was marred by a number of distortions. One was the networks' effective endorsement of the claim made by Eugene McCarthy, the Democratic insurgent running against Lyndon Johnson on an antiwar platform, that even though he polled 42 percent of the vote to Johnson's 49 percent in the New Hampshire primary, he was nonetheless the moral victor and deserved to be considered the front-runner for the nomination. Television news largely bought this version of the New Hampshire story by giving McCarthy the coverage normally accorded to a winner. The networks paid lots of attention to him, they focused on the positive aspects of his campaign that were winning the voters' support, they minimized or ignored his negatives (since thematically these ran counter to the success story), and they paid less attention to his opponents or dwelled on the opponents' negatives. To judge from the theme of television news, Eugene McCarthy in the wake of New Hampshire was a candidate starting out on what looked to be a triumphant sweep of the Democratic nominating process.

In fact, he'd only embarrassed Johnson and Johnson's war. McCarthy's chances of winning many of the big primaries ahead, let alone carrying the Chicago convention, where most of the delegates would come from nonprimary states, were extremely slim. In the event, McCarthy won only a quarter of the convention vote, while Hubert Humphrey took the overwhelming majority.

During the general election campaign in the fall, the networks took a similar approach. Nixon, well ahead in the polls but slowly losing his lead, ran a cautious, defensive, negative campaign. After a shaky start Humphrey regained his old happy-warrior exuberance and came on strong, rapidly narrowing the gap with Nixon and raising the possibility that he'd win in a photo finish. Television news covered the process as if it were a repeat performance of its misconceived version of McCarthy vs. LBJ. Coverage of the Nixon campaign was overwhelmingly negative, particularly in the crucial closing weeks; Edith Efron's study found that negative material about Nixon exceeded positive material by a factor of ten. By contrast, TV news gave equal exposure to the negative and positive sides of the Humphrey campaign. Nixon hung on to eke out a slender victory, but had the campaign lasted another few days and had television persisted in its effectively anti-Nixon coverage, Humphrey might have won.

In the years that followed, there was much discussion of the distortions of television's campaign coverage. While in public the networks flatly rejected criticisms and insisted their coverage was beyond reproach in every respect, in private they took a less adamant posture. In 1976 TV news covered an equally hotly contested presidential campaign with vastly improved balance and fairness. It obviously had learned a lot from the mistakes of 1968.

Underdog candidates who did much better than expected against front-runners but still didn't win weren't presented as moral victors. As Bruce Morton, then with CBS, wryly reminded his viewers in a pre–New Hampshire *tour d'horizon*, "It's the fella with the most votes wins."

Candidates who, like McCarthy in 1968 and George McGovern in 1972, attracted intense support among liberals were covered, not as consensus heroes in the making, but as sectarian candidates whose liberalism might help them in the Democratic primaries but probably made them unelectable in the general election. Television news withheld the McCarthy-McGovern treatment from liberal candidates such as Jerry Brown or (at least with respect to domestic issues) Henry Jackson. The candidate TV news thought could do well in 1976 was Jimmy Carter, the Washington outsider, born-again evangelical Christian, and big-government agnostic who promised he'd never lie to the American people. They didn't think Carter made much sense (ABC's Sam Donaldson, then a newcomer to the network news campaign coverage game, was unmerciful in exposing Carter's vacuities), but they thought his mild conservatism and outsider posture could make him a winner.

They were right, of course. Television news wasn't neutral in 1976—it helped some candidates and hurt others; it always does—but its biases in this case were aligned with those of the electorate, which the networks pretend to reflect. In 1968 the networks glorified liberal losers and savaged conservative winners. Eight years later, with a clearer picture of the electorate and firmer rein on its own political enthusiasms, TV news glorified centrist winners and trashed liberals as losers. By 1980 the networks were able to allow a conservative to enjoy the benefits of the front-runner's position and didn't succumb to the temptation to savage Ronald Reagan as they had savaged Johnson and Nixon.

This pattern of falling into error, then recoiling to reject the error and embrace the opposite mistake by adopting a heroic adversary posture against the problem in question is recurrent in modern journalism. A classic example is the way the press covered the 1968 Tet offensive in Vietnam. Previously, as Peter Braestrup's masterful *Big Story* demonstrates, the press had largely accepted the highly positive, optimistic, light-at-the-end-of-the-tunnel accounts of the war effort's progress being given by President Johnson and the military command. The implication of these upbeat assessments was that a successful, all-out offensive by the Viet Cong was a military impossibility. When such an offensive occurred, the press coverage shifted 180 degrees. Tet, the stories argued and implied, showed that the war effort was failing. Tet was a defeat. Tet was a military disaster.

In fact, as Braestrup's book shows, while Tet was indeed clear evidence that the previous accounts of the war's progress had been highly misleading, it wasn't a military defeat for the United

States. To the contrary, once the U.S. military recovered from the surprise and applied its superior force, Tet became a massive U.S. victory. However, the adversary mind-set of the working journalist when dealing with proven, undeniable, embarrassing journalistic error prevented that reality from making much of an impression in press dispatches from South Vietnam. The military victory disappeared amid news stories reporting the details of a political disaster.

The reporter's tendency to become the adversary of old errors sometimes leads to attempts to change not just lines of coverage but the very structure of journalism. This impulse was clearly at work behind the invention of the tabloid newspaper.

The first American tabloid was the *New York Daily News*, created in the wake of World War I by Joseph Medill Patterson, a scion of the journalistic family that owned the *Chicago Tribune*. The rich, Yale-educated army officer was alienated from the upper-class background from which he came—he had been a socialist in his college years and was known to show up at the opera dressed in blue jeans and chewing huge wads of gum—and with the *Daily News* he declared his independence of the stuffy, manipulative world of respectable journalism, whose Orwellian deformities had reached a high-water mark with massive wartime censorship and propaganda. Patterson identified with and idealized the common man and built his newspaper on a populist antagonism to big institutions and middle-class propriety and a cynical resignation over the possibilities and appeals of citizenship in twentieth-century America.

Patterson's journalism dealt with pseudoevents in Washington and City Hall mostly by ignoring them. The *Daily News* simply wasn't interested in most politics and government, and the political material that did get its attention was mostly local and personal. The *Daily News* focused on human interest stories, celebrities, sex, sports, and the police blotter.

The paper was a smashing success in business and cultural terms, raising the circulation of the largest American news publications to well over two million and earning vast profits. It broadened prevailing patterns of news coverage somewhat and, at its best, added a slick, sassy, sardonic voice to the conversation of the big city. Yet within a generation of its birth, the tabloid reached a peak from which it slipped, slowly at first, into a spiral of irreversible decline.

Network television, the ultimate mass medium, began to displace it as a way of reaching the city's consumers. The postwar movement of ever-growing numbers of New Yorkers into middle-class respectability made the paper's perverse, working-class angle on life less and less relevant and palatable. Moreover, that angle itself became less working-class and more perverse. The *Daily News*'s professions of populist independence of the establishment were harder to take seriously as the paper slipped into bed with—and began to retail the lies of—an array of institutions every bit as pompous, self-serving, oligarchical, and manipulative as any the *Times* and *Tribune* espoused, notably the more conservative trade unions, the Democratic machine, and some of the older ethnic groups. In a city whose masses were increasingly black, Hispanic, foreign-born, and non-English-speaking, Patterson's *Daily News* became a hopeless contradiction, disconnected both from the new urban masses and from the descendants of the old.

The adversary journalism that arose in the 1960s traced a trajectory similar to that of the tabloid, but at the opposite end of the political and social spectrum. It, too, began as a reaction against the excesses of wartime news management and propaganda, only this time the journalists' target was the cold war that involved the United States in Vietnam, and the reaction came from the left rather than the right.

The inaugural event was the declaration in a 1967 speech by Clifton Daniel, the executive editor of the *New York Times* and the son-in-law of President Harry Truman, that the *Times* had been wrong in 1962 to succumb to intense pressure from the Kennedy Administration not to publish information the *Times* had acquired about the impending, soon-to-fail Bay of Pigs invasion of Cuba sponsored and commanded by the U.S. Central Intelligence Agency. Reflecting Daniel's signal, American journalists were soon busy exposing lies, failures, and abuses in high places on a wholesale basis.

The Tet offensive in Vietnam in 1968 was the first major

example, when adversary journalism redefined a major U.S. military victory as evidence that U.S. war policy had failed disastrously. The ability of the North Vietnamese to mount a big attack, the coverage suggested, showed that the United States hadn't achieved the total dominance in South Vietnam that Lyndon Johnson had been claiming. This was followed by the exposé of the My Lai massacre, publication of the Pentagon papers, and the press's pursuit of the Watergate scandals.

But in these adversarial efforts to expose old errors and get the truth out, journalists remained in their old, dependent, submissive, narcissistic, courtiers' roles vis-à-vis official sources. What was new was the diversity of official views and positions. A once stable bipartisan, consensus-oriented approach to foreign policy collapsed amid the growing opposition to the Vietnam War. Suddenly, new choices were open to the traditional journalist—he could choose between hawk and dove newsmakers, perspectives, stories. Either would happily provide information, stories, political validation, personal patronage, or whatever else the journalist or his news organization might seek. And each in this instance took a strongly adversarial posture toward the other side of the foreign policy debate.

Adversarial journalism, then, didn't reflect a new independence on the part of the journalist. It reflected the journalist's continued dependency together with a new adversarial diversity among newsmakers. This was true even of the *Washington Post*'s famous Woodward and Bernstein exposé of the Watergate scandals. As Edward Jay Epstein showed in a famous essay that made the grandees of the *Post* very uncomfortable indeed, Woodward and Bernstein didn't develop their information independently. Virtually all of it had been amassed and validated by congressional and other official investigators. The *Post*'s stories essentially retailed the investigators' version of the story. Woodward and Bernstein were taking their handouts, in a way that was formally much the same as the way that the reporters who gave favorable coverage to the early phase of the Vietnam War had accepted the Johnson Administration's handout stories and information on the subject.

Thus, adversary journalism in the national press wasn't the radical change many hoped or feared it would be. It involved the press not just in resisting the manipulations of incumbents but in lending support to the stratagems and ploys by which congressional Democrats and liberal interest groups hoped to dominate public policy and return to power. And so it tended simply to exchange one side's lies for another's, and in the event it was no more substantial and had no more staying power than its political allies' prospects for victory.

What was definitive about adversary journalism, in other words, wasn't that it was adversarial but that it was derivative, dependent, and displaced in the grand Pulitzerian tradition. While it pitted the news media against stories, newsmakers, and institutions they once idolized, it did so on the basis of the same uncritical, manipulated posture that gave rise to the original mistake. It reversed rather than corrected errors, creating new alliances that were just as abusive as the old ones they were meant to discredit and replace and demonstrating the continuity of the Pulitzerian tradition that makes the news worker the prisoner of the newsmaker and of his own courtier's character.

CHAPTER 7

Stupid Politics

Over the past several decades Americans' traditional faith in the
essential fairness and goodness of their politics has declined
sharply, and an emerging consensus has begun to depict American
politics as a largely ineffective, unfair, harmful, unrepresentative
enterprise. Many theories are put forward to account for the
change. The problem is too much idealism and ideology, argue
some. The problem is too much servicing of special interests, say
others. The problem is too much power for high officials and
other elites, goes another argument. The problem is too little
leadership by elites forced against their will to demagogically
curry favor with a pampered, fickle, uppity, overexpectant populace, runs a further viewpoint. The list could be extended; there
is hardly an institution or political value, it seems, whose exces-
sive presence, or weakness, hasn't been deplored as the source of
the new American distemper.

In my experience, all these theories are true as far as they go.
All the problematic phenomena cited by analysts, contradictory

though they may be, are in fact depressingly familiar to close observers of the Washington scene. And that, I would argue, is the point. In a media age American politics is characterized, not by a single dominant pathology, but by a profusion of diverse pathologies, all of them routinely and more or less randomly present in the environment. Pulitzerian journalism leads to a random profusion of pathological outcomes because the emergency power it evokes weakens or suppresses the political immune system that is built into constitutional government to defend it against the many diseases, disorders, and parasites to which bodies politic have historically been vulnerable.

Media politics has a specific ability to deal with urgent threats to life and limb. That is what the emergency power is for; not coincidentally, it is the one area in which American government has genuinely distinguished itself, from the astonishingly effective three-and-a-half-year response to the Japanese attack on Pearl Harbor in 1941, to the more demanding and longer-running crash program to contain the political, military, and cultural aggressiveness of the old Soviet Union after World War II, to the massive help provided to victims of disasters and misfortunes of many kinds, to the remarkable forbearance of the populace during urban blackouts and riots and earthquakes and other crises. In the wake of such disasters, the press routinely congratulates community members on rising to the occasion with exemplary displays of public-spirited, self-sacrificing behavior. These encomiums should go on, but usually don't, to add a note of self-congratulation. If there is one thing American journalism can pride itself on teaching the American people, it is how to behave in a crisis—how to put political and partisan differences aside for the duration, how to be appropriately self-sacrificing, how to focus on what works now. That is what our news media are all about, with their big stories and urgent headlines and special reports and videotape at eleven of plane crashes and hurricane damage and tenement fires and African famine victims.

However, when the news-based emergency power is applied to the normal business of constitutional society—when it is asked to sustain the complex enterprise of creating and managing a legitimate liberal social order—things go awry. The emergency power is utterly unsuited to the longer-term, proactive exercises of representing the members of society, deliberating issues, making policy, and eliciting informed consent. Accomplishing these difficult and partly conflicting tasks on an ongoing basis is what a constitution is all about. It is something, however, that emergency politics can't do. By extricating itself from constitutional structures and the ideals they reflect, by abandoning the effort to formulate general rules generally applicable, emergency government takes issues out of a format designed specifically to enable people to deal with them comprehensively and addresses them in a framework in which dealing with issues comprehensively is impossible.

Media politics is an exercise in the absence, or avoidance, of legitimate order. It is a politics of chaos. The one general statement that can be made about it with confidence is that whatever is happening in a media-influenced system—whether things are going well or badly—it's rarely for a good reason; things usually aren't what they seem, and anyway a fresh pattern will be along in a minute, or else it won't, as the case may be. News institutionalizes a stupid and dysfunctional way of conducting society's business, public or private. Public values give way to private privilege, and the long-term well-being and independence of individuals and organizations are sacrificed for fleeting, short-term, often costly advantages. Despite its energizing summons to citizenship and political life, Pulitzerian journalism functions as an engine of drift and decline.

That, at least, is the way media politics looks from a constitutionalist point of view. To people who believe in the rule of law, freedom, the individual's duty to serve the community, economic markets, and other liberal ideals, media politics looks like a failed and pathological enterprise. However, to those who operate within the moral and political framework of the media-created system itself, media politics is a natural, workable system of individual and organized group advantage. It creates the kind of order that the classical political scientists called oligarchy—rule of the rich and powerful few in their own special interest and at the expense of the large majority, but always in the name of the common good and high social values.

A good example of the constitutional stupidity and chaos—and oligarchical order—promoted by news is the politics of acid rain.

I first ran into acid rain back in 1974, when an Ohio-based utility holding company called American Electric Power Company was raising a ruckus over some directives by the brand-new Environmental Protection Agency concerning sulfur dioxide emissions. The Clean Air Act of 1972 had designated sulfur dioxide a target pollutant, and the EPA was, in effect, ordering utilities to outfit existing coal-fired power plants with scrubbers to cleanse flue gases of sulfur dioxide.

American Electric, which, with access to cheap, high-sulfur midwestern coal, was the biggest, lowest-cost, privately owned power maker in the country, was pushing the EPA to accept an alternative antisulfur strategy. AEP had been developing ways of reducing sulfur emissions that didn't use scrubbers, which the company didn't like because they were expensive, produced sludge, and degraded plant efficiency. AEP had invested in naturally low-sulfur coal from the mountain states and had built extra-tall stacks and emissions-management technology for diluting and dispersing sulfur dioxide so that the atmosphere around its plants met the EPA's air-quality standards. The company was pressing the EPA to accept its sulfur strategy with a series of newspaper and magazine advertisements ridiculing scrubbers and attacking the EPA as a bureaucratic juggernaut hell-bent on its own program and beyond the reach of reason or outside information.

To me the company's approach made sense. It was reducing its overall sulfur emissions by almost as much as scrubbers would have and without the disadvantages of scrubbers. It was switching away from a fuel high in a seriously harmful substance, an inherently desirable move. The emissions management program had brought the sulfur pollution levels around AEP's plants below EPA's ceilings on nearly all days.

Yet the company's entire campaign was a lie. AEP, I learned, had already fought and lost its war against scrubbers—first in Congress, then in the courts. The law required "continuous technological controls" of emissions, that is, scrubbers. The EPA wasn't the crazy bureaucratic malefactor AEP was pretending, it was merely carrying out the provisions of the law. The company, willing neither to give up nor play fair, was putting out a blitz of dishonest publicity in the hope of forcing EPA to ignore the law and accept a good business and antisulfur strategy that public policy had perhaps mistakenly but nonetheless officially rejected. The effort was coming along nicely; I wasn't the only journalist covering the story.

On the other side, the EPA and environmentalists were fighting the power company tooth and nail. Yet their position, too, misrepresented the truth. Instead of simply saying that the issue was closed and AEP was playing fast and loose with the facts, the environmentalist side set out to demonize AEP as a shameless corporate despoiler. The plan to switch to low-sulfur coal was an environmental disaster, they said; using high-sulfur coal in combination with scrubbers was the only real solution. The notion of managing and dispersing sulfur emissions to keep the local atmosphere in compliance with EPA pollution limits was an outrage, they said. Dilution is no solution to pollution, and anyway there was reason to think that sulfur dioxide, floating about in the atmosphere, eventually turns into sulfates and acidic mists, which come back to earth as acid rain and snow. Scientists had only begun to study the problem, they said, but there was some suggestive evidence that a local sulfur dioxide pollution problem had given way to a regional sulfates and acid-precipitation problem. If so, AEP's super-tall stacks were making things much worse by injecting the pollutant into the jetstream that would carry it hundreds or thousands of miles downwind to wreak God only knows what havoc on the biosphere.

I wasn't impressed with these arguments. They casually equated sulfur dioxide, a well-known toxin for which standards had been issued—and as recently as the 1950s the active ingredient in occasional "killer fogs" that had left dozens dead in London and some American cities—with sulfates and acid rain, about which almost nothing was known and for which the EPA hadn't (and, twenty years later, still hasn't) issued standards because, while harmful to flora and fauna, they appear not to hurt public health.

Moreover, the activists' arguments conveniently glossed over a crucial political fact. Behind Congress's scrubber mandate lay a strategic political alliance between environmentalist groups and the United Mine Workers Union. The greens had agreed to support a scrubber requirement in an effort to save the market for high-sulfur coal even though, as AEP recognized, the sulfur pollution problem meant that high-sulfur coal was a fuel whose time had passed. In return for the greens' help in saving the market for an inherently environmentally harmful form of energy that should logically have been phased out as soon as possible, the UMW and the coal-mining industry had agreed to back sulfur dioxide controls.

What enabled these unlikely bedfellows to stay together was the political efficacy, in a media age, of the image of a looming acid rain catastrophe. The notion of an invisible plague of acid rain sweeping death and destruction across wide swaths of the planet was the perfect image for a news bandwagon to put the costly, perverse, pro-sulfur scrubber requirement across. The image was so powerful that it shaped the way government was handling this problem despite both a paucity of mature scientific data demonstrating the hypothesis and at least some contrary evidence indicating that scrubbers, while removing sulfur dioxide, actually created and emitted the sulfates from which acid rain is supposed to evolve in the sky.

It was a spectacle of utter lunacy. AEP was creating a dishonest media bandwagon to discredit the EPA as crazy for enforcing a law that illegalized an environmentally sound approach to sulfur problems. The high-sulfur coal industry was lending its political clout to a media bandwagon against acid rain that eventually was going to devastate the market for its product, in a deal it figured would put off high-sulfur coal's day of reckoning for years. And environmental groups were gaining political power for their projects, including the cause of eliminating sulfur pollution, but in a way that harmed the very environmental values and sulfur-reduction goals they were in business to pursue. It was a coalition of chaos given a false patina of good sense by the news genre's crisis-and-emergency-response scenario.

A decade later, when I was in charge of *Fortune*'s Washington bureau, my writers and I revisited the acid rain movement. In the intervening years it had become bigger and even crazier. Now the acid rain coalition was teeming with Canadians. Some were owners of resorts on Ontario lakes harmed by rain-borne acidification, they said, and requiring reparations by the Yanks. Others represented Quebec Hydro, a vast hydroelectric and construction-jobs project growing rapidly to a size far in excess of Canada's electric-ity needs. These people figured that if super-strict acid rain controls were imposed on America pronto, electric utilities in the American Midwest and Northeast would soon be closing down a lot of coal-fired power plants and deciding not to build any new ones and would be feeling that contracting for a lot of long-term Canadian power imports was the way to go. While seeking to make the Americans do something about acid rain, the Canadians didn't count it as a problem that their own country imposed no controls on sulfur emissions and that the biggest sulfur dioxide source in the world was a smelting plant in ... Ontario. These people were indignantly resisting American suggestions that they practice what they preach as a condition of U.S. cooperation. (After much high-level haggling, they eventually acceded as part of the price of a Yank acid rain control program.)

What happened in the acid rain affair is repeated nearly every time Washingtonians venture to address a question of public policy by means of the news-activated emergency power. The effort to stage persuasive images of crises and emergency responses soon leads people farther and farther afield of reality. Fictional events soon come to be in the saddle, reason and truth take a holiday, and a lot of stupid, unfair, self-destructive things end up taking place.

There are, it should be noted, other modes of politics in play in Washington. For instance, farming areas—puny in population but potent in geographical sweep and political organization—give an annual object lesson in the capabilities of an old-fashioned interest-group coalition that has the votes and the strategic position (control of the right committees, for instance) to grab some $100 billion a year in federal subsidies with scarcely a media event or news story in their corner. But these other modes of political action, once dominant in Washington, are the exception, not the rule.

The politics bandwagons make possible has its moments. Some problems and issues that lend themselves to headline treatment are inscribed on the public agenda. Officials are forced to exercise leadership. Events build toward a climactic burst of public action in which crises are managed, problems are addressed, scandals are set right, rights are vindicated, malefactors are brought to justice, and the needs of the people are served.

The Civil Rights Act of 1964 was unquestionably the finest

hour of modern media politics; if ever there was an episode that vindicated the media's way of conducting public business, this was it. The civil rights revolution, especially at the national level, was made by and for the media. National TV news's focus on the sights and sounds of black citizens and their white supporters peacefully petitioning for their constitutional rights in the face of the violence and injustice of the Jim Crow South made the civil rights laws of the mid-1960s possible. It was a magnificent and inspiring moment. A nation belatedly opened its heart to the better angels of its nature, remedied a historic injustice, owned a burden of guilt, spoke the electrifying language of human rights, and experienced a renewed sense of community as people realized that they were doing the right thing together and that it felt good.

Four years later, the civil rights revolution lay in collapse. "We shall overcome" had given way to "Burn, baby, burn," Lyndon Johnson had renounced the presidency that had brought the Civil Rights Act into being, Martin Luther King was dead of an assassin's bullet, and Americans were turning to presidential candidates who accommodated racism rather than facing it down. Not least, the authority created four years earlier to end racial discrimination was starting to be used by judges and bureaucrats to impose a new set of racial distinctions on schools and businesses in the name of justice and equality.

How a revolution could have happened so quickly and completely, then been all but reversed in even less time by people acting without a shred of legislative or juridical authority is a mystery to most Americans. It shouldn't be. The process of making public policy in a blaze of urgent, televised glory, then quietly unmaking and twisting it to ends different from the ones originally conceived is what media politics is all about.

Public policy is established as a response to media-highlighted crisis conditions. At the moment of its creation, the policy is clearly defined and usually broadly supported. The moment passes, and the policy's purpose and occasion disappear. Then the crisis passes; the seeming threat to society's survival that energized the president, press, and legislators to act quickly is no longer present; the source of its popular political backing disappears. Thus, crisis-oriented public policy is always more or less still-born. The act of creating it guarantees that almost as soon as it comes into existence, it finds itself bereft of the public purposes and political support that occasioned its creation.

To be sure, the policy remains on the books and continues to define a source of authority and funding for bureaucrats to use. Official activities continue to be undertaken in its name. But now the purposes to which it's put are not the ones involved in its creation. They are specified or sustained by special interests; slowly the policy is co-opted by interest groups and officials.

The Civil Rights Act, for instance, was sold as a way to hold the country together. It defined the civil rights and race relations problem as one created mainly by official Jim Crow segregation in the South. Accordingly, it took the position that the solution to the race problem was to be found in official nondiscrimination of the sort that had dominated public policy outside the South. Minnesota Democrat Hubert H. Humphrey, the bill's floor manager in the Senate, was doubtless sincere when he pledged that the legislation was an antidiscrimination measure, period, and wouldn't establish compensatory racial preferences or entitlements.

After the bill became law, the legislation's identity changed. The bill having been passed, there was no more civil rights crisis; the law's main purpose had been achieved. Yet the legislation was on the books and a bureaucracy was in place, dismantling Jim Crow and setting up programs to achieve racial representation or balance in schools, places of employment, and other venues—just the sort of thing Senator Humphrey appeared to be saying the bill wouldn't entail. Was this a result of the capture of the civil rights bureaucracy by groups with racialist agendas? Or was it a result of the bureaucracy's decision that racial representation was a sine qua non of the elimination of de facto discrimination on the northern model? Or both? Whatever the answer, it's clear that officials promulgating affirmative action were taking steps not contemplated, and officially rejected, by legislative decision makers.

Contrary to Woodrow Wilson's hopes, emergency government can't govern. Not only does public support for emergency policies evaporate the minute they're in place and the crisis passes, but officials acting in the emergency mode can't make meaningful public policies. According to the classic textbook definition, government is the authoritative allocation of values, and emergency government doesn't authoritatively allocate values.

In the first place, crisis government isn't authoritative. It operates in urgent circumstances that don't permit deliberation and choice in the traditional legislative sense. The only legitimacy it can claim is that it got society out of a bad scrape at the moment. That isn't a very authoritative posture, not even at the time it takes place and certainly not later, when the crisis has passed and everyone can once again contemplate issues in their true context. Thus, the achievements of media politics have a short life expectancy. No sooner is an exercise in this kind of policy making over than the decisions are revisited and the issues reopened.

Neither is emergency government reliably linked to public values. Crisis managers, concerned only with survival and pressed hard to meet the exigencies of the moment, do whatever it takes to get themselves and their countrymen through, by fair means or foul. As time passes and the crisis fades, the connection to the community's political values, never strong, fades, in some instances to the point of disappearing.

Crisis government can't allocate anything. It can't make meaningful decisions. It acts by preempting the deliberative and legislative functions. Even when the executive branch's crisis actions receive the legislative branch's sanction, they typically are authorized by vast, uncritical majorities acting in an atmosphere in which everyone insists on acting first and thinking later. In such circumstances the central action of governing—the framing and making of choices among competing values—isn't undertaken. There's action but no decision or responsibility.

Moreover, crisis government works poorly in the long run. It is, necessarily, focused on the danger of the moment, committed to doing whatever it takes to bring the community through, and indifferent to the long-term and broader effects that the solutions it comes up with, while they work in the short run, often work only in the short run. As time passes, the long term arrives, the costs and other drawbacks of the quick fix become glaringly obvious, and actions that once seemed highly satisfactory in urgent circumstances look more and more like a permanent fiasco.

With the passing of time, then, the policy virtually disappears, leaving, like the Cheshire cat, only the smile behind—that is, the pot of power, organization, and funding assembled to implement the policy. People or groups then try to turn the policy to their own goals, as indeed they have been doing all along. The policies' public identities are compromised or obliterated entirely, and then the policies are revived as juridical zombies serving the ends of private privilege. When public programs are perverted gravely and persistently, they are sometimes reborn as scandals, reentering the news genre's crisis-and-emergency-response scenario and retracing the century-old cycle of revelation, investigation, punishment, and reform; in other words, the scenario-tropism is recast in moral rather than practical existential terms.

The odd, insubstantial barrenness of public policies enacted under the news-activated emergency power is symbolized and underscored by the bizarre experience the working journalist encounters in trying to report a story at the White House. From a distance the White House seems a profound, substantive, vital source of vision and energy dominating government's handling of a policy issue. Up close and personal, however, the place is a fog bank.

When I first began reporting *Fortune* stories on business-government issues, I was naturally interested to know what presidential staffers covering the subject had to say. After interviewing a few such people, however, it was clear I wasn't learning much. They generally confined themselves to the White House's line du jour, which is whatever the West Wing grandees have concocted to serve the president's strategic needs of the moment, usually an obvious minimalism of no real interest.

When I pressed them on the substance of issues, I discovered they often didn't know any more than I did, for the simple reason that they'd learned about them in much the same way I had, by talking with agency and private experts. The one thing they did know a lot about—the inside politics of the issue at hand—they didn't disclose. Their job was to help the president play the hero, not to deconstruct his performances. The closer they were to the president, the less they tended to say. When they did talk about internal politics, their comments were highly unreliable, generally self-serving, and often unverifiable. Sources, knowing they were writing on a clean sheet of paper, routinely took large liberties with the truth. The place was a zoo.

The White House I got to know, in short, wasn't a source, it was a performance. There was no substance there, only appearance. A reporter almost never needs to interview people there. The performance is available in handouts and the conventional press. Real facts about real issues and events, by contrast, are available in the agencies and among the experts and lobbies, where people are much better in touch with reality and have a narrower need for political lies. A journalist who nevertheless goes a-reporting at the White House is asking to be lied to.

The ironic fact that the White House, the biggest story in town, is the least productive place a working reporter can find himself is explored, by implication, in the one Washington novel that illuminates the world I got to know as a journalist: Douglass Cater's *Dana: The Irrelevant Man*. In this insufficiently appreciated work, Cater, himself a former Washington journalist, author of a seminal book about the press (*The Fourth Branch of Government*), and a senior aide in the Johnson White House, tells the story of a Harvard graduate history student commissioned to write a biography of a Clark Cliffordesque senior White House aide named Dana, who had played a central role in the management of his president's war policy. The novel records the would-be biographer's slow realization that, no matter how deeply he delves into the record, Dana remains the enigmatic figure he appears on the surface. The man is all performance and no off-stage identity. Dana's secret is that, deep down, he is as insubstantial as he appears to be.

Behind the theatrical mask the White House shows the press, there lies a process of calculation, maneuver, and artifice that translates the president's political objectives into the vocabulary of the emergency power. Of these, as we've seen, the public objectives begin to fade as soon as they're achieved. By contrast, the private ones—mostly desires for public benefits and privileges—are more authentic, longer lasting, and more consequential. Thus, behind the rhetoric and posturing, what media politics generally boils down to is a virulent form of interest group foraging.

The old-fashioned kind of interest group politics celebrated by civics textbooks was generally stable and moderate and tended to converge on the public interest. In it organized interests of all sorts vied with one another within a framework created by the two political parties and many congressional committees. The parties and committees were powerful and stable enough to make members answerable for the consequences of their decisions. As a result, government tended to work the way the Founding Fathers intended, refining the views and interests expressed and encouraging groups to find common ground with one another and to take account of future public costs and risks as well as private benefits.

In the Washington I got to know, parties and committees were weak, and most major policy decisions were made in near unanimous votes. Answerability was minimized both by the news-enabled convergence on legislative bandwagons and by the closely related absence of discussion of and public information about who would benefit at whose expense. As a result, legislators had a large opportunity to inject special interest provisions into the details of the law, and the incentive for anyone to find common ground or anticipate future consequences was small. Media-driven bandwagon politics had no center of gravity; it seemed capable of almost any excess. Each interest group tended to cooperate with the bandwagon, no matter what else was written into the fine print, as long as the costs were offset by some special compensation or were passed on invisibly to someone else. It was a system that tended to intensify and multiply interest group demands rather than refine and restrain them.

The result was a pattern of policy making that was positively schizophrenic in quality. On the one hand, policies would have a sweeping, radical, whatever-it-takes grandiosity about them, corresponding to the crisis-and-emergency-response scenario by which they were sold to the public and pushed through the legislative process. On the other hand, the laws would be riddled with exemptions, special timetables, one-time payments, tax breaks, and all manner of goodies and deals tailored to the special requirements and agendas of the many interests that would be affected by the sweeping declaration of policy. But there was no meaningful policy-related connection between the two sets of provisions. The effect wasn't one of balance or precision, but of dual, equal, and opposite extremisms, similar to the pattern of the past decade's fiscal policies, which have doubled the deficit while conducting a dramatic, uncompromising crusade designed singlemindedly to eliminate the deficit.

I ran into a good example when I reported a story for *Fortune* about the Office of Noise Control at the Environmental Protection Agency. The agency was beginning to apply a typical media-politics statute regulating noise pollution. On the one hand, the law authorized a sweeping noise ceiling based solely on the exposures that produced hearing loss (no attention to economic effects or other considerations allowed) and a second, even more drastic, but nonmandatory ceiling based on the exposures scientific studies showed to have an adverse effect on human welfare. These ceilings were so low, I realized, as to invalidate industrial society as we know it.

On the other hand, the law was a Swiss cheese full of exemptions and special deals. For instance, the one genuine large-scale danger to public hearing were the subways in New York, where hundreds of thousands of regular straphangers were (and still are) incurring deafness due to the extremely high noise levels. But as the price of winning the votes of the New York delegation—fixing the New York subways would have cost billions that the city and state didn't have and that its elected representatives didn't want to take responsibility for—the sponsors of the Noise Control Act agreed to specifically exempt all existing subways from the standards. Most of the other big nonoccupational sources, such as trains, highways, trucks, and military aviation, also wangled special indulgences of one sort or another. The one major noise source category that didn't get a loophole and had to meet some tough new standards was jet aircraft. While no danger to anyone's hearing, they had become a problem in some big-city airport neighborhoods—and more to the point, I discovered, Boeing, Pratt & Whitney, and General Electric had decided to acquiesce in the noise protesters' and noise regulators' activities in the hope of inducing the government to order the airlines to buy a new generation of quieter, more efficient jet aircraft and jet engines. (The airlines, not yet deregulated, were still in the grip of their old passion for new equipment and still able to afford the luxury of being indifferent to many issues of cost.)

The media politics I got to know in Washington was not, however, any simple matter of public pretense and private rapacity, of empty gestures to serve the public interest and substantial, effective efforts to turn public matters to private advantage. That was indeed generally the intention, but it was not always the outcome. A lot of media politics ended up being as ineffective and sometimes counterproductive in advancing private interests as it was in serving the public interest.

A key reason why is the scarcity of big news stories that play out for long enough to produce the desired substantial changes in public opinion and public policy. Media politicians, aware of this fact, know they can't be picky when it comes to deciding which news stories they'll hitch their wagons to. They try to take a ride on more or less anything plausible that comes along and labor opportunistically to find some way to derive personal or organizational benefit, even if this means changing business strategies, political affiliations, or personal beliefs in order to gain advantage from the potential benefits that happen to be present in the environment.

This practice of jumping aboard every passing bandwagon, laboring to make it yield personal advantage, and jettisoning such elements of the would-be beneficiary's long-term personal, political, or organizational self as were necessary to make a virtue of necessity was the most characteristic and bizarre aspect of the media politics I got to know in Washington. It was a spectacle of individuals and groups in powerful positions who enjoyed advantages in profusion, but at the expense not just of others and of society as a whole but of their own integrity, competence, and independence. It was a form of taking a ride on the tiger's back and ending up inside. It was the quest for personal privilege pursued so systematically and with such heedlessness of the consequences, personal as well as social, as to be self-abnegating.

A good example of the politics of self-abnegating privilege occurred during the first weeks of the Bush Administration in 1989, when the U.S. Senate took up the question of advising and consenting to the new president's nomination of former Texas senator John Tower to be secretary of defense.

The Tower hearings had begun routinely as the nominee responded reassuringly to gentle questions on his policy views (conservative, but toned down for the hearings) and personal habits (he denied rumors that he was a hard-drinking womanizer). On the third day, however, a New Right activist and former Senate staffer named Paul Weyrich charged that Tower was unfit to be defense secretary on the ground that he had an apparent habit of drinking to excess and conducting liaisons with women. Weyrich supported the claim with his own eyewitness observation of Tower on a number of Washington social occasions when the senator appeared to be inebriated, in the company of a woman not his wife, or both. Weyrich's direct accusation touched off a firestorm of controversy. The press covered the allegations massively, the committee extended its hearings to look into them, and the Democrats found themselves eyeball to eyeball with an opportunity to defeat Tower. Eventually the ex-senator was rejected for the defense post by a straight party line vote, 53 to 47.

The Senate Democrats voted against Tower mainly, they said, because a reexamination of his FBI dossier, in light of Weyrich's charges, persuaded them that the man had a history of problem drinking. This claim, however, was media-politics hypocrisy. If Tower, who'd been a member of the Senate for twenty-four years, had an alcohol problem substantial enough to warrant rejecting him, it should have been apparent to his colleagues back in the days when they worked with him on a daily basis. Moreover, if they believed Tower's drinking was really the problem they were saying it was, they should have been doing something about it during his Senate days, when he served as chairman and ranking member of the Senate Armed Services Committee.

The Democrats' real reason for opposing Tower, of course, wasn't his drinking. They were against him for reasons of politics and ideology. George Bush, having just trounced his Democratic opponent, was riding very high just then, and the Democrats were very much in the market for a way to take him down a peg or two. Moreover, in a period of easing East-West tensions and growing budget deficits, the Democrats were returning to their Vietnam-era enthusiasm for lower defense spending. Defeating a hard-liner like Tower would further that end and possibly help frame an issue that would resonate with the electorate in the next election. But the Democrats were unlikely to get anywhere with either argument. Bush and his Republican allies would counter that a president has the right to name whoever he wants provided he or she is qualified, the public would accept this view, and enough Democratic senators would be persuaded to confirm Tower.

Thus, the Democrats kept quiet about their real reasons and co-opted Weyrich's charges and the confidential FBI reports to create a news-based crisis defining Tower as a disaster waiting to happen, the American people and global peace as his potential victims, and the Democrats in the Senate as their saviors. With such large dangers in prospect, people would feel constrained to focus on them and to ignore the presumptions of normal politics—that a president's nominee with two decades of successful high-level experience in the Senate can expect confirmation and that in America people are considered innocent of wrongdoing until proven guilty.

President Bush and the Senate Republicans naturally stood up for Tower and insisted he'd be an outstanding defense secretary, but the arguments with which they defended their man were as hypocritical in their way as those with which the Democrats attacked him.

When President-elect Bush picked Tower, he was of course aware of the drinking and womanizing issues. The rumors (and actual behavior patterns behind them) were old and well-known; Bush chose Tower in spite of them, not in ignorance of them. A full account of why Bush named Tower awaits the historians, but the president's reasons appear to have included Tower's knowledge of defense, political skill, hard-line views, and the president's personal feelings for an old friend and Texas ally. In appointing Tower, Bush was effectively saying that these considerations outweighed the negative of Tower's drinking or reputation for drinking, and that the negative, though real, wasn't big enough to be dispositive.

If, however, Bush responded to the charges by openly describing this reasoning, giving his candid personal judgment of Tower's strengths and weaknesses in comparison to other candidates', he could count on nothing but trouble. Not only would he be unselling his own candidate and embarrassing an ally and friend, but by framing the confirmation issue in a political context, he'd be giving the Democrats all the ammunition they needed to turn the Tower confirmation into a partisan vote of confidence on Republican positions on defense issues.

So instead of insisting on the political reality and political merits of the appointment, Bush joined Tower's detractors in denying them. He responded to the media-fueled firestorm over Tower with a short, pithy defense. He'd known Tower for years, Bush said, and had full faith in his judgment. The FBI had found no history of problem drinking and had given Tower a clean bill of health. The Democrats were doing Tower and all fair-minded Americans an injustice by repeating isolated, uncorroborated allegations by unnamed people against a distinguished public servant.

This, however, was at best an exaggeration. While Bush didn't make the dossier public, senators who were allowed to read it noted that since the FBI's report consisted of raw field data, all the information about Tower, favorable and unfavorable, was presented in a format that left it isolated and uncorroborated and the people who provided it unnamed. The FBI dossier didn't try to confirm or falsify the charges. Thus, the President wasn't in a position to make the claim that Tower had been given a clean bill of health by the FBI. He was dismissing anonymous charges as arbitrarily as the Democrats were dignifying them.

The pro-Tower position was, then, the mirror image of the other side's position. Where the Democrats feigned an innocence about an old colleague's drinking to attack conservative defense politics, Tower's defenders feigned a similar innocence about Tower's drinking in order to repel his critics and stymie the bandwagon they were building. To the Democrats' hypocritical "What about Tower's drinking problem?" they replied, equally hypocritically, "What drinking problem?" To the Democrats' self-serving alarm over the danger that the public might be victimized by appointment of an alcoholic to the second highest position in the military chain of command, the pro-Tower side responded with a dishonest denial that the entire hypothesis had any basis in fact.

The press, in keeping with its historic commitment to the news genre's scenario of crisis and emergency response, played both sides' claims at face value. Every experienced reporter in Washington knew, or with ten phone calls could have found out, whether Tower drank too much. They also knew that both the Democrats and the Republicans, in pursuit of personal and political advantage, were playing fast and loose with that problem and the FBI's report on it. To acknowledge these realities, however, would have been to contradict the basic worldview of journalism and to throw a great story to the winds.

It was a typical case of bandwagon politics' self-abnegating quest for privilege. Each side was fighting over an issue it didn't care about (drinking) and pretending not to care about issues it cared a lot about (defense spending and political advantage). Thus, each side was working to win in a way that sacrificed important elements of its own political and cultural identity for the sake of victory and victory's advantages. The Democrats, historically the party of civil liberties and personal tolerance, dropped their usual latitudinarianism with respect to personal behavior and vices and lit out after a rumored drinker and womanizer with the censorious gusto of a religious fundamentalist. George Bush and the Republicans, for whom Tower's attraction was precisely his political competence and realism, threw competence and realism to the winds in a desperate doomed defense based on the transparent fib that there was no evidence of an alcohol problem and indeed that they'd personally never seen the man take so much as a sip of white wine.

Thus, the issue was fought in a way that guaranteed that, whoever won, the victory would be narrow, personal, and fleeting and would entail substantial costs and disadvantages. For the Democrats the defeat of John Tower led to the appointment of a much better and no less conservative man (Richard Cheney) to the Pentagon post at a time when the Soviet empire, and thus the pertinence of the hard-line position, was collapsing. They also got themselves committed to a position on dealing with alcoholism that few of them really believed in and that someday could come back to haunt them. Not least they called attention to their hypocrisy in a period of rapidly intensifying pubic anger over the Washington problem. As for the Republicans, they fought for their man in a way that compromised the ideological positioning and leadership he could provide in office and their own reputation for honesty and competence.

The phenomenon of the bandwagon-based quest for the self-abnegating privilege wasn't confined to officials in Washington. It was clearly evident in the way private interests related to the policy process as well. One can discern it in most regulatory issues, for example.

Thus, media politics not only sacrifices public to private, it also often ends up weakening its private beneficiaries. It is a politics of decline and ruin. People and groups routinely ride media bandwagons to short-term advantages that bring with them longer-term costs and disabilities and count on a fresh round of future media-won benefits to offset the costs when the bill comes due for payment. In the Washington I got to know, people were lobbying and winning themselves into growing personal dependency and risk.

Jean-Jacques Rousseau said there'd be societies like the one I got to know along the Potomac during the Reagan years. But I never realized, as a graduate student studying the works of this most brilliant and profound of modern political philosophers, that the day would come when I'd recognize my own among them. Rarely, however, has there been a more perfect fit between text and reality than the fit between the analysis of modern liberalism set forth by Rousseau in the mid-eighteenth century and the Washington that Ronald Wilson Reagan inherited from Woodrow R. Wilson.

In their economic livelihoods, Rousseau observed, people were closely integrated with and interdependent on one another; the simple, self-reliant life of the solitary forager was a distant and forgotten bit of the past. But the freedom to jointly prescribe for all wasn't yet present. There was a pretense to such a form of prescription in the form of constitutional government. But this system, Rousseau held, was based on individuals' self-interest rather than their mutual commitment to the ideal of freedom. It promised justice but delivered manipulation and exploitation as everyone sought to use the system to his own immediate advantage.

In short, Rousseau argued, the philosophy of Hobbes, Locke, and Bacon had brought forth what he called a new bourgeois society. It was based on fear of death and a new science of self-preservation and personal comfort, and amid its idealistic promises of individual freedom and social harmony, it was a recipe for hypocrisy. People professed devotion to law, freedom, and the common good. But these promises were opportunistic, based on an expectation of advantage. It was a society that taught privilege and injustice.

The Washington I came to know in the Reagan years was precisely the world Rousseau described. It was a place of seeming enlightenment, freedom, material comfort, and personal cultivation dominated, ironically, by the politics, economics, social relations, and ethics of the jungle. The Founding Fathers had labored heroically to create institutions that would enable America and its capital city to escape the fate Rousseau had anticipated. Pulitzer and Wilson, with their Progressive-era ambition and vanity, had ignored the founders' ideals, displacing arrangements they had carefully designed to make popular government principled, coherent, far-sighted, and competent with a crude method of conducting the public business that had no answers to the problems Madison and Jefferson had toiled so inspiredly to deal with and that was certain to come a cropper. Their innovations had opened the way to a politics that had no institutional defenses against, and so was prone to, all the pathologies the Founding Fathers had sought to give American government an immunity to. They had paved the road back to Rousseauville.

At the center of this paradoxical world stood the press. It was the day-to-day broker of the political and social psychology of *amour propre*, conveying the information and images needed for the successful exercise of the psychology of privilege and priority. The late Allan Bloom wrote that the bourgeois is defined by the fact that, when dealing with others, he can think only of himself and that, when trying to satisfy himself, he can think only of how others will see him. News evokes a stage for the enactment of *amour propre* on a national or global scale. With its images of what the whole world is watching, with its promise of nonideological practicality and problem solving, it gives cues as to how others are reacting and offers a means of manipulating the sociability of others to one's advantage and of trading one's future well-being for a short-lived present benefit.

CHAPTER 8

Constitutional Journalism

Sooner or later, most people who write about the press issue a stirring summons to greater professionalism on the part of journalists or express gratitude for the high level of professionalism already manifested by the press. The critics take for granted the basic concept of news that prevails in the industry and focus on the success or failure of newspeople to live up to that concept. Thus, they urge news organizations to be more balanced politically and newspeople to write more objectively. They advocate more and better education for journalists. They wish for the maintenance of a higher ethical tone in news organizations. Alternatively, they express satisfaction with the balance, objectivity, educational levels, and ethics already visible in journalism.

This instinctive, unconsidered embrace of the professional idea in journalism is the main reason why decades' worth of press criticism and vast hurricanes of public rage against the media have come to so little over the years. Professionalism isn't the solution to our journalism problem, it *is* our journalism problem.

The point at which otherwise intelligent observers and critics of journalism begin to advocate professional kinds of solutions is the point at which our thinking about journalism departs from our experience of it and public discourse about journalism disappears into the intellectual black hole that is the culture of lying.

The true cure to what ails media and politics today is to be sought, not in professionalism, but in an *alternative* to professionalism and its corrupting notion of news as crisis and emergency response and the journalist's perverse pretense to a special relationship with newsmakers. In particular, the cure for the culture of lying is to be found in a revitalization of the journalist's role as a nonexpert and lay person and a remaking and remoralizing of his relationship with the reader or viewer.

This remedy is a simple one in the sense that, when put into practice, it works easily and well.

One of the tricks I learned during my years as an editor was that when a story was troubled and neither the writer nor I seemed to be making much progress with it, often the best solution was to extend the due date a bit and send the writer off to do some more reporting. Sometimes I'd make a suggestion about what to focus on, but I learned it didn't matter if I didn't. Instructed or not, the writer would go off, memories of our editorial conferences fresh in mind, and when he or she returned a day or two or a week later, the usual result wasn't merely a debugged manuscript but a genuinely good story. Once-wobbly facts would become crisp and compelling, quotes would sparkle, meandering thinking would go straight, insight would prevail where muddle had reigned, tired writing would find energy and conviction— all thanks to the magic of the reporter-newsmaker and reporter-editor encounters.

It wasn't a strategy one invoked lightly. More reporting took time. You never knew what the story would end up saying. There was a good chance that the art would have to be redone and the story rescheduled, and you also needed something to run in the hole you were making in the original issue. But if a story wasn't coming together and it had to be saved, sending the writer back to his notebooks and sources was the way to go. It was practically a panacea.

In another sense, however, restoring the journalist to his true role as a citizen with an editor and an audience is an extremely difficult task. It puts the journalistic reformer on a collision course with basic features of the modern world, including the business strategies of news firms and the needs of high officials in government and business. Such a goal, especially when taken as an absolute, may well be impossible in many cases, and attempting to push ahead with it regardless of practical difficulties could easily make matters worse by weakening good but flawed journalistic institutions, such as the *New York Times* or NBC News, without putting anything better in their place.

Happily, however, reuniting the journalist with his true destiny in a constitutional world can be approached in small, pragmatic steps; we are not talking here about an all-or-nothing-at-all proposition. In the pages that follow, I will describe nine directions journalists and newsmakers might take in their efforts to remedy the present situation. While, in my opinion, all nine changes are desirable, I don't offer this as an integrated agenda that has to be adopted more or less in its entirety for any significant improvement to take place. Even very modest changes along any of these lines will often bring noteworthy benefits.

Reporters would dope out what was an empty performance and what was real, and their stories would reflect that awareness. Performances would be deconstructed, lies exposed, officials' vain self-inflation ignored. Officials, seeing how little they were gaining by playing to the press gallery, would start to drop the whole charade and begin focusing on their real jobs. Authentic actions and views would slowly come to dominate public discourse again.

The first step the press can take to put the dysfunctional heritage of Joseph Pulitzer behind it is to redefine news.

1. COVER CRISES AND DISASTERS LESS.

The first step in eliminating the culture of lying is to drastically cut back on coverage of natural disasters, fires, crashes, political and social crises, revolutions and coups d'état, wars, crimes, and the sexual, romantic, marital, familial, and financial lives of the rich, powerful, and famous. The vast majority of news stories dealing with such events in today's media have no place in the journalism of a constitutional society. The news industry should drop them like the bad habit they are.

The basic reason to do so is that crisis-and-scandal journalism is at odds with the entire concept of liberal democracy. Constitutional society is based on the ideals of the free individual, voluntary social activity, and a government of laws. The essence of such a society is that its public business takes place within the frameworks created by its formal institutions, from small businesses or local churches and schools to giant corporations and the legislative branch of the central government. Crises and scandals, we've noted, push public attention and action away from those frameworks and tend to weaken and supersede them. Crisis and scandal are in this sense irrelevant to public affairs in democratic society. They are an inappropriate focus for constitutional journalism.

To be sure, crises happen, and the media should cover what happens; I am not arguing for repression of the journalistic function. But in real life, crises are events of a sort very different from the events portrayed by Pulitzerian front pages. In real life, when an emergency or disaster takes place, we don't fixate on it, at least not for long. When a friend is killed in a car crash, or a tornado devastates our neighbors' houses, or we go through a divorce, or we're laid off from our job, or a child is victimized by a molester, or a loved one is gravely sick, we turn immediately to family, friends, church, medicine, courts, and government at first for healing and thereafter as an alternative to the chaos and injustice of the emergency. In other words, real-life crises and scandals are so painful and repellent that they lead us to redouble our sense of involvement in the settled social frameworks that constitutional society is all about. In this sense the experience of crisis hardly exists; it is a fleeting prelude to a lasting desire for and rededication to normal life.

In the world according to Pulitzerian journalism, by contrast, crisis is a simple, permanent, unvarying reality. It leads, not to a rediscovery of the values of normal life, but to the ad hoc autocracy of the emergency power and to the often successful efforts of special interests to turn other people's misfortune to their own advantage. Thus the crises news covers aren't the hard realities we automatically take them to be. They are, or soon become, a highly artificial propaganda in which what the media covers is a fabrication and the impression it conveys is unreal. For example, half a dozen commercial airplane crashes a year killing a few hundred people a year are big, big news in America. By contrast, two million car crashes a year killing forty thousand people are treated as a much smaller, even insignificant story. Activities surrounding illegal drugs that kill a few thousand Americans a year are a very big story. By contrast, two legal drugs that kill several hundred thousand people a year are scarcely covered or are ignored altogether. Such coverage does not paint a picture of reality, it bamboozles.

Finally, crisis news, and its newly popular kissing cousin, scandal journalism, are ethically reprehensible. They treat the heroes of their stories as objects to be exploited and as beings with no rights to privacy or claims to our respect. In precisely the same spirit, they define the audience as objects to be titillated by the media and their clients, the advertisers. Insofar as it focuses on crises and scandals, the journalism Pulitzer created is in fact a kind of social pornography, and it plays on the same prurient social psychology that undergirds racism—the sense of aggrandizement one person or group feels at the dehumanization, devaluation, and victimization of another.

The media should put themselves on a strict crisis-and-scandal diet. A limited amount of such coverage is healthy and should be continued, but the gluttonous binging and gorging at the crisis-and-scandal table has got to stop. A good place to begin is with foreign news. Nearly all of it deals with crises and emergencies of various sorts. A reader of the best American newspapers today is capable of going years on end without encountering a single story from the capitals of Africa or Asia that isn't about coups, wars, ethnic riots, droughts, floods, and terrorism. That being the case, why bother at all? A coup qua coup isn't much, and when one knows nothing of the people, cultures, and issues involved, they all look and sound pretty much the same, anyway. I propose a modest rule: There should be no coverage of wars, coups, violence, or the like in a country unless at least a few noncrisis stories have also run lately. If a country is judged not to merit noncrisis coverage, then this should be taken for what in fact it is—evidence that the place doesn't merit crisis coverage, either. The notion that we might somehow want to know about illegal transfers of power in a distant country but not legal ones or food riots there but not the growth or decline of its leading industries is crazy, and it shows how quickly the Pulitzerian view of the world leads off into irrationality and unreality. The media should drop this unjustifiable, pathological approach to events abroad.

At home they should do much the same. Crises should be covered insofar as they are truly important. Huge negative local experiences impacting large numbers of people—big earthquakes, Force 4 hurricanes, major urban riots on the scale of Los Angeles in 1992 or Detroit in 1967, and the like—merit the massive treatment they're getting now. Major misdeeds or crimes warranting pursuit by official agencies should be covered, but with a restraint and circumspection suitable to the sensitive issues of the individual's presumption of innocence and other rights. Where the scandal unfolds in abuse-prone, nonjuridical contexts like an investigative hearing by a congressional committee or a leak by a local prosecutor's office, the story should pay suitable attention to the backstage, out-of-frame behavior and thinking of the investigators, who almost always derive—and expect and seek—personal career advantage out of the story. That is as much a part of the real event as the scandal is, and news should find ways to reflect it.

Otherwise, however, emergencies, crises, and scandals should not be covered, or at least the coverage they do receive should be limited to brief items and perhaps confined to a special emergency-news section. If the event involves few people, if it's being dealt with adequately by public and private crisis-management authorities, if it represents a wild and self-serving accusation by one competitor against another, if it doesn't put large numbers of people in immediate danger, or if it isn't something that a news firm would investigate and fire its own executives and directors for, it shouldn't be reported. I mean that last point so emphatically I'm going to repeat it: *The news media shouldn't report a scandal that they wouldn't investigate and fire their own employees, executives, or directors for.*

It was not just unfair, it was arrant hypocrisy for the *Miami Herald* in the 1988 presidential campaign season to seek out and report a story about ex-Senator Gary Hart's extramarital affair.

This was behavior the *Herald* and the Knight-Ridder chain would, quite rightly, never tax their own executives and employees for, and they had no business taxing the Harts for it. By the same token, all the media were wrong to cover the *National Enquirer's* press conference to promote Gennifer Flowers's *Enquirer* story alleging she had had a long-term affair with Bill Clinton while he was governor of Arkansas and married to Hillary. In a liberal and constitutional society such matters are private not merely in the sense that they should be protected from publicity but also in the larger sense that they can be understood and dealt with only by the people immediately involved. To a distant stranger who knows nothing of the people and issues and intentions and context, such events and stories can mean anything and so mean nothing. Thus, they become a media-made propaganda. The fact that the media covered the Hart and Clinton matters the way they did was another brick in the wall of media-based injustice and unreality separating America from her liberal heritage and aspirations.

2. COVER NORMAL, FORMAL POLITICAL, SOCIAL, AND ECONOMIC EVENTS MORE.

As emergency events lose the limelight, the focus of journalistic attention should shift to significant normal events taking place within formal institutional contexts. The deliberation and policy-making activities of the legislative branch, the moral core of constitutional government, should be front and center on the media's stage. State and local government, accounting for half of public-sector spending and nearly all of government's morally and politically sensitive functions, from education to policing public order, should be much more prominent in the news. Key actions of private formal associations, from big corporations and unions to professional groups, should also be well covered.

The rule should be that whatever key institutions spend time and effort on, the media should cover. If raising and spending public funds or creating and maintaining streets and highways or holding public hearings is preoccupying a legislature, department of public transportation, or school board, that's what the story should be. It was wrong but typical of the media not to cover the taxing and spending decisions that generated the $400 billion annual federal deficit. Focusing on the normal routine actions of major institutions within their own frameworks, not the media's, will ensure that in the future, taxing and spending actions that create deficits will be covered, not ignored.

Many media critics and scholars count an institutional focus as a weakness in journalism that empties news of reality and injects into it a conservative (or centrist, or pro-establishment) bias. This is mostly a semantic confusion, however. In current journalism there is a bias *in favor of top officials* that is inherent in the crisis-and-emergency-response scenario; this bias is indeed conservative, or, as I've called it, pro-privilege. There is also a bias *against institutions*, whose frameworks and perspectives are largely obliterated by the scenario. This bias leads to the same effect.

In contrast to crisis journalism's rejection of institutional frameworks, which creates a theater of privilege, a journalism that embraces institutional events creates a theater of constitutional democracy. Putting events and news back into their constitutional boxes, where each has a meaningful, intended, institutionally elaborated, independent existence, enables both to be real. The actions are taken with reference to the institutions' procedures and goals, not just to making a favorable impression in the news. These institutional frameworks are products of legislators acting with a view toward performing specific public tasks and avoiding well-known problems. They are means of improving public policies' chances of succeeding. They create responsibility; people outside formal structures usually are less answerable and thus less trustworthy.

Reporting stories for *Fortune*, I was always struck by how quickly my efforts to understand a particular issue or problem or official or bureaucracy led to the core activities of constitutional government. Almost whatever my ostensible subject might be, I found, the story soon ended up being about the laws, the debates behind the legislation, and the ideas shaping the debates. In other words, the closer my reporting took me to the institutional frameworks and procedures of constitutional politics in America, the more information was available and the more real my stories became. The farther I strayed from those frameworks, the less real information was available.

Lest there be any confusion on this point, let me add that in urging journalists to cover crises and scandals less and constitutional events more I am not suggesting that the news should drop the element of story or that newspeople should seek to make themselves and their work product boring. The element of story, one of the most basic and fruitful modes of human discourse, should and will remain. I am saying, rather, that the *kind* of story news specializes in should change—from the superficially exciting but often misleading story of crisis and emergency response to the more meaningful and constructive constitutionalist story of representing society, framing choices, resolving issues, and conducting the rest of society's business.

3. CUT BACK FORMATS IMPLYING THAT THE WHOLE WORLD IS WATCHING.

At the root of much evil in journalism are the advertising-related devices created over the years to impute a high level of public interest in news events, particularly the front page and headline in newspapers and the omniscient narrative of TV news. These devices, which focus on crises, have created the illusions of emergency and unanimity that have made journalism a theater of lies and privilege and should be greatly pruned back.

The graphic vocabulary that imputes rank and magnitude to events should be eliminated or curtailed. Newspapers could usefully reformat their front pages on the model of the first page of the *Wall Street Journal*, with its unvarying grid, routinization and rotation of the topical uses of front-page spaces, and rigorous withholding of graphic imputations of public interest or importance to news events. A freer but still highly routinized and unhierarchical model is provided by the front page of *USA Today*, which usually has space for only a few breaking news stories a day and which often uses it for noncrisis events. *USA Today* also shows how nongraphic page makeup elements can eliminate the crisis-community illusion by, for instance, devoting substantial front-page attention to matters that are so clearly incommensu-rable with emergency public events—such as stories about pro-fessional sports and show business—as to break the illusion that is projected so emphatically by the front pages of the *New York Times* and the *Washington Post*.

I am not arguing against all graphic representations of story size or priority. On the contrary, I am arguing that news graphics should begin to convey more accurate, less misleading images of news events. Most such events are, or should be, occurrences taking place within the frameworks of constitutional society, in which meaning and importance are in the eye of the beholder. News graphics should convey that reality.

And when an unambiguously big emergency event occurs, news graphics should reflect that reality, too. Northern California newspapers were right to run the story of the San Francisco earthquake in 1906 in the same banner headlines and enormous typefaces that, six years later, the New York newspapers were right to use in covering the sinking of the steamship *Titanic* or that, in 1917, American newspapers were equally right to use in reporting Congress's declaration of war against the German and Austro-Hungarian empires. Truly big events are quite rare, how-ever, and on the vast majority of days, layouts and headlines should be conveying an image of public affairs as a participatory, open-ended affair in which people are encouraged to develop and contribute their own perspectives and in which the press doesn't prejudge what is big news and what isn't.

News firms should also drop the closely related device of the headline and inverted-pyramid story structure, which bring events into a tight focus commensurate with their detailed rank-ing and sizing on the front page. The conventional headline that describes—and, inevitably, prejudges—the event by specifying what in the editor and reporter's judgment is its essential or most newsworthy feature should give way to a wider range of formats and styles. In addition to the headline, which should be used when the event is simple rather than complex or when the central action really is clear, the head based on a noun phrase should also be in widespread use (as it is in my local paper, the *San Francisco Chronicle*). When a presidential press conference covers a wide range of important material, the story should cover all of it under a head such as "Presidential Press Conference." When a congressional subcommittee holds a hearing to develop information on an emerging issue or problem, a similarly generic summary, "Congressional Hearing on X," should be standard.

In television news the demotic narrative style that prevails should be dropped. Television newspeople could model their way of presenting the news on the relatively cool, emotionally uninflected voices of the readers on the news programs of the BBC. Or they could go the other way, discard all the accoutrements of authoritativeness, and seek to become personal, reflexive, even modest in their presentations of self.

Together, these de-Pulitzerizing reforms add up to a substantial reshaping of the essential character of news. For this redefinition of the media product to "take" in the news industry and news markets, some correspondingly fundamental changes should be made in the social and economic role of journalists and the media firms in which they work.

4. JOURNALISTS SHOULD DEFINE THEMSELVES AS CITIZENS, NOT PROFESSIONALS.

To create a theater of democracy rather than privilege, the news media should create a corporate and occupational culture that is genuinely geared toward the liberal, constitutional, and democratic values they now only pay lip service to. To that end, journalists should give up the notion that they are professionals or experts who survey events from a vantage point different from and superior to that of the audience. They should abandon the habit of identifying with officials and authorities. They should seek to recover their true identity as citizens.

The journalist exercises, not a special expertise, but everyman's right, duty, and innate inclination to participate in public discussion and community affairs. What is enduringly valid about journalism is that it is the record compiled by a *non*expert as he engages the events and institutions and personalities and issues of the day and reports what he observes and thinks to his fellow citizens. The journalist is a soldier serving on the front lines in the war for experience, pitted against the claims of superior knowledge and authority of experts, hierarchs, and specialists. The journalist doesn't represent or serve the citizenry, he *is* a citizen. He goes forth, has a citizen's experience or simulation thereof, then comes back to share it with his fellow citizens. The core of the job is to be and remain a citizen. He should identify with his fellow citizens. He should accept an obligation to be truthful and responsible to them.

Journalists should maintain a distant, independent, mistrustful posture toward officials. The halfhearted effort during the late 1960s and 1970s to define journalists as the adversaries of officials who lie and manipulate should be revised and extended to apply to all officials, not just those associated with the center and right. Journalists' efforts to be independent should extend to a rigorous social self-segregation; the spectacle of reporters and officials socializing with one another, or even sitting down together at mutually flattering, pseudosatirical banquets and roasts, is something constitutional society would do much better without.

Insofar as there are deals with authority—and of course there will be many; cooperation is in the interest of both sides—the journalist must observe an ethic of strict disclosure. Everything he does in the making of a story that is pertinent should be disclosed. He shouldn't pledge secrecy to any source, he should promise all sources that they can expect publicity and disclosure. His responsibility is to perform the citizen's role and tell what he observes as he performs it. He isn't answerable for officials' secrecy or candor. If they won't talk, he should report it even though it may not make much of a story. If they talk nonsense, he should report that, but not in a way that implies it's real and, if possible, in a way that signals the reader of the writer's impression that it's nonsense.

Journalism education should be refocused as liberal education for citizenship, with healthy doses of political theory, ethics, and theology as well as technical courses and the history of journalism. In keeping with this shift, the Pulitzer Prizes should be eliminated. They are at odds with the journalist's identification with the audience. They deny the constitutionalist conviction that journalistic excellence is ultimately a quality for readers or viewers to judge for themselves in light of their experience and needs, not a means of usurping the readers' or viewers' primacy and glorifying people who ought to see themselves and be seen as the audience's humble servants. At the very least, the Pulitzer Prize program should be restructured to give a larger role to nonspecialists and outsiders in picking winners, and most of the prizes should be given to journalists and news organizations for *resisting* tempting fabrications by big newsmakers. Prizes should not be given for exposés and feature stories told mainly from the viewpoint of this or that special interest group.

5. ESTABLISH A CULTURE OF RESPONSIBILITY AND DELIBERATION INSIDE THE NEWS ORGANIZATION.

Discussion, debate, and an ethic of personal responsibility should prevail in the newsroom. Editors and reporters should air their views openly and take personal responsibility for their decisions. Editors should clearly establish and own up to the particular angle or style of their publication. The imperial editocracy should go; top editors and top writers should receive roughly the same pay and prestige.

Reporters should be rewarded for rejecting newsmakers' efforts to get pseudoevents played as if they were real, even though this may mean that more stories they're assigned to will be killed or played down. The traditional postures of objectivity, designed to give news a specious aura of reality and public validation, should go, since they are tools by which audiences are manipulated, lies are propagated, and journalists deny responsibility for their stories' faithfulness to real life. While reporters should still seek and report facts, they should also take responsibility for point of view and disclosure of pertinent facts about the making of the story.

Thus, newspapers and news programs should own up to their point of view. Journalism, like every other form of communication, can't exist in the absence of a point of view; the author's point of view is what makes it possible for him to see and respond and understand and communicate. And journalism about public affairs can't go forward without some location in the spectrum of political opinion. To pick a subject or to focus a story is to express a notion of, among other things, what's interesting and valuable to large numbers of people, and that in turn is a function in significant part of both the journalist's and the audience's politics.

But to do their job properly, news media need not only to have and to clearly express a point of view but to develop and clarify and improve it, to turn it into a selling point, to conduct ongoing debates and forums with readers and others about it. Point of view, including but not limited to political point of view, is one of the things that makes journalism interesting. I would insist even that it is one of the great pleasures of journalism. But it is only a pleasure and point of interest when it's owned up to. Our newspapers and TV news shows should start doing that.

They can usefully start in small ways. When Walter Cronkite stepped down as anchorman of the *CBS Evening News with Walter Cronkite*, the program dropped Cronkite's sign-off line, "And that's the way it is." The statement suggested that in twenty-two minutes everything that had happened that day had been covered and that the coverage itself had been a disembodied reflection of reality. It was widely agreed the line was incredible and misleading. When Dan Rather took over from Cronkite in 1981, it was discontinued; now Rather signs off by saying, "And that's part of our world tonight." Much better.

Now other media should make similar changes. The *New York Times*, for instance, should drop its misleading, dishonest, destructive Adolph Ochsian motto, "All the News That's Fit to Print." It's not possible for any newspaper to print *all* the news that's fit to print, because what news is depends on point of view, and it isn't possible to have all points of view, it's possible only to have the point of view you do have. And it's dishonest to suggest that the only limitation on what's printed is fitness and, by implication, that whatever you don't print *isn't* fit, making a tacit equation between your point of view and fitness on the one hand and other points of view and unfitness on the other. If the *Times* wants a motto (and I think a motto is an excellent idea), it should find one that reasonably conveys its real viewpoint. Maybe "A Great

Liberal Paper for a Great Liberal City" or whatever the owners and managers of the *Times* decide they are or want to be.

The most important thing in this respect, however, isn't just the way the news operation describes its point of view but the spirit in which the operation expresses and develops it. A model one could usefully emulate would be the great newspapers of Europe—the *Neue Zürcher Zeitung* or *La Corriere della Sera* or the *Manchester Guardian* or the *Times* of London or *Le Figaro*—newspapers that, coming in effect out of the pre-Pulitzerian tradition of journalism, both have and own up to more or less clearly defined political identities, whether broadly ideological or more narrowly partisan.

6. REORIENT MEDIA-FIRM BUSINESS STRATEGY TOWARD READERS AND AWAY FROM ADVERTISERS.

To reposition the journalist as a citizen, align him with the audience, further distance him from the newsmaker, and create a culture of responsibility, the media firm needs to sharply reorient its business strategy. It's no accident that non-responsible journalists and non-justifiable stories are widespread in an industry that makes a business of renting access to its audience and authority to an advertising industry that produces responsibility-dispersing communications for products sold by privilege-seeking manufacturers in a market whose disciplines they would rather evade than submit to. Lasting improvement in the news industry won't be possible until firms deemphasize ad sales strategies and commit themselves to developing their reader sales business.

Media firms should slowly raise prices to subscribers so that reader purchases are the main source of revenues. They should reposition their advertising sales business so that the resulting shrinking of the rate base won't devastate their bottom lines. They should study their readers. They should divert their capital spending away from programs to maintain or inflate the rate base and redirect it to improving the product, since their business is going to be more and more dependent on readers' satisfaction with the product and willingness to pay more for it. Subscription sales packages should emphasize the product; premiums and other nonproduct inducements should be dropped.

These efforts will not only align the product with the interests of the audience, they will also disconnect the product from the needs of the advertiser and of maintaining advertiser revenue streams, which can distort coverage and investment patterns.

A final trio of proposals define steps to be taken outside the news business by people and other institutions who would like to encourage and support a constitutional journalism.

7. DEREGULATE, DESUBSIDIZE, AND DEMONOPOLIZE THE NEWS INDUSTRIES.

If journalism is to get back in touch with readers and reenter constitutional society, it needs help from government—not in the sense of subsidies or protection, but precisely to eliminate the subsidies—help in managing markets and other anticompetitive, pro-oligopolistic benefits that the corporate state has bestowed on the media industry over the decades. While there are substantial elements of competition in the media firm's environment, the news industries are far from being the free and level playing fields we imagine. They need to become free and level. The reforms described above won't happen, at least not satisfactorily and lastingly, if media firms continue operating in a regulatory hothouse that insulates them from the information and benign influences of the marketplace.

The place to begin is the obvious one: with the massive government regulatory presence in the TV, radio, and, to a lesser extent, cable industries. Along with the airlines, which grew up in the same nurturing and protective regulatory environment, the broadcast industries are a classic case of a new industry seeking and getting the systematic help of the government in controlling entry, limiting product diversity and innovation, and otherwise managing its affairs as an official cartel. Given the inherent social-psychological clout of the television medium and the substantial national political influence of network news since its inception in the 1960s, the oligopolistic character of broadcast journalism has been a crucial factor behind the growth of the culture of lying. Government, which has made a modest start at decartelizing broadcasting, should move strongly to deregulate and deoligopolize TV, radio, and cable across the board. Increasing frequency availabilities, auctioning access to them, eliminating content supervision, de-guilding the Hollywood program production industry by removing the limits on broadcaster entry, freeing the cable alternative, and removing entry barriers to fiber optic, digital audiotape, and other new technologies are necessary and beneficial steps that should be taken immediately. The objective should be to radically downsize and restructure government's presence in this industry so that it resembles the presence government now has in, say, apparel retailing.

The print news industry has also been shaped by the subsidizing, protective presence of the corporate state, but in a much quieter and more indirect way. Special low mail rates and expedited mail delivery constitute a huge public subsidy to newspaper and magazine publishers that should be eliminated immediately. They have pushed media firms toward a pro-advertising sales business strategy and away from their original pro-reader sales strategy by lowering the cost of the massive direct mail needed to maintain the vast, artificially inflated circulations sought by advertisers. Mail subsidies and privileges have also lowered the inherently high cost of delivering magazines made thick and heavy by hundreds of advertising pages. All these mail privileges should be withdrawn. The natural cost advantages of sparse, light publications and magazines should be restored, and publishers should not be spared the delays unfortunately experienced by ordinary private users of the postal system.

Another subtle but influential public support for the culture of lying has been the bias built into the tax code in favor of investments in marketing assets such as brand or manufacturer name recognition or wide and rapid dissemination of new product or price information. The business tax code permits the writing down of the entire value of such investments in the year in which they are made even though the results, in the form of public perceptions, often have very long lives. By contrast, investments in tangible capital goods such as plants and equipment must be written down much more slowly, over the anticipated useful life of the asset, often many years. These policies have had the effect of advantaging spending on marketing, especially advertising, which in turn has artificially inflated the ad sales market that has drawn media firms away from their reader connection. Making the tax treatment of intangible marketing assets more consistent with the tax treatment of tangible manufacturing assets would put the media firm's reader sales market on a fairer footing vis-à-vis the advertising sales market.

Public policy has also supported the culture of lying and the underlying concept on which it rests (that is, that the journalist is a professional with a quasi-official role and authority vis-à-vis the general public) by giving accredited representatives of the media special privileges. A small example are the so-called shield laws under which most states exempt journalists from part of the normal citizen's obligation to give evidence in criminal court proceedings. Much more consequential is the massive public information and public relations apparatus maintained by government at all levels at a cost to taxpayers of billions of dollars a year. Journalists complain about the self-serving, fiction-spinning, truth-bending, generally low-life character of these enterprises and the people who staff them, but we also know them to be very useful. Usually a single call to a single press-relations person is enough to produce an entire day's or week's worth of interviews and inspection tours, supplemented by nearly any amount of official information, often on extremely short notice. Doing it yourself would take days if it could be done at all.

This is a subsidy that isn't available to all comers. An ordinary citizen seeking interviews and observation opportunities out of mere personal interest wouldn't get the time of day. A representative of a nonaccredited or out-of-field medium is also apt to consider press relations a way of providing some journalists with protections against competition from other journalists. Congress, for instance, restricts access to the press gallery to accredited journalists and denies accreditation to publications of groups taking positions on policy issues or providing consulting services to private clients. These special privileges should be eliminated.

Shield laws should be eliminated; they are a direct attack on the concept of the journalist as an ordinary citizen and on the ethic of disclosure that I urge as key antidotes to the culture of lying. The benefit of news coverage made possible by the journalist's shield law–backed promise of anonymity to whistleblowers vulnerable to retaliation from the powerful people whose crimes they are bringing to light is real. But such cases are the exception, not the rule. The vast majority of whistleblower stories are based on information developed inside rather than outside the context of official law enforcement. More important, the journalist's sense of having a special, privileged status, reinforced by such things as shield laws, is a key element of the culture of lying, and its negative consequences extend to nearly every story and official context. Giving up the benefit of an occasional whistleblower exposé for the vastly larger benefit of curtailing the culture of lying is a bargain well worth making.

Public information operations should either be eliminated or made to work on a fairer, non-privilege-giving basis.

Last but not least, the First Amendment protections of the media business should be strengthened by rescuing the constitutional doctrine involved from its current utilitarian purgatory, in which it's used to justify vast government intrusions on the broadcasting industry and small government privileges such as shield laws, as well as to justify the concept, clearly intended by the Founding Fathers, of strict noninterference by government with the free expression of the press, period.

8. REFORM GOVERNMENT AND BUSINESS ALONG LIBERAL CONSTITUTIONALIST LINES.

While this book and the program of reform I'm laying out in the present chapter are about the journalistic side of the culture of lying, the news industry isn't the only place where people should be rethinking and reshaping the role they play in the world. The culture of lying is as much the doing of officials and institutions as it is of the press, and its curtailment requires that some changes be made on the official side as well as on the media side. This is a matter that takes us far afield of the focus of this book, so I'll confine myself to two broad points about what other institutions should be doing about the culture of lying.

On the one hand, institutions and officials should disinflate their oligarchical ambitions and imperial style. Business firms, especially big corporations, have large appetites for power over markets and for privileges from government, and these objectives, as noted, lead them to lie, manipulate, and generally fabricate news personae designed to help them wrest from a society that still speaks the language of Locke and Jefferson benefits more in keeping with the traditions of Napoleon and Mussolini. Public officials, driven by an insistent careerism and an ideology of pragmatic government problem solving, comply with group agendas for privilege, piling onto their clients' lies an additional layer of their own. For the culture of lying to be scaled back on a meaningful scale, these antimarket, anticonstitutionalist vocations for privilege need themselves to be scaled back. Business firms should restructure business strategies in keeping with market principles and market ethics. Government officials should find new government-limiting ways of addressing public and constituent needs. Everyone needs to rediscover new relevance in the classical liberal notions of individual self-responsibility and limited government. Government needs to be scaled back in many areas, and public policy's commitment to markets should be strengthened.

On the other hand, the ability of government to conceive, discuss, refine, adopt, elaborate, and put into practice public purposes through public policy needs to be strengthened. The culture of lying is a reflection of the weakness of public intentions and public decisions, as distinct from private intentions masquerading in political drag. For the culture of lying to be pared back, public institutions need an injection of the institutional, intellectual, and moral resources required to speak sincerely and act efficaciously in behalf of public values. To make itself politically more limited, in other words, government, paradoxically, needs to make itself morally stronger. As readers will have become aware by now, I sympathize with the classical liberal approach to political life, but I emphatically part company with my libertarian friends on the issue of the moral strength and coherence of government. Many latter-day classical liberals think that depreciating and weakening political institutions are ways of confining them to a narrower, more properly constitutionalist role in society. I believe, by contrast, that our institutions need to be strengthened so that they *both* satisfy society's legitimate needs *and* limit themselves. How to do this is a vast topic that goes far beyond the scope of this chapter or book. I will say only that a wide range of reforms and constitutional issues should be considered, including such fundamental changes as switching to a parliamentary form of government. It's just possible that Woodrow Wilson was right the first time around.

9. Readers and viewers should pointedly stop using Pulitzerian media and seek out congenial non-advertising-oriented, nondaily, non-journalistic information services.

Arguably the single most important step anyone can take to encourage the above changes is one he or she can take by himself or herself: stop watching, reading, and subscribing to Pulitzerian news sources and write the broadcasters, publishers, and major advertisers involved a note stating that you are pulling the plug on them, explaining why. The main reason to take this step is to disconnect yourself from the lies and illusions the newsmaker-and-media system is currently foisting upon you. A subsidiary reason is that your defection, especially if announced and explained in a personal communication, may help push the media involved to reconsider and redirect their approach to the journalistic function.

I would encourage people to experiment with a wide range of other sources of information about public affairs. Take a good newsletter or trade magazine in an area of special interest. Watch C-SPAN or get a subscription to the *Congressional Record* or *Congressional Quarterly* or *National Journal*. Subscribe to one of the weekly or biweekly opinion magazines, such as the *New Republic*. Follow the minutes of your local city council or zoning commission or school board. Read current novels or poets or go to the theater or opera. All of these are rich sources of information about and criticism of current events. A quick reading of some sonnets by black poet Claude MacKay or Ralph Ellison's *Invisible Man*, or an hour with one of the arresting rap albums of Public Enemy is worth all the black-related news coverage in a year's or even a decade's worth of *Washington Post*s.

Get personally involved in a community institution or activity that interests you. Careful comparative test-drives of cars from Japan and Korea and Detroit will probably tell you more about the auto industry and the state of the big American corporation than all but the most sophisticated specialized publications. A hands-on, in-person familiarity with the affairs of your local high school is likely to be more informative about the state of the community than anything published by a Pulitzerian newspaper.

I suggest all the above measures because I believe they are correct. I believe that, if put into practice, they would move the press a long way away from the current pro-oligarchical posture and a long way toward recovering the central elements of journalism as it was in the constitutionalist age that preceded Pulitzer.

I would favor the above measures even if I thought that putting them into practice would be extremely difficult and the chances of succeeding in the effort quite dim. As it happens, however, I believe that in practice several elements of this agenda would prove to be surprisingly easy to implement. In other words, the agenda, in addition to its merits, could have the further virtue of offering media firms a low-cost way to deal with some of the problems that plague the news business and a high-reward response to the opportunities present in the marketplace.

The economics of the conventional, advertising-oriented news firm has come under growing strain from the rise of specialized media that efficiently target specialized audiences and from the growing interest among consumer product firms in market-segmenting approaches. As a result, ad revenues are increasingly subject to fluctuations, whereas subscriber-derived revenues are steadier. And amid the fluctuations of ad revenues, maintaining huge, expensive rate bases and production volumes has become more and more difficult. Even small downturns in ad revenues are capable of putting the whole house of cards in danger of collapsing, as efforts to compensate by cutting costs undermine the artificially pumped-up rate base, which in turn brings ad rates down (or pushes the practice of under-the-table discounting up) and raises the question in advertisers' minds of whether they would be better advised to spend their marketing dollars elsewhere. By contrast, selling real information to real readers who have an investment in the product, while generally taking more time and capital to mature, is often a more secure strategy, is less subject to fads and whims, and has a very substantial upside.

Moreover, the news-industry action in recent decades has clearly been on the side of innovations embodying the concept of smaller, more reader- or viewer-regarding, more specialized products. The most successful new products, from *USA Today* and CNN News to lower-volume products like the *MacNeil-Lehrer News Hour* embody many of the features I'm advocating: less demotic formats, more commitment to a deliberative vision of public affairs, less imposition of journalistic formats on institutional ones. Specialty media, which serve audiences with significant independent sources of information about the subject matter and so have little choice but to maintain more sophisticated, less lie-infested information services, are on the upswing. Suburban and nondaily news media are doing well. The old general-audience, big-city newspapers are diversifying and innovating in promising directions as they respond to the public's growing alienation.

The news markets today remind me of nothing so much as American automobile markets in the late 1970s, on the eve of the second oil crisis that enabled Japanese car manufacturers to transform themselves in the American context from anonymous producers of bottom-of-the-line miniboxes to the trusted creators of the most desirable products in the market. More and more, things in the news business seem poised—or at least to have the potential—for dramatic change.

Signs of how near at hand true alternatives to the culture of lying already are and how potentially revolutionary our present media environment has become can be found in two of the brightest stars in cable television's fin-de-siècle firmament—QVC and C-SPAN. Together, they embody in prototype form a complete alternative to the culture of lying. QVC is advertising-merchandising without the usual piggyback ride on news and the audience's sense of citizenship, and C-SPAN is journalism without the distorting presence of news themes and formats designed to enhance advertising appeals. What is startling is how utterly far removed from the puffery and fraudulence of conventional media a viewer of both programs feels. The culture of lying is nowhere to be found in either; it has simply disappeared.

QVC, of course, is the Quality Value Channel, on which a wide variety of consumer products is offered for direct and immediate sale via telephone or other interactive electronic media. The viewer sits in front of his video screen at home, watches and listens to the products, prices, and pitches, and decides whether or not to take the deals offered. It is a real-time video catalog service, and in recent years it has been growing rapidly. What is important about QVC, for purposes of the present discussion, is that there's no noncommercial programming. The selling part of the service isn't appended to a nonselling part; it doesn't assume or invite the viewer to be uninterested in buying merchandise. To the contrary, the selling is the programming in its entirety, selling that doesn't pretend to be something other than what it is. It is selling without the culture of lying.

C-SPAN is national public affairs journalism without the mediation—and distortion—of an advertising-oriented news format. Founded in 1979 as a public affairs service supported by cable operators, C-SPAN began by televising the daily sessions of the House of Representatives, then added a second channel for the sessions of the U.S. Senate when it voted to let the cameras in. C-SPAN has supplemented these basic services with coverage of a growing array of public affairs events, including congressional hearings, presidential campaign rallies, public-policy conferences, interviews with newsmakers and journalists, and viewer call-ins.

Over the years C-SPAN has developed an approach to covering national public affairs that exemplifies the institutional-event-oriented, constitutionalist journalism envisioned earlier in this chapter. The focus is always on the actual event. Typically there is no reportorial presence whatsoever. When C-SPAN's own reporters are physically present on the screen, they are usually cast in a neutral, fact-gathering, reportorial posture. They virtually never express personal views or pursue obvious themes. In fact, so different is C-SPAN from conventional television that the C-SPAN personnel who appear on camera are not even professional reporters in the usual sense. Most are officers of the C-SPAN corporation, and the one who appears most frequently or in connection with the most important events is Brian Lamb, the network's founder and CEO. Prior to conceiving and selling the idea for C-SPAN, Lamb was, among other things, a business lobbyist. On camera, he is intelligent, matter-of-fact, unfawning, self-effacing, and profoundly neutral on the issues at hand.

There is no culture of lying on C-SPAN. The culture of lying has magically vanished; indeed there's no place on C-SPAN for it to exist. The program simply reproduces what happens on the Hill; it covers what happens in constitutional institutions and in constitutional frameworks. C-SPAN provides no substantial independent framework on which an official could hang a manipulative pose. The channel shows how close we are, conceptually and historically, to having workable alternatives to the culture of lying.

It isn't exciting fare, but it is deeply engrossing, and it has acquired a significant audience. It reaches some sixty million households, or roughly half of the national total, and according to public opinion surveys it is watched regularly—that is, several times a week—by 23 percent of the population. Those who are the heaviest watchers are typical upscale Americans—that is, typical with one exception. According to a doctoral dissertation by Maura Clancy at George Washington University, C-SPAN viewers are somewhat more active citizens than nonviewers *even controlling for education, income, and other relevant factors*. In other words, this is a journalism for people who identify as citizens, and it's associated with a higher level of voting, participating in official processes, communicating to public officials, and so on.

It may be asked if the constitutional journalism I'm sketching would really be such a blessing in practice. In particular, with its less sensational and more institutional focus, might it not create the circumstances in which growing public inattention led to a resurgence of political machines or bureaucratic excess or any other abuse that intense press scrutiny and exposure would curb? The answer is that it might, but at any rate, as far as I'm concerned, the particular political outcomes of who's helped and who's hurt are beside the point.

By reverting to a more constitutional form, in which media would record the proceedings of deliberative institutions without trying to impute public reactions to them, journalism would be putting the institutions on better display and enabling citizens to participate in and respond to them as actively—or as inertly and ineffectually—as they are moved to. In other words, the media would be enabling people and institutions to take responsibility for their own actions and failures. It might be that institutions and people would fail. But at least it would be clear what had happened and who was responsible.

The only cure for our current system of constitutional oligarchy is to take away from the political system as it exists the communication structures that give citizens the illusion that they're participating when they're being manipulated, that they can participate passively rather than by actually taking part. There's no such thing as a cure for the ills of constitutional oligarchy within the framework of journalism. The cure is activity in the constitutional and institutional arena.

Where journalism went wrong a century ago was in getting mixed up with a notion of citizenship and consumership that assumes it's possible to exercise either of these roles in a passive mode. Advertising that was addressed to strangers with zero commitment to the product and that treated the consumer as passive led business astray by inviting manufacturers to think they could take their eye off the customer and his experience. News, structured in advertising's image, enabled public officials and organized private interests to take a similar perspective.

Liberal democracy isn't automatic. The pursuit of self-interest wherever it might lead, subject only to the requirements of the laws against fraud and violent crime, isn't enough. Constitutional democracy requires a positive commitment throughout the society to the values of constitutional democracy itself. It requires a willingness to make appropriate sacrifices in an effort to see to it that those values become a reality. The cure for the journalism and journalistic politics that are displacing liberal values is an effort on everyone's part to recover the largely but by no means entirely lost perspectives and skills of active citizenship.

NOTES ON SOURCES

CHAPTER 1. FABRICATIONS

On the emergency power, see John Locke, *Second Treatise on Civil Government*. A recent analysis of the prerogative power, as Locke called it, is Harvey C. Mansfield, Jr., *Taming the Prince* (Free Press, 1990).

For more on the definition and ethics of lying, see Sissela Bok, *Lying: Moral Choice in Public and Private Life* (Vintage, 1979) and *Secrets: On the Ethics of Concealment and Revelation* (Vintage, 1989).

The full citation for my vinyl chloride story is Paul H. Weaver, "On the Horns of the Vinyl Chloride Dilemma," *Fortune*, October 1974.

Business's support for the rhetoric of the free market and the reality of big government is discussed in Paul H. Weaver, *The Suicidal Corporation* (Simon & Schuster, 1988).

A pro-market critique of the New Deal myth is Ronald Radosh and Murray N. Rothbard, eds., *A New History of Leviathan* (Dutton, 1972).

The Warren Commission's limited investigation is described by Edward Jay Epstein, *Inquest: The Warren Commission and the Establishment of Truth* (Viking, 1966).

On public cynicism and alienation, see Seymour Martin Lipset and William Schneider, *The Confidence Gap: Business, Labor, and*

Government in the Public Mind (Free Press, 1983). A more recent analysis from a less technical perspective is E. J. Dionne, Jr., *Why Americans Hate Politics* (Simon & Schuster, 1991).

The *Washington Post* editorial ran on page A27, October 14, 1981.

CHAPTER 2. PULITZER'S REVOLUTION

The account of Pulitzer's life and achievements derives from W. A. Swanberg's biography *Pulitzer* (Scribners, 1967) and George W. Juergens's outstanding social history *Joseph Pulitzer and the New York World* (Princeton University Press, 1966). The analysis of evolving news formats borrows broadly from Michael Schudson, *Discovering the News* (Basic Books, 1976), and specifically from Helen Mahin Douglas, *The Front Page* (University of Michigan Press, 1938). For a discussion of epideictic, see Aristotle, *Rhetoric*, esp. 1366a–1368a. Michael Schudson's study of press coverage of the state of the union address is "The Politics of Narrative Form" in *Daedalus*, March 1987.

The discussion of the rise of the corporation is based on Alfred D. Chandler's *The Visible Hand* (Harvard University Press, 1979); Martin J. Sklar, *The Corporate Reconstruction of American Capitalism, 1890–1916* (Cambridge University Press, 1988); and Richard S. Tedlow, *New and Improved: The Story of Mass Marketing in America* (Basic Books, 1990). These topics are also discussed in Paul H. Weaver, *The Suicidal Corporation* (Simon & Schuster, 1988). For more on concentration in the media industry, see Ben H. Bagdikian, *The Media Monopoly* (Beacon Press, 1987).

The discussion of advertising is based on Michael Schudson's superb scholarly study, *The Advertising Persuasion* (Basic Books, 1981). See also Philip Gold, *Advertising, Politics, and American Culture: From Salesmanship to Therapy* (Paragon House, 1987). My view of advertising owes an intellectual debt to the political psychology expounded by Alexis de Tocqueville in *Democracy in America*.

Ivy Lee's career and contributions are discussed in Richard S. Tedlow, *Keeping the Corporate Image: Public Relations and Business, 1900–1950* (JAI Press, 1979). Also see Alan R. Raucher, *Public Relations and Business, 1900–1929* (Johns Hopkins Press, 1968).

Material on the life insurance scandal of 1905 is from Morton Keller, *The Life Insurance Enterprise, 1875–1910* (Harvard University

Press, 1965), as well as from Swanberg's lively chapter. The mention of a "revelation, investigation, punishment" tropism is a reference to Benjamin Ginsberg and Martin Shefter, *Politics by Other Means: The Declining Importance of Elections in America* (Basic Books, 1990).

On Woodrow Wilson's wartime presidency, see David M. Kennedy's *Over Here: The First World War and American Society* (Oxford University Press, 1983). The material on the rhetorical presidency is from Jeffrey K. Tulis, *The Rhetorical Presidency* (Princeton University Press, 1987).

The story of how Pulitzer endowed the Columbia Journalism School is told by Richard Terrill Baker, *A History of the Graduate School of Journalism, Columbia University* (Columbia University Press, 1954). The discussion of Lippmann borrows from Ronald Steel, *Walter Lippmann and the American Century* (Atlantic-Little, Brown, 1980). On the sources of government growth, see Robert Higgs, *Crisis and Leviathan: Critical Episodes in the Growth of American Government* (Oxford University Press, 1987).

CHAPTER 3. HOW A NEWS STORY LIES

The story about the Sproul Hall bust appeared on page A1, the *New York Times*, December 5, 1964.

The analysis of the news genre owes a debt to Aristotle's *Poetics* and to Wayne Booth's seminal *Rhetoric of Fiction* (University of Chicago Press, 1961) and *Rhetoric of Irony* (University of Chicago Press, 1974). A witty analysis of journalistic and other voices is Walker Gibson, *Tough, Sweet, & Stuffy: An Essay on Modern American Prose Styles* (Indiana University Press, 1966). My own writings on the news genre include Paul H. Weaver, "Is Television News Biased?" *Public Interest*, Winter 1972; "Newspaper News and Television News," in Douglass Cater and Richard P. Adler, eds., *Television as a Social Force* (Aspen Institute, 1975); and "The Politics of a News Story," in Harry Clor, ed., *The Mass Media and Modern Democracy* (Rand McNally, 1975).

CHAPTER 4. WAYWARD HEROES

The story of Paul Volcker's disinflation policy at the Fed is told by William Greider in *Secrets of the Temple: How the Federal Reserve Runs the Country* (Simon & Schuster, 1987). The experimental study of media-led bandwagons was described by Shanto Iyengar and Donald R. Kinder, *News That Matters* (University of Chicago Press, 1987).

CHAPTER 5. EDITOCRACY

On front-page topics, see David Shaw, *Press Watch: A Provocative Look at How Newspapers Report the News* (Macmillan, 1984).

On A. M. Rosenthal's reign see Joseph C. Goulden's unflattering *Fit to Print: A. M. Rosenthal and His Times* (L. Stuart, 1988).

On cursory reporting, see Stephen Hess, *The Washington Reporters* (Brookings Institution, 1980).

Edith Efron's study of anti-Nixon bias in network news coverage of the 1968 presidential campaign is reported in *The News Twisters* (Nash, 1971). The article that apparently invited the CBS News targeting study of me was Paul H. Weaver, "Captives of Melodrama," *New York Times Magazine*, Sunday, August 29, 1976.

Benjamin Bradlee's *Conversations with Kennedy* was published by Norton in 1975.

Chris Argyris's monograph is *Behind the Front Page* (Jossey Bass, 1974). The list of "living system" traits is from chapter 1, the discussion of shrillness on the editorial page is from pages 173–174, and the long concluding quote is from pages 236–237.

CHAPTER 6. TRAITORS TO THEIR EXPERIENCE

On the courtier spirit among journalists, see the insightful and witty observations of Lewis H. Lapham, *The Wish for Kings: Democracy at Bay* (Grove, 1993).

The notion that reporters seek vicarious experience of real-world professions is commonplace in journalists' accounts of their careers and lives. See Gay Talese's sometimes autobiographical account of the *New York Times, The Kingdom and the Power* (World, 1969), or Norman Mailer, *The Presidential Papers* (Bantam, 1964), p. 219.

On the political affiliations and character structure of journalists, see S. Robert Lichter, Linda Lichter, and Stanley Rothman, *The Media Elite* (Adler & Adler, 1983).

Peter Braestrup's study of the media's coverage of the 1968 Tet offensive is reported in *Big Story* (Westview, 1977).

Joseph Medill Patterson's role in creating the *New York Daily News* is recounted in John Chapman, *Tell It to Sweeney* (Doubleday, 1961); Burton Roscoe, *Before I Forget* (Doubleday, 1937); Alice Albright Hoge, *Cissy Patterson* (Random House, 1966); and Frank C. Waldrop, *McCormick of Chicago* (Prentice Hall, 1966).

On the *Washington Post*'s sources on Watergate, see Edward Jay Epstein, "Did the Press Uncover Watergate?" *Between Fact and Fiction: The Problem of Journalism* (Vintage, 1975).

CHAPTER 7. STUPID POLITICS

This chapter owes a general intellectual debt to the writings of Theodore Lowi, particularly *The End of Liberalism* (Norton, 1969) and *The Personal Presidency* (Cornell, 1985). It also connects with themes sounded by William Greider in *Who Will Tell the People: The Betrayal of American Democracy* (Simon & Schuster, 1992).

My story on the business strategies and political strategies in the acid rain issue is Paul H. Weaver, "Behind the Great Scrubber Fracas," *Fortune*, January 1975. For more on the economics and politics of acid rain, see Bruce A. Ackerman, *Clean Coal/Dirty Air: Or How the Clean Air Act Became a Multibillion-Dollar Bail-Out for High-Sulfur Coal Producers* (Yale University Press, 1981).

The concluding point about Rousseau is inspired by Allan Bloom's essay, "Rousseau: The Turning Point," reprinted in Allan Bloom, *Giants and Dwarfs: Essays 1960–1990* (Simon & Schuster, 1990).

CHAPTER 8. CONSTITUTIONAL JOURNALISM

The study of C-SPAN viewers' citizenship behaviors is Maura E. Clancy, "The Political Knowledge, Participation, and Opinions of C-SPAN Viewers: An Exploratory Assessment of Mass Media Impact," Doctoral dissertation, University of Maryland, 1990.

ACKNOWLEDGMENTS

The Hoover Institution at Stanford University provided the fellowship that enabled me to write this book. I'm grateful to Glenn W. Campbell, who was Hoover's director at the time of my appointment and whose leadership over three decades had created an environment for research and writing that was supportive, comfortable, and efficient beyond all previous experience and imagining. I want to express warm personal thanks to John Raisian, whose support as associate director was instrumental in bringing me to Hoover and whose continued backing as Campbell's successor as director kept me going through successive drafts of a project that turned out to be much harder and more time-consuming than either of us expected.

My editor at the Free Press, Adam Bellow, and his boss (and my old friend), president and publisher Erwin Glikes, believed in what this book could become, contributed crucial ideas about structure and style, and refused to settle for anything less than my best. Loretta Denner was a rigorous yet warmly supportive production editor. My agent, Arthur Klebanoff, president of the Scott Meredith agency, was, as always, a source of impeccable guidance and dazzlingly articulate help.

I want to thank the several friends new and old who read the manuscript at various points of a long and transformative evolution. In a book that takes seriously, among other subjects, the issue of authorial responsibility, it seems appropriate not to name names. Not all the readers liked everything they saw, and I want to avoid shanghaiing them into a covert advertisement for either the book or the author.

I am grateful, too, to the many people and organizations that over the years have furthered my education in journalism and politics: the scores of reporters, editors, and business-side executives at the *New York Times, New York Daily News*, and *Boston Globe* who in the second half of the 1960s allowed themselves to be interviewed by a callow young political scientist; the friends and colleagues I shared the journalistic life with at *Fortune* magazine from the mid-1970s to the mid-1980s; the public affairs staffers and senior executives at Ford Motor Company with whom I worked from 1978 to 1980; the courageous investors and venture journalists who made my *Fed Fortnightly* newsmagazine launch in Washington, D.C., in 1986 an outstanding, though unhappily short-lived, reality; the editors of the magazines that over the years have encouraged and published my writings about the press, including *New York*, the *Public Interest, Commentary*, the *American Spectator, Fortune*, the *New York Times Magazine*, and *Reason*; and not least, my teachers at Cornell and Harvard, whose voices, examples, and precepts are still very much with me three decades later.

Toward the end of the writing phase, I was saddened by the death of one of those teachers, Allan Bloom, whose memory I will treasure always. My sense of indebtedness to this most brilliant of mentors, whom I learned from when he was a resident faculty member at Telluride House at Cornell, grew with the passing years. The more I've seen of the real world, the more I've found myself using, and needing, the perspectives I learned from this loud, funny, sympathetic, astonishingly learned professor of political philosophy. Bloom became famous in the 1980s as the neoconservative social critic who wrote the bestselling *The Closing of the American Mind*, but I remember him as an incomparable teacher who, over a diet of Cokes and cinnamon toast and Gauloises consumed in the Telluride House pantry after the libraries had closed, entered enthusiastically into the lives and thoughts of the young people in his vicinity, hewed to no ideological line, and argued over and over again that man is by nature a political being, that political reality is constituted by political ideas, and that he who denies these truths is cruising for a metaphysical and existential bruising. Little did a fascinated nineteen-year-old imagine that the bull-session backchat of this passionate intellectual was planting seeds from which a theory of journalism might spring.

My daughters, Ashley Augusta de La Harpe Weaver, eleven, and Samantha Signa Weaver, nine, continue to be my inspiration. I also want to thank my parents, Cecile T. Weaver and Harold F. Weaver, for their untiring support from the beginning, through the time I first encountered journalism as a graduate student, and now to these years just past in which, as an aging journalist and parent myself, I have completed a book on the subject, with growing awareness that whatever merit readers may be charitable enough to find in it is but a dim reflection of a mother's compassion and commitment and a father's high standards of intellectual achievement.

INDEX